Revolutionary Spies

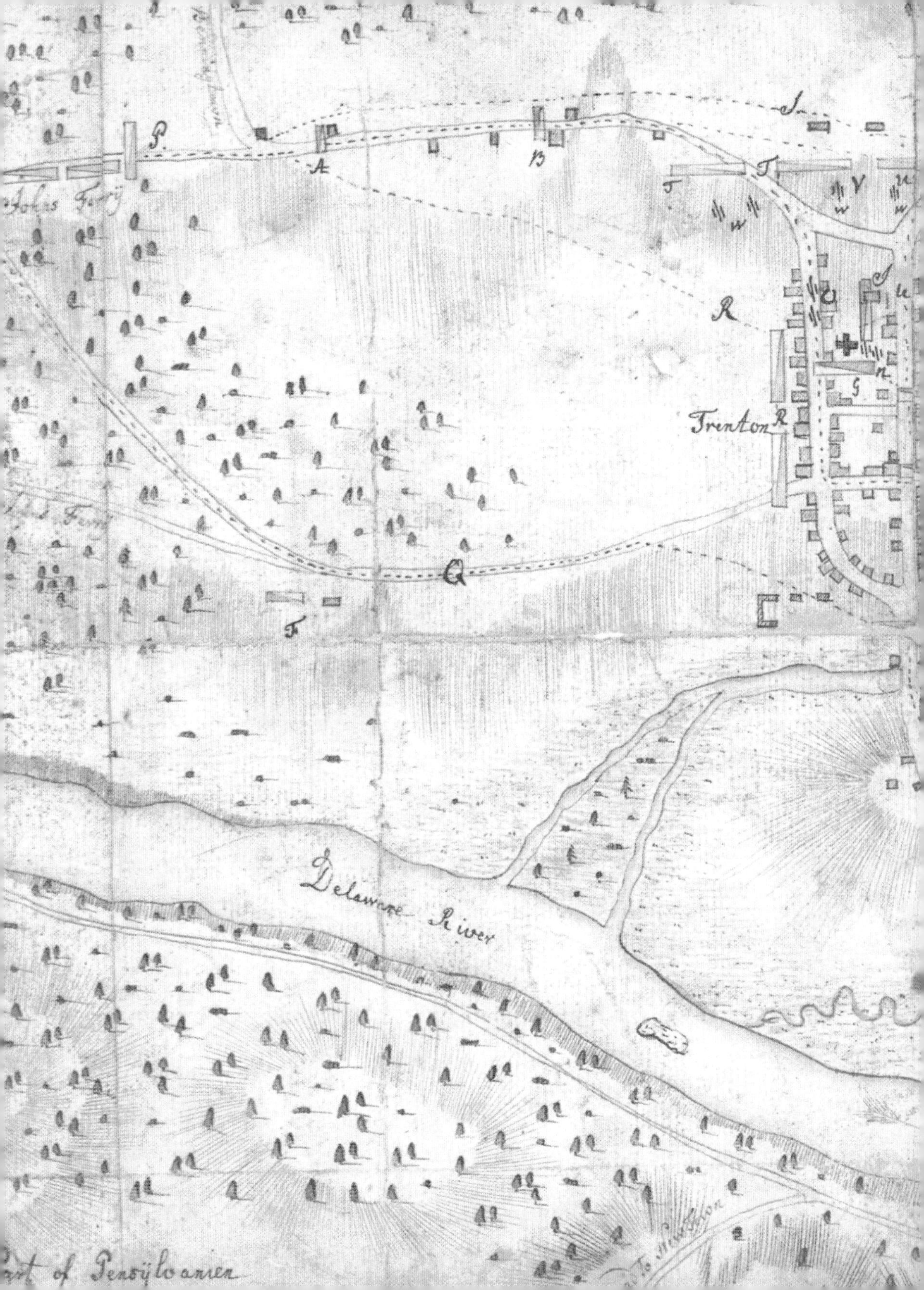

Johns Ferry

P

A

B

S

I

V
w

R
C

Trenton R

Q
S

Delaware River

Part of Pensylvanien

To Maidenhead

Revolutionary Spies

INTELLIGENCE AND ESPIONAGE
IN AMERICA'S FIRST WAR

TIM MCNEESE

FALL RIVER PRESS

New York

FALL RIVER PRESS

New York

An Imprint of Sterling Publishing
1166 Avenue of the Americas
New York, NY 10036

Cover design by David Ter-Avanesyan
Book design by Gavin Motnyk

ISBN 978-1-4351-5621-0

For information about custom editions, special sales, and premium and corporate purchases,
please contact Sterling Special Sales at 800-805-5489 or specialsales@sterlingpublishing.com.

Manufactured in China

2 4 6 8 10 9 7 5 3 1

www.sterlingpublishing.com

Contents

Preface

ear sunrise, on a warm and windless Massachusetts morning in the spring of 1775, between seventy and eighty anxious citizen-soldiers formed a ragged skirmish line on the village green in Lexington, muskets at the ready. They belonged to a training band of militia, a system of organizing local men to military arms that dated back to the previous century when their Puritan forefathers had founded the Massachusetts Bay Colony. The men were tired and nervous, many having spent much of the night without sleep. The alarm rider Paul Revere, Boston silversmith and leader among the secret dissident group the Sons of Liberty, had roused everyone with warnings that British soldiers, the well-trained regulars known as "Redcoats," were bound for Concord. Lexington lay in their path.

Captain John Parker stood at command on the green. In the insular world of rural New England, Parker could count one out of four of his men as a relative, either by blood or marriage. He was not a well man, tuberculosis ravaging him internally. The disease sometimes made it difficult for him to speak and barking orders could hardly be done without a twinge of pain. As he and his men waited, Parker understood clearly that they would soon face the fearsome specter of nearly a thousand professional British soldiers. He also knew that fighting was not a necessity. The British were moving on neighboring Concord, not his small town. The weapons, powder, and ball the British were after in Concord had already been whisked away to safety. The Americans were not even at war with the British, at least not yet. Parker also knew that other British units had previously engaged in similar marches out of Boston in search of munitions, foodstuffs, and even rebel leaders, which had failed to result in clashes between Massachusetts militiamen and British forces. Perhaps today would be no different.

But such a hope would not come to pass. Shots would be fire, blood spilled. The political and military trajectory of years of rebellion, boycott, pamphlets of protest, and myriad acts of civil disobedience had finally landed in Lexington.

British troops lined up by the hundreds opposite a line of Lexington farmers, shopkeepers, artisans, and common laborers. Parker (at least, according to tradition) spoke words that are today immortalized on a stone monument commemorating the first shots of the American Revolutionary War: "Stand your ground. Don't fire unless fired upon, but if they mean to have a war, let it begin here."

When the smoke of the minutes-long encounter cleared, eight colonists lay dead or dying. Captain Parker was among them, his body marked by crimson patches delivered by a host of British bayonets.

On that morning in Lexington, the future of America changed forever. After the first spilling of blood, the war began in earnest. The fight soon transmogrified from a theoretical conflict of street mobs and paper petitions to the real combat of armies, militias, rifles, and cannons. Through the American Revolution's eight long and anxious years, Americans fought hard against unlikely odds to gain their independence from Great Britain. They fought to free themselves of all the abuses, real and imagined, that the British Empire represented to the eighteenth-century colonists whose world had hugged the rugged Atlantic coast from Maine to Georgia for more than a century and a half.

Yet although the story of the American Revolution commonly focuses on military matters and political decision making, it is a story with a shadowy element. Both before and after the Battle of Lexington, the Americans consistently relied on a critical and secret weapon, one often overlooked in textbooks and military histories: secrecy. The Revolutionary Army's fight against the British included the efforts of scores of individuals who served as spies, saboteurs, code makers, and couriers. Some served only very briefly or on solitary missions. Others, such as the now well-documented Culper Ring of Long Island, worked for years gathering intelligence for the Continental Army's commander, General Washington.

But each one, from field agents to spymasters, represents part of a larger framework of American espionage. The risks of clandestine operations were high. They moved in a world of mysteries and aliases. They peeked around darkened street corners, listened intently to gossip, secretly read mail, bought British officers drinks in taverns and coffeehouses, inveigled themselves into the ranks of the enemy, hid in haystacks and closets and beneath windowsills, and constantly gathered any scrap of information that might be of service to the American cause.

The British had spies, too, of course. Many of them were aristocratic Redcoat officers and gentlemen or American Loyalist officials. But most espionage operatives for the revolutionary cause were a more mixed bag. They included Quaker midwives, butchers, and bakers; everyone from farm girls and whalers to ministers and militiamen. There were rascals and privateers among their number, as well as slaves and tavern keepers, artisans and mechanics, printers and coffeehouse workers. They were shot at, tortured, kidnapped, mugged, imprisoned, hanged. Each of them took risks and gambled lives and livelihoods, all in the name of a revolution they could never be certain would be won until the absolute end.

Presiding over much of this secret service was a gentleman farmer from Virginia. George Washington, the Founding Father later immortalized as the man who couldn't tell a lie, told his share of tall tales, engaged in disinformation and subterfuge, and encouraged others to do the same.

The story of this curious collection of agents and double agents is one filled with intrigue, close calls, and derring-do, even as much of the work of spying remained out of sight, in the shadows. In this book, I hope to push back the shadows and bring the stories of these brave revolutionary spies to light. Some have remained in the darkened corners of American history for far too long.

～ ※ ～

CHAPTER ONE

George Washington: Spy Apprentice

FRONTIER FLASHPOINTS

t was not surprising that two of Europe's most expansive colonial powers, England and France, would clash in the Ohio Valley's primeval forest halfway through the eighteenth century. The Ohio Valley—a region that included western Pennsylvania and the future states of Ohio, Indiana, Illinois, and Kentucky—was considered a land worth fighting for, a hunter's paradise over which indigenous American nations had fought for thousands of years.

Both the French and English had been extending their reach into this region, largely through trade—the most common European tactic for convincing Native Americans to accept their presence. Indians not particularly enamored with having land-hungry white farmers as neighbors often longed to maintain connections with colonial traders, who bore a highly mobile inventory of calico, alcohol, and metal (including cooking kettles, butcher knives—and guns).

The English began increasing their trade into the Ohio Valley during the 1740s. Such encroachments forced the French to make countermoves designed to block the advance of their longstanding opponents, which ultimately led to a rapidly developing and increasingly confrontational cold war in the region.

In 1749 the French took a bold step. That year, a flotilla of thirty-three French canoes moved quietly along the valley's tangle of rivers and backwater streams. It stopped at a half-dozen watery confluences and buried lead plates engraved with a jingoistic claim of ownership. Effectively, the French were marking their territory (see "Buried Plates," following page).

Over the next few years, the frontier representatives of the British and French empires vied for the best treaties they could get out of Indians willing to bargain away their sometimes tenuous land claims. Both sides dumped trade goods in the laps of tribal chiefs and plied them with vast quantities of alcohol. Then, in 1753, the French upped the ante.

That year, new French outposts were built in the western portion of modern-day Pennsylvania. These forts—named Presque Isle, LeBoeuf, and Machault—were each erected with a combination of strategic and geopolitical presence in mind, intended to control the section of frontier that stretched from the southern banks of Lake Erie and south through the Pennsylvania forests.

With these three forts, the French created a daring national presence, forming the first links in a chain of western military outposts that would eventually connect to the region's defensive anchor—a massive fort at the most strategic location in the entire region, at what is now Pittsburgh. Established in 1754, Fort Duquesne would dominate the confluence of three rivers—a site known as the Forks of the Ohio—including the Allegheny to the north, the Monongahela to the south, and the mother of eastern frontier rivers, the Ohio. And it was the French occupation of this location that precipitated a showdown between the colonists of King George II and those of King Louis XV.

Buried Plates

Once the French decided to solidify their claim to the Ohio Country following the Treaty of Aix-la-Chapelle (1748), they began constructing a string of forts across the region. However, they also sought to confirm their claim in an unusual way, one that was more symbolic than substantive: they buried a series of lead plates in the ground.

In the spring of 1749, the Marquis de la Galissoniere, governor of New France, sent Captain Pierre-Joseph Celoron de Blainville into the Ohio Country, along with more than two hundred troops and a Jesuit chaplain. The party paddled up the St. Lawrence River in thirty-three birch-bark canoes, then portaged around Niagara Falls to Lake Erie. Reaching the confluence of Conewango Creek and the Allegheny River (today's Warren, Pennsylvania), Celoron first nailed a metal panel displaying King Louis XV's coat of arms to a tree, and then, beneath its branches, he buried the first of six lead plates, each to serve, according to their inscription, as "a monument of renewal of possession which we have taken of the said river Ohio, and of all those [rivers] which fall into it, and of all those territories on both sides as far as the source of the said rivers."[1]

Throughout the summer, Celoron and his men buried these plates at key locations in the Ohio Country, including the site that would one day be Fort Venango. But as the French party moved through the region, they continually encountered a decided English presence, including trading posts and settlers' cabins, as well as Indian villages that traded with the English. Lead plates aside, the Ohio Country was anything but a French stronghold. This was English country.

A Scot Weighs In

With the sound of French axes ringing through the wilderness, information about their movements could not help but reach one of King George's men. Since Virginia claimed much of the Ohio Valley at the time, and the colony's governor resided in England as an absentee politician, the real political force in the region was Lieutenant Governor Robert Dinwiddie. A Scotsman who weighed in at over three hundred pounds, Dinwiddie was alarmed by the deft moves of the French into the Ohio Country. At that time Virginia extended over a much larger area than it does today, so these new French forts now stood virtually at the colony's back door. With the erection of each new *en pile* wall, Dinwiddie responded with hand-wringing alarms. In May 1753, he zipped off a communication to the governor of Pennsylvania, James Hamilton, warning about "the French designs to settle the Ohio" and adding, "I have sometime ago heard of their robberies & murders."[2]

Dinwiddie wasted little time making certain his voice was heard—all the way to the seat of English power itself, Whitehall. By October 1753, his call for action received a response. The king's instruction was clear: if the French were building forts, so must the English.

The Virginia leader was to order the construction of competing fortifications. But first, he was to send a man into the wilderness to reconnoiter the region. This designated agent was to spy out the Ohio Valley and verify whether the French were actually fortifying it. He was also supposed to make contact with them and deliver a political ultimatum—that they leave the region and abandon the forts they had constructed on what the British considered to be George II's lands. In the words of the king, the agent was to "require of them [the French] peaceably to depart." In case the French chose to rebuff England's emissary to Lake Erie, the king advised that "we do strictly command and charge you to drive them out by force of arms."[3]

~ ※ ~

An Imbalance of Population

By the mid-eighteenth century, the French and the British were sharp rivals, both wielding significant power on the European continent and abroad in far-flung colonies. As the two powers began to vie for control of the Ohio Country, the British appeared to hold a distinct advantage: population. The Canadian census of 1754 reveals that New France was home to just 55,000 white inhabitants, nearly all of them French. (Another 25,000 lived in Acadia and Louisiana.) Compare this to the thirteen English colonies hugging the Atlantic Coast, where the population included a burgeoning 1.16 million white inhabitants, as well as 300,000 black slaves. Not all of the whites living in the English colonies were English, however. Some were French, including Huguenots (Protestants), who immigrated to various British colonies, since French laws only allowed French Catholics to migrate to New France.

AN AMBITIOUS YOUNG MAN

The agent sent to spy on the French was an ambitious twenty-one-year-old neophyte named George Washington. A Virginia militia officer whose family came from second-tier Virginia aristocracy, Washington had some frontier experience. He had previously worked as a surveyor's assistant in western Virginia on behalf of his neighbors, the Fairfax family. Once young Washington had experienced the challenges and excitement of the frontier, one that included crossing paths with an Indian war party bearing a scalp from a recent fight with a neighboring tribe, he was smitten. He was taken with its far-flung landscapes and its potential, both for his colony and himself.

Yet Dinwiddie's selection of Washington was curious. True, the young man had his positive traits—he was eager for the responsibility, had a sense of the logistics required for such a wilderness expedition, was a military man, and seemed a bit more mature than his years. But even young George was surprised to be named to the post. He wrote: "It was deemed by some an extraordinary circumstance that so young and inexperienced a person should have been employed on a negotiation with which subjects of the greatest importance were involved."[4]

OPPOSITE:
Robert Dinwiddie, the veteran British colonial administrator and lieutenant governor of Virginia who sent George Washington on his intelligence mission into French territory.

But, doubts aside, Washington was chosen, and he became Governor Dinwiddie's field agent. The young Virginian showed up in Williamsburg on October 26, 1753, and called at the Governor's Palace, which handsomely commanded the town green east of Gloucester Street. The following day, Dinwiddie informed the King's Council that Washington, the militia major currently serving as adjutant of the Northern Neck military district, "had offered himself to go properly commissioned to the commandant of the French forces."[5] The council's approval was immediate (after all, there were no other willing candidates). Dinwiddie waited a couple of weeks before informing the House of Burgesses, the legislative body of Virginia, of his plans, by which point Washington was already on his way.

On October 30, as Dinwiddie faced Washington across a green baize–covered table in the Governor's Palace, his instructions to the young major were clear. He spoke directly about "a body of French forces being assembled in an hostile manner" in the Ohio Country, Virginia's own backyard.[6] Dinwiddie wanted Washington to find the French and present his papers as though he were an emissary traveling through French-occupied lands under diplomatic cover. He was to be polite, but was expected to determine the French justification for trespassing on British soil. Beyond these orders, Washington was also ordered to seek out other intelligence and make mental note of all he saw: What were the French forts like? Where were they located? How many men were garrisoned in each? What were the French up to, ultimately?

Washington understood this element of his mission and willingly accepted it, dangerous though it was. Diplomatic "immunity" did not guarantee his safety (see "Right of Embassy," page 34). After all, the French had already taken British subjects in the region hostage. Nor was that the only concern. If the wrong tribe of Indian warriors encountered Washington, they would have no understanding of his mission or diplomatic status—nor would they care.

A Tenuous French Claim

As the French began building forts in the Ohio Country during the early 1750s, these military outposts were intended to solidify—literally, with boots on the ground—a claim to the region that extended back to the days of seventeenth-century French exploration. But a more direct claim arose after the French and English signed the Treaty of Aix-la-Chapelle in 1748, which followed the War of the Austrian Succession (the portion of that conflict that included fighting in North America was referred to by the British as King George's War). Under that treaty, French dominance was recognized over a vast, crescent-shaped swath of North America extending from the western Great Lakes to the mouth of the Mississippi River. In between, French lands included the long-standing trade and portage routes, as well as corridors that ran through what is now Illinois and Indiana.

But a closer look at the map reveals a gap in the geographical reach of France. East of Indiana's Wabash River and extending further on to the Appalachian Mountains, the French claim ended. These lands, which stretched out for hundreds of miles in every direction from the Forks of the Ohio (today's Pittsburgh), were not included under the Aix-la-Chapelle Treaty. It is no wonder then that when English colonists began to trickle into the region after the war, the migration set off alarm bells in Paris and Montreal, leading to a French counter-response—the building of forts in the Ohio Country.

INTO THE WOODS

As Washington left the familiar streets of Williamsburg for the unknown world of the frontier, he went with absolutely no diplomatic experience under his belt. He didn't even speak French. But the following months provided the young Virginian with training he could not at the time appreciate. In fact, Dinwiddie considered Washington more than a simple courier, a carrier of diplomatic dispatches. He expected him to serve as an intelligence-gathering agent—in effect, a spy.

With diplomatic papers tucked safely away in an oilskin packet, Washington departed on October 31 for Fredericksburg. There, in need of a French translator, he sought out an acquaintance, a Dutchman named

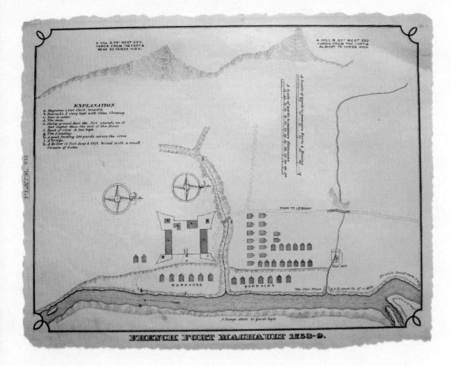

FRENCH FORT MACHAULT 1758-9.

Jacob van Braam. Just three years older than Washington, van Braam had only arrived in the colonies the previous year. Together, they continued on to Winchester, where they gathered packhorses. After two weeks on the trail, they reached Wills Creek (today's Cumberland, Maryland). By this point, civilization was behind them, and the wilderness closed in from every direction.

There at Wills Creek the young major made contact with someone who knew much more about the frontier than himself, a man named Christopher Gist, who would serve as a guide for the mission. No better man could have been selected. Gist was a veteran of the Shenandoah Valley and the west beyond. He had explored and hunted in the Ohio Country since the early 1750s, and had been employed by the Ohio Company as a surveyor. Washington wrote of Gist: "He has had extensive dealings with the Indians, is in great esteem among them; well acquainted with their manners and customs, is indefatigable, and patient: most excellent qualities indeed, where Indians are concerned!"[7] Washington gave Gist a written request from Dinwiddie to join the party, and the seasoned frontiersman eagerly agreed. Along with van Braam and Gist, four others signed on, including three packers and one John Davison, who could speak a variety of Indian tongues.

During the weeks that followed, Washington and his six men met various difficulties. From Wills Creek, the elevation increased by three thousand feet, as the party passed from rivers that flowed to the east to those that ran to the west. Along this leg of the trek, they reached the remote cabin of English trader John Frazier, near where Turtle Creek flowed into the Monongahela River. Frazier's cabin served, in effect, as a frontier "listening post"[8] through which intelligence regularly passed. He had stories to tell. Frazier cautioned Washington to watch his step,, both figuratively and literally. First, he explained that three Indian nations in Washington's path had decided to side with the French if a future conflict were to unfold. Second, the Monongahela was at high water and dangerous—"quite impassable" Washington noted in his journal.[9]

From Frazier's cabin, Washington and his cohorts followed the Monongahela River toward the Forks of the Ohio. Due to "the excessive rains and a vast quantity of snow which had fallen,"[10] progress was slow. It took a full week to travel approximately seventy-five miles. The weather was typical for late November in western Pennsylvania, with snow covering the uneven and heavily forested landscape. Washington remarked that the men were making their way through "a most inclement season."[11]

But the intrepid Washington proceeded undaunted. Anxious to reach the Forks, the young major left his party with the horses and took off in a canoe, scooting along with the current to the confluence of the region's three great rivers: the Allegheny, the Monongahela, and the Ohio. Dinwiddie wanted to build a competing fort here, and Washington immediately understood the Forks' value. He spent two days reconnoitering the important locale and determining where best to situate the fort. As strategic as the site was, however, his true mission lay ahead along the banks of another body of water, French Creek.

A Hunter's Paradise

The Native Americans who inhabited the northeastern region of what is now the United States relied heavily on hunting as one of their primary food sources. When Europeans arrived, they eagerly traded animal furs and hides for European goods, including cloth and metal items.

Fortunately for hunters, the region teemed with animals. Today, it is difficult to imagine just how crowded North America's eastern forests were with wildlife. Experts estimate that 10 square miles of forest, in the mid-eighteenth century, was home to approximately five black bears, two or three mountain lions (a common term at the time was a "catamount"), a pair of gray wolves, two elk, nearly three dozen red foxes, a couple hundred turkeys, four hundred deer, and a whopping twenty thousand squirrels. As far as trade with Europeans went, many of these animals were money on the hoof.[12]

So common was the frontier trade between English traders and native hunters that a single deerskin gained a monetary value equal to a Spanish dollar. This gave rise to a term still used today for the American dollar—a buck.

INTELLIGENCE GATHERING
AT LOGSTOWN

Within a few days of Washington's proceeding ahead of his men, the main party caught up with their commander. Washington and his men soon reached Logstown, an unimpressive collection of Indian dwellings, including Iroquois longhouses and a smaller scattering of Algonquin huts. Dinwiddie's instructions were for Washington to find leaders of the British Empire's tentative allies, the Iroquois, and request of them "a sufficient number of their warriors to be your safeguard."[13]

At Logstown, Washington caught an intelligence break. On November 25, four Frenchmen arrived from the west. According to Washington, they had "deserted from a company at the Cuscusas [Kaskaskia in the Illinois Country]."[14] The French deserters had allegedly broken off from an original detachment of one hundred soldiers who had left New Orleans—the southernmost French outpost in North America—with orders to aid the French expansion in the Ohio Valley. (It is unknown whether there actually had been a party of one hundred Frenchmen or if the story was only meant to intimidate Washington or the local Indians.) These four had abandoned their comrades to seek their fortune elsewhere, and landed at Logstown, right in the backyard of the British. From them, Washington learned about France's outposts along the Mississippi and Ohio.

The following day, another visitor arrived. It was a man Washington had been intent on meeting. Tanaghrisson, also known to the local British as the Half-King, was a Mingo leader around fifty-five years old. (The name "Half-King" came from his being not a full chief, but a representative of the Mingo, an Indian nation dominated by the Onondaga Council of the Six Nations of the Iroquois.)

From the Indians with whom he parleyed, including Tanaghrisson and Shingas, the leader of the Unalachtigo band of the Delaware, Washington discovered that the French had a fort on Lake Erie (Presque Isle) connected by a wilderness path to the outpost along French Creek (LeBoeuf). He was even handed diagrams of the layouts of both military posts.

The Indians dropped another important piece of information in Washington's ear—that the French were intent on going to war with the British if necessary, in order to keep control of the Ohio Country. Washington had accomplished a coup as a frontier field agent—he had found native allies. Tanaghrisson, Shingas, and a pair of additional sachems (native leaders) named Jeskakake and White Thunder were now among his party.

By engaging native leaders in his fight against the French, Washington was following standard operating procedure for the British Empire, which rarely had enough soldiers to sufficiently guard its far-flung provinces and often needed the help of local allies and surrogates. In fact, the U.S. military has continued this practice in its recent campaigns in Iraq and Afghanistan, befriending local tribesmen and clan leaders to establish intelligence networks, just as Washington did.

$\sim$ ※ $\sim$

Tanaghrisson's Early Life

As Washington trekked off toward the French forts in the late fall of 1753, he would soon encounter a key Indian representative in the region, a Mingo named Tanaghrisson, whom the English referred to as the "Half-King." He was his mid-fifties when Washington met him, and little is known with certainty concerning his early years. He may have hailed originally from the region of modern-day Buffalo, New York, born into the Catawba tribe, but later adopted into the Seneca nation after being captured by the French.

From his youth, Tanaghrisson hated the French and claimed in his later years that they had captured his father, whom they boiled and ate. By the time Washington was introduced to him, Tanaghrisson was already poised to play a pivotal role in the events leading to the French and Indian War.

Early English and French Claims

More than a century would pass between October 12, 1492—when Christopher Columbus's ships first dropped anchor off the shores of a small island in the Bahamas—and the first tentative colonizing efforts of the French and English in North America. While both European powers dispatched ship captains to the East Coast during the half-century following Columbus's first New World voyage, neither put down roots.

Then, during the early years of the seventeenth century, French and English colonists arrived. In 1604, a French colonizing company that included Samuel de Champlain—who would eventually be recognized as the "Father of New France"—threw up a trading post on the St. Croix River (between Maine and the maritime province of New Brunswick). Following the harsh winter of 1604–05, the post was moved to more hospitable environs along the coast of Nova Scotia, only to be abandoned by 1607. That same year, three English ships arrived at the mouth of Chesapeake Bay, filled with 144 male colonists who would soon found Jamestown. In the meantime, Champlain and a small group of French colonists and traders sailed up the St. Lawrence and built a trading post at a site the Indians called Kebec (now Quebec).

LEFT:
An etching of the French explorer Samuel de Champlain, from the book A Popular History of France from the Earliest Times.

A Paper Ultimatum

Washington and his men left Logstown on November 30. After five days of travel, Fort Venango loomed into view. Its white flag bore the French imperial insignia: a trio of fleur-de-lis. Nearby, the waters of French Creek joined the greater course of the Allegheny. As Washington's native allies headed off into the neighboring Delaware village, the Virginians were greeted by three officers. One of them, who looked more like an Indian than his comrades, turned out to be the fort's commander, Captain Daniel Joncaire.

Washington presented himself and his papers to Joncaire, but was told he would need to continue on to the next military post at Fort LeBoeuf, the most important of the French forts in the region. That was where he needed to submit his demands. But before leaving, he and his men were invited to spend the night and enjoy an evening of food and French wine.

What happened next would reveal just how adaptive the twenty-one-year-old George Washington was to the constantly shifting circumstances of his mission. He took advantage of the flow of alcohol while sharing a meal with his French adversaries. In the pages of his journal, the scene is set. Washington's wine glass was filled repeatedly, but he seems to have consumed but a trifle, even as his French hosts "dosed themselves pretty plentifully with it."[15] George Washington, serving in effect as a British secret agent, listened eagerly and registered all the details. It was an intelligence-gathering night to remember.

In his book, *Spies, Patriots, and Traitors: American Intelligence in the Revolutionary War*, former CIA operative Kenneth Daigler notes the intelligence technique so keenly utilized that evening by young Washington. Called elicitation, it is one of a spy's most important skills. The practice involves cunning and subterfuge, and requires a significant degree of subtlety. Elicitation happens when two or more people are engaging in a way that seems natural and even mutually advantageous to both participants, but one party is actively trying to gather important information from the other. Alcohol is often used to stimulate conversation, but the key for the spy is not to imbibe too much of the intoxicant. Perhaps Washington's age helped lower the French officers' guard. Perhaps they saw before them an unintimidating boy courier sent on a man's mission. After all, the young

Virginian was even ignorant of their language. They ate, they drank, they talked too much. But Washington, once he found himself behind closed doors, copied their words down in his journal.

Washington learned that evening that Dinwiddie's concerns were well founded. The French had constructed Venango as a forward operating base to stave off English settlers, traders, and land agents. He also learned the locations of the other French military outposts to the north and their links to Canada and Montreal specifically. French Canadians could deliver supplies into the Ohio Country by leapfrogging from one fort to another. The young major's mission was accomplishing more than Dinwiddie might have expected.

～ ※ ～

STRIKING OUT FOR HOME

Once Washington was informed that he would need to deliver Dinwiddie's missive to the commandant at Fort LeBoeuf, which lay another sixty miles up the icy waters of French Creek, he was ready to continue on in his mission.

The next morning Half-King presented Joncaire with a special wampum belt he had been carrying for several months, a gesture that meant their alliance was severed (see "Native American Wampum Belts," page 21). This belt was a token he and the other sachems had received from the French during an earlier council, symbolically binding them in allegiance to the Canadians. But Half-King and his associates had changed their minds. The French had promised not to encroach on Indian lands, and now they had broken that promise. That morning Tanaghrisson delivered a speech he had practiced many times, Washington noted. He handed the belt to Joncaire, who refused to accept it. Joncaire explained that such a serious token of separation would need to be delivered to his superior, the same commandant Washington was planning to meet at Fort LeBoeuf. For the moment, the Virginia major could breathe a sigh of relief. He and Half-King would be proceeding to their destination not at cross-purposes, but as allies.

On December 7, Washington and his party left Venango and struck out for LeBoeuf, escorted by a party of four French soldiers. The soldiers

The Six Nations of the Iroquois

Even as the French and British prepared to contest one another for control of the Ohio Country, this area was home to a third group of inhabitants—the Indians. Although dozens of Indian nations or tribes lived in the Ohio region, the dominant group was a confederacy of tribes, a union of six nations—the Mohawk, Seneca, Oneida, Onondaga, Cayuga, and the Tuscarora. They held land that extended from the Upper Hudson River west to the banks of the Ohio River. By the 1750s, the Iroquois Confederacy was so powerful it was able to dominate other tribes, including the Mingo, Shawnee, and Delaware—the so-called "Ohio Indians"—who had encroached on Iroquois lands, as ever-increasing white settlements pushed them farther west.

ABOVE:

An unidentified chief of the Six Nations of the Iroquois, painted by John Trumbull, c. 1792.

had arrived at Venango on December 7 under the command of an officer named Michel Pepin. Again, the weather remained uncooperative, as the group slogged along for nearly five days through "excessive rains, snows, and bad traveling through many mires and swamps."[16] A horse went missing along the way. As the sun began to sink along the treetops toward evening on December 11, with Washington and his men having trudged a full fifteen miles since sunrise, Fort LeBoeuf finally came into view. Snow was swirling in from the north, a full storm in the making. Van Braam announced their arrival to the garrison's commandant. As Gist wrote, the Dutchman "gave the commandant notice of our being over the creek; upon which he sent several officers to conduct us to the fort, and they received us with a great deal of complaisance."[17]

Soon Washington and his party were the recipients of a new round of French hospitality, even if the cordiality seemed strained. Commandant Jacques Legardeur de Saint-Pierre was a French marine officer in his early fifties, a veteran of the frontier. (Washington described him as "an elderly gentleman" who reflected "much the air of a soldier.")[18] He had commanded similar military posts stretching across North America, including Acadia in Eastern Canada; Fort Assumption along the banks of the Mississippi at present-day Memphis; and Fort La Jonquiere, where the Canadian prairie city of Winnipeg would one day stand. He had battle experience, including several clashes with Native Americans. To this seasoned French veteran, the young courier from Virginia probably seemed out of his element.

In a sense, Legardeur proved somewhat cavalier concerning the young major in his midst. Washington presented himself to the commandant early on the morning of December 12 and went straight to the business at hand, delivering Dinwiddie's letter. (It may have been sent by the Virginia lieutenant governor but it carried the full weight of the British Crown.) Legardeur ordered a captain who spoke passable English to translate the document. In the meantime, he informed Washington, through his translator van Braam, that he was free to have a look around. This was Legardeur's opportunity to impress his visitors with the "shock and awe" of the French military occupying the Ohio Country. Likely such license was intended to discourage Washington, and thereby the British.

If the move was meant to be tactical—even strategic—in giving Washington unfettered access to the fort, he was providing the Virginia militia officer with an invaluable opportunity to, again, collect intelligence, only this time firsthand. Washington took his opportunity as it was offered, walking around the French facility, taking in the length and breadth, "the dimensions of the fort, & making what observations I cou'd."[19] He could not fail but be impressed with what he saw. He made mental notes of the fort's situation, its layout, measuring in his mind the size of its buildings, estimating the bore of its cannon. Although he could not pinpoint the number of men, he noted the presence of "an hundred exclusive of officers."[20]

As he calculated within the walls of the fort, he sent others down to the river to count the number of canoes, the modern-day equivalent of taking inventory of a garrison's trucks, Humvees, and other vehicles. An exact number made its way into his journal, including "50 of birch bark, & 170 of pine."[21] In addition, Washington's men saw a construction yard where many other canoes were being built to add to the French flotilla.

Native American Wampum Belts

As Washington delivered Dinwiddie's message to the French, so too would Mingo leader Half-King deliver his own message, even if both were quite different in form. Tanaghrisson's message consisted of a wampum belt, which carried a potent political message.

Such belts were fashioned by the Iroquois from beads made of two different clamshells—one white, the other dark purple. Wampum belts came to have a value of their own in trade with fellow tribes, who offered animal furs, flint, and other items in exchange. Early on, wampum represented a form of communication, a tangible means of recording agreements between negotiating parties. They were used in ceremonies and council meetings. Traditional stories credit the legendary Hiawatha with making the first wampum necklaces as symbols of peace and healing between warring Indian nations.

Tanaghrisson sought to return a wampum belt to the French commandant, Captain Joncaire, at Fort Venango, when Half-King and Washington arrived in November 1753. Joncaire refused to accept it. Tanaghrisson would finally hand it over to the commandant at Fort LeBoeuf. By doing so, he was renouncing the earlier agreement he had made with the French. His motivation? First, the French had violated their promises of leaving the Ohio Indians free of European influence. Second, he was by that time intent on pushing the French and British into a military showdown over the Ohio Country, believing such an event might make an opportunity for him to advance in power as a native representative.

ABOVE:
An example of a wampum belt.

Washington interpreted the numbers for what they clearly represented: the French were making plans for something big. Such a large number of canoes meant the French would soon have the means for rapid deployment.

Following a conference with his officers, Legardeur gave Washington his reply to Dinwiddie's demands. The commandant informed Washington that the entire Ohio Valley belonged to the French and that the English not only had no right to settle there, but no right to engage in trade in the region. Legardeur then handed Washington a letter for Dinwiddie, stating firmly that the French intended to remain in the region.

Tanghrisson's December 14 meeting with Legardeur did not go as he had planned, either. The Indian leader attempted to hand the symbolic allegiance wampum to Legardeur, but the French leader had refused to receive it, promising instead continuing friendship, peace, and more French trade goods. All this was meant to represent his good faith and intentions. Tanaghrisson was so swayed by Legardeur, Washington had a difficult time convincing him and his fellow sachems to leave with him. After his party's chilly farewell to Commandant Legardeur, Washington strategically had the Indians take the lead, in part, to keep an eye on them. The return trip back to Williamsburg proved more treacherous and fraught than the trek into the Ohio Country. The party was nearly swept away by strong river currents. When the Indians killed three bears, they refused to continue the journey until all the meat was consumed. Although the snow stopped falling, this meant the water level in the river did as well, making it difficult for the party's canoes—the French had loaned them a pair—to proceed. Washington made a difficult decision—he would continue without Half-King, the sachems, and his Indian guides.

As Washington's canoes scraped along the river's rocky bottom, progress on the trail was slow for him and his remaining party. Ice had begun to spread out from the river's banks to the middle current. Three days of struggle passed, and then the ice fanned out from shore to shore forming a great impassable sheet. For Washington, the only moment of levity came when four canoes filled with Frenchmen and a cargo of alcohol steered past his party, only to overturn, resulting, as Gist described later, in "the brandy and wine floating in the creek."[22]

↝ ※ ↜

"ARE YOU SHOT?"

A week after leaving LeBoeuf, Washington returned to Venango. (By then, the Indians had caught up.) After three days at the fort, they set out for the long journey back to Virginia. Again, the Indians were reluctant to continue with the Virginians, since this portion of the trip held no importance for them. Washington decided to depart anyway, leaving them in the hands of Joncaire and his promises of wonderful gifts and future friendship.

As the party continued, the punishing elements continued to press in on them. Though he had worn his uniform in the presence of his French military hosts, Washington now turned to dressing like an Indian, replete with Indian walking dress, deerskin leggings, a leather over-jacket that extended to his knees and cinched at the waist with a leather belt, and a pair of moccasins.

The cold slowed their progress even further. Frostbite attacked some of the men, taking fingers and toes. By Christmas, the horses had given out, and Washington made a desperate decision to abandon the horses, leaving them with the bulk of the party, with instructions for the packers to get the horses to Wills Creek when they were able. The Virginia major now intended to press ahead on foot with Gist, both men laden with backpacks. The two comrades did manage to make better progress alone, putting nearly twenty miles behind them their first day on the trail.

But a new danger lay ahead. Just two days after abandoning their main party, Washington and Gist were hailed by an Indian warrior, one Gist believed he had seen at Fort Venango. He offered to guide them along their way, even proposing to carry Washington's pack. Gist was suspicious from the moment he laid eyes on the mysterious man, and his instincts proved correct. On the claim that he was leading them to his cabin just up the train, the Indian took the two farther north than Gist thought reasonable, and the men quarreled.

Then, suddenly, the brave bolted ahead, only to wheel around at a distance of fewer than fifty feet, brought his rifle to his shoulder, took aim, and fired in Washington's direction.

Both Washington and Gist turned to one another as the man ran ahead and hid behind a white oak tree, working feverishly to reload his gun.

"Town Taker": A Washington Family Nickname

As young Washington and the Mingo leader, Tanaghrisson, shared exploits during their trek across western Pennsylvania in the winter of 1753–54, Half-King gave the young Virginian a nickname of sorts—"Town Taker." Since Washington had not yet captured any villages during his frontier travels, the name seemed odd to him. Not until years later did he understand why the Indians used the strange moniker. A century earlier, they had given this name to Washington's great-grandfather, John, who had settled lands previously held by Native Americans. That the Indians identified the two men as distant relatives likely reflects their sense of community and shared oral traditions.

"Are you shot?" cried Washington to his companion.[23]

Gist answered he was not.

Both men rushed forward and seized the would-be assassin before he could fire another shot.

Although Gist was ready to kill the assailant, Washington could not allow it. He had never seen a man die violently, much less by his own hand. Suggesting to their captive that his shot might have been accidental, they freed him and told him to go ahead to his cabin where they would join him soon. As their attacker ran ahead, Washington and Gist waited until he was out of sight and then escaped themselves.

The final leg of their journey went tolerably better, as Washington bartered a coat and a bottle of rum with Delaware Indians, all as a continuing part of his frontier diplomacy to encourage Indian allies. As 1754 opened, the two frontiersmen were heartened to come upon a party of fellow Virginians transporting building supplies intended for the construction of a fort at the Forks of the Ohio. A week later, they reached Wills Creek and floated down the Potomac nearly to Washington's home, stopping by neighbor William Fairfax's house, Belvoir, for a day of rest before arriving back in Williamsburg on January 16 where Washington reported to Lieutenant Governor Dinwiddie. In Washington's words, he sat down with "his honour the governor with the letter I had brought from the French commandant."[24] He had much to tell.

REPORTING TO DINWIDDIE

After seventy-eight days Washington had accomplished his mission, He wasted no time in writing out the details in a report of nearly seventy-five hundred words, most likely because Dinwiddie had given him only one day to write it. The details of his report reveal a young man who believed he had succeeded despite great difficulties. For more than two months, Washington and his small band of brothers had trekked from Williamsburg nearly to Lake Erie and back again through hundreds of miles of challenging frontier terrain and meteorological menaces. Most importantly, he had delivered the ultimatum to the commandant at Fort LeBoeuf—the whole purpose for which his mission had been organized, even if the French response had not been one the Virginians had hoped for.

Writing with a boyish braggadocio, Washington recounted that he and his group found their way back to Virginia "after as fatiguing a journey as it is possible to conceive, rendered so by excessive bad weather: From the first day of December 'till the 15th, there was but one day, but what it rain'd or sno'd incessantly & throughout the whole journey we met with nothing but one continued series of cold wet weather."[25]

Washington had carried out his mission as an agent of the common-wealth and the Crown. He had been shot at by a gunman possibly hired by the French. He had met with tribesmen representing numerous different allegiances and had convinced them, at least for the moment, to support his mission in the field. From these native contacts, he had gained what modern espionage agents term "strategic intelligence," including the extent of the enemy's military presence across a wide area of disputed territory.

Perhaps more impressively, he had entered the enemy's camp and gained intelligence through deft social interaction. As French tongues wagged under the influence of alcohol, Washington kept his cool. Under the guise of delivering a political message—a practice known today as "cover for access"—he obtained valuable information for the British. The letter delivery gave him an opportunity to see the French fortifica-tions, take mental measurements of everything he saw, and collate it as intelligence data—the number, size, and location of forts; the number of available troops; the number and location of canoes; the size and field implementation of cannon. In spy parlance, Washington had engaged

Samuel de Champlain's illustration of a fight on the shore of Lake Champlain in July 1609. His Iroquois and Huron allies are at left, and a larger force of Mohawks are at right, with Champlain himself in the center firing the harquebus that decided the skirmish in his favor.

in "casing," the observation of a target to determine the best means of responding and meeting the challenge it represents without drawing undue suspicion.

As he cased the French forts, Washington committed the relevant numbers, facts, and figures to memory until he could safely write them down. Washington gathered much of his intelligence by witnessing it with his own eyes. As such, he served as a "collection agent," one who gains access to intelligence through secondary activities, such as social or political interaction. His report provided Dinwiddie with "actionable intelligence," information that could be used to counter an adversary's intended actions, such as France's plan to completely dominate the Ohio Country. Washington accomplished this with no intelligence training or field experience, and without the ability to even speak the language.

French and Indian Depredations

One concern Virginians had regarding the expansion of the French into the Ohio Valley was the security risk posed to the English living in the region. In the early summer of 1752, a raiding party of close to 250, including a small core of French Canadian militiamen, plus dozens of Ottawa and Ojibway warriors, had descended on the English trading post at Pickawillany, armed with muskets, broadswords, tomahawks, and razor-sharp scalping knives. Their mixed-blood leader, born of an Ottawa mother and a French father named Charles-Michel Mouet de Langlade, like Washington was only in his early twenties.

The victims, including local Miami women, were brutally killed or taken hostage. The aged Miami chief, Memeskia, was not only killed and scalped, but sliced up into parts that were thrown into a cooking pot, boiled, and then consumed by his killers. An English trader was tomahawked and scalped, then his chest was sliced open, his heart removed, then passed around with each victorious Indian warrior eating a piece of the warm, bloody organ. Pickawillany represented just the sort of dark and bloody frontier depredations Dinwiddie and others feared would become more common if the French were not stopped.

The conclusion of Washington's report revealed his hopes that he had done well in Dinwiddie's name: "the most remarkable occurrences that happen'd to me. I hope it will be sufficient to satisfy your Honour with my proceedings; for that was my aim in undertaking the journey: & chief study throughout the prosecution of it."[26]

Washington's efforts would not go unnoticed, despite the fact that most secret agents remain out of the spotlight. Instead, his lengthy, handwritten report was actually printed in newspapers throughout the colonies. Soon the name "Washington" became well known. At the news of Washington's success the men of the House of Burgesses were ecstatic, voting him a fifty-pound stipend in support of "his journey to the Ohio."[27] Further, the major's report would help convince the Burgesses to open up the colony's coffers for defense funds to counteract the French. This was only the beginning of Washington's exploits in the Ohio Country.

⚮ ※ ⚮

A New Mission

Even as Washington appeared to have accomplished his mission, the French response did not prove to Dinwiddie's liking. Dinwiddie then sent Washington back into the region on a second mission, one more military than diplomatic. In early April 1754, Washington—now a newly minted lieutenant colonel—left for the west again, this time with 150 men under his command, rather than a half dozen. They comprised two "companies of foot," meaning they were infantrymen, including 120 privates, a variety of officers, a drummer, a surgeon, and a "Swedish gentleman, who was a volunteer."[28]

Washington reached a site called Great Meadows in south-west Pennsylvania and built a small, unimpressive post he called Fort Necessity. In the meantime, he was joined, once again, by Tanaghrisson, who informed him that the French were already building a fort at the Forks of the Ohio (what would become Fort Duquesne). Then, in late May, after receiving intelligence from the Indians that a small party of French soldiers were encamped nearby, he and about forty of his men, plus Half-King and a dozen Mingos, stole a night march on the French party, located approximately ten miles from Fort Necessity. They attacked at dawn, catching many without even their shoes on as they were preparing their breakfast.

This was Washington's first taste of battle, even if it was only a small skirmish in a heavily wooded thicket of trees. The undergrowth in the shadow of rock outcroppings provided the Virginia militia officer and his men, including their Indian allies, with cover and the advantage of the high ground. The French party numbered a few dozen, with approximately one in three killed, which the Indians scalped, then mutilated. Others were taken prisoner and a few managed to escape. Among the dead was their commander, Joseph Coulon de Villiers, Sieur de Jumonville, a thirty-six-year-old French marine officer. Tanaghrisson personally killed Ensign Jumonville, a calculated move that shocked Washington, who was still a newcomer to this kind of wilderness warfare. Although Jumonville had surrendered and was on his knees among the other French prisoners, the Half-King strode forward and killed him with a tomahawk blow to the head.

Immediately, Washington needed to justify what had happened to his superiors, as he was ostensibly the current commander of the Indians. He discovered that the Jumonville party was similar in purpose and intent to his first mission. Jumonville was en route to Dinwiddie to tell him what he already knew—the French were not going to abandon the Ohio Country. Likewise, his prisoners also confirmed that their mission, or "cover to access," was to collect military intelligence from the British, or at least from their representatives in Williamsburg. Jumonville had already sent back actionable intelligence to French officials about Washington, his presence at Great Meadows, the fort, and the garrison that occupied it.

During the weeks that followed, with every assumption the French would learn of the skirmish and the death of Jumonville, and return for vengeance, Washington prepared his men for military engagement. He also engaged in intelligence activities. When native allies delivered nine French deserters to him, he invented a bit of propaganda, a common intelligence weapon that relies on using information to misdirect an enemy. He wrote a letter for the deserters to use to convince additional French troops to abandon their allegiance to Louis XV and fight for George II. Additionally, Washington fell back on his successful connections with Indian allies. In late June, he met with the leaders of several Indian nations in the area, his purpose being to gain their trust and support. At the same time, he also sought to use them for counterintelligence purposes. As Washington counseled with them, he knew some were in the paid service of the French, working as spies themselves and gathering intelligence. Using an intelligence tactic called disinformation, Washington told the Indians intentionally false things that he knew would get back to the French. In his journal, he noted the native agents, "who had been sent by the French to act as spies, returned, though not without some stories prepared to amuse the French, which may be of service to make our own designs succeed."[29] Here is Washington, caught on a steep learning curve, operating as an espionage agent, relying on disinformation to turn the enemy's strategy and response. Twenty years later, it was a trick he would use on the British time and time again.

But Washington's time in the field was nearly at an end. By early July, the French had returned to the vicinity of Fort Necessity en masse with a party that included French regular troops, many French Canadians, and

FOLLOWING:
Robert Griffing's painting The Crossing *illustrates the moment on July 9, 1755, when General Braddock's troops forded the Monongahela River; George Washington can be seen in blue at the side of Braddock, sitting on a bay horse.*

Right of Embassy

It might seem strange for Washington, as a technical representative of the British, to enter French forts on the frontier and even engage in activities that might constitute intelligence gathering. Washington enjoyed the privilege through the "Right of Embassy"—the framework was ironed out by Dutch legal expert Hugo Grotius in 1625—a longstanding set of rules between European nations that protected such representatives of European powers as ambassadors, emissaries, "deputies sent from provinces, cities, and other places," and even their servants.[30] In effect, the French had no choice but to protect the life of Washington and his men and allow, within reason, him to meet with the French on their turf and even get a good look around their forts.

several Indian allies. The ensuing battle left Washington defeated and a bit chagrined. Forced to sign a surrender document—in French, no less, which Washington could not even read—he unknowingly confessed to the assassination of Jumonville, an unfortunate admission that soon thrust him on the world stage as a veritable villain. They had violated the same right of embassy that had earlier protected them (see "Right of Embassy," above).

In a year, the French and British—and their colonial counterparts—would be at war, a conflict referred to as the Seven Years' War, except in North America, where it became known by England's enemies as the French and Indian War. What had been developing over the previous five years as a cold war on the frontier, erupted into a white-hot conflict with global implications. Through this crucible of war and wilderness fighting, Washington would emerge as a recognized leader. The conflict would help prepare him for the Revolutionary War, in which he would play a singular role. While his legacy is today typically weighed in terms of his military leadership and presidency, his days spent along the Indian paths of the Ohio frontier also prepared him for another role, one often overlooked, yet one that would prove crucial to the success of the Patriot cause. Major Washington had learned the spy game in the forests of western Virginia and Pennsylvania. During the Revolutionary War, General Washington would become his own Dinwiddie, a spymaster who repeatedly outfoxed the British.

CHAPTER TWO

Dr. Benjamin Church: Patriot Double Agent

The BLOODY MASSACRE perpetrated in King Street Boston on March 5th 1770 by a party of the 29th Regt.

BUTCHER'S HALL

Engrav'd Printed & Sold by PAUL REVERE BOSTON

Unhappy BOSTON! see thy Sons deplore,
Thy hallow'd Walks besmear'd with guiltless Gore:
While faithless P—n and his savage Bands,
With murd'rous Rancour stretch their bloody Hands;
Like fierce Barbarians grinning o'er their Prey,
Approve the Carnage, and enjoy the Day.

If scalding drops from Rage from Anguish Wrung,
If speechless Sorrows lab'ring for a Tongue,
Or if a weeping World can ought appease
The plaintive Ghosts of Victims such as these;
The Patriot's copious Tears for each are shed,
A glorious Tribute which embalms the Dead.

But know, FATE summons to that awful Goal,
Where JUSTICE strips the Murd'rer of his Soul:
Should venal C—ts the scandal of the Land,
Snatch the relentless Villain from her Hand,
Keen Execrations on this Plate inscrib'd,
Shall reach a JUDGE who never can be brib'd.

The unhappy Sufferers were Messrs. SAML. GRAY, SAML. MAVERICK, JAMS. CALDWELL, CRISPUS ATTUCKS & PATK. CARR

Killed. Six wounded; two of them (CHRISTR. MONK & JOHN CLARK) Mortally

Published in 1770 by Paul Revere Boston

MISPLACED POLICIES

n the stillness that followed the end of the French and Indian War, the balance of power in North America experienced a seismic shift. Simply put, the French were out, at least officially, although many French-speaking *inhabitants* and *métis* did not pack up and leave even as British overlords appeared. It meant the recently crowned king of England, George III, now reigned supreme from Canada to the Gulf of Mexico. Britain's star certainly appeared on the rise.

Yet British policies soon proved unpopular with English colonists in America, signaling a great political shift in the relationship between Crown and colonists. King George, typically with strong support from Parliament, began passing a series of badly considered pieces of legislation that could only be interpreted by colonists as oppressive. One motivating factor in this great shift in British policy was the war itself. It had been an expensive venture, with England shipping thousands of troops to battle the French and their allies. When the account books were opened, royal officials were stunned at what they saw. Effectively, the national debt had doubled almost overnight, from roughly £67 million to £137 million. Talk in the halls of Parliament and Whitehall amounted to little more than anguished handwringing. In spite of the victory, the conflict put Britain on the verge of bankruptcy.

To avoid this outcome, officials developed a plan they thought made extraordinary sense. If the Crown had gone into debt fighting a war to liberate English colonists from the encroachments of the French, then why should the king's subjects not cheerfully accept paying a portion of that bill? Customs duties were increased, including the Sugar Act of 1764, by which England imposed a tax on molasses and attempted to stop the colonists from smuggling it. But they typically refused to pay such duties. Colonists soon began to believe they saw tyranny everywhere.

～ ✖ ～

OPPOSITE:
An engraving of the Boston Massacre of March 5, 1770, that was printed and sold by Paul Revere (copying a design by Henry Pelham) several weeks later. The lines of verse underneath begin: "Unhappy Boston! see thy Sons deplore, Thy hallowed Walks besmeared with guiltless Gore." Listed afterward are the names of the civilians killed and wounded in this skirmish with British soldiers.

An Extremely Sticky Tax

When Parliament passed the Sugar Act, it included a tax on imports of molasses into the British colonies. Although colonists protested, the new act actually lowered the tax from six pence per gallon (this had been established under the Molasses Act of 1733) to three.

In reality, the tax was extremely small, especially in light of the profits a gallon of molasses represented to a colonial rum distiller. Typically, a gallon of molasses cost sixteen pence. Once distilled, a gallon of rum sold for 192 pence, representing a tidy profit even after accounting for transport, bottling, and other overhead. Even under the original Molasses Act, the tax of six pence per gallon of molasses had only a trifling impact on the business's generous profit margins.

But for many colonists, the amount of the tax placed on them by Great Britain was not the point. Their anger was due to the fact that such taxes were forced on them without having any say in the matter.

THE SONS OF LIBERTY

In 1765, Parliament passed the Stamp Act, which required that any paper documents be written or printed on a special government-stamped paper—at a cost, of course. The act effectively created a paper tax. Everything ephemeral went up in price—newspapers, broadsheets, contracts, marriage licenses, even playing cards and dice (see "Gambling Doesn't Pay," page 40). The Stamp Act raised a howl among colonists from the most learned and outspoken (lawyers who handled paper on a daily basis) to the disgruntled, lower-class that frequented taverns, where they smoked, drank, and played cards and dice.

The Stamp Act elicited a variety of colonial responses, including street-level demonstrations and mob actions. The year 1765 had not only spawned such unpopular legislation as the Stamp Act, it also gave birth to a savvy protest organization centered in Boston—the Sons of Liberty. Today, many Americans think of the Sons of Liberty as little more than a group of rabble-rousers bent on poking a sharp stick in the eye of British authority through mob actions. They were, however, a cadre of political organizers, thinkers, writers, and ralliers. Their name came about through a less-than-likely source.

During an exchange on the floor of Parliament concerning American Stamp Act protests, member Charles Townshend—who would later become chancellor of the exchequer and squeeze the colonists with more taxes—spoke out against the organization's members (known first as the Local Nine), claiming they were "dependent" on England for their livelihood, to which fellow member, Isaac Barré, responded instead by calling them "sons of liberty." When the story surfaced in Boston, the group's leaders were only too happy to take the name for their own. Ultimately, the efforts of the Sons of Liberty would prove extraordinarily effective. Through intimidation and harassment, and well-played episodes of violence, such as the Andrew Oliver incident, the Sons of Liberty managed to bring about the resignations of every designated stamp agent they set in their sights. With such pressure, plus a well-coordinated boycott of British goods sold on American shop shelves, the Stamp Act proved too controversial and even unenforceable. By March 18, 1766, Parliament repealed it.

$\sim$ ※ $\sim$

Gambling Doesn't Pay

While the Stamp Act appeared to target lawyers especially—what attorney doesn't handle papers regularly?—the scope of the act hit other groups hard as well, including the tavern crowd, the likes of whom were prone to drink and gamble. The act taxed both playing cards and, oddly, dice. In fact, the tax on dice was much higher than for playing cards. As stated in the act: "And for and upon every pack of playing cards, and all dice, which shall be sold or used within the said colonies and plantations, the several stamp duties following (that is to say): For every pack of such cards, the sum of one shilling. And for every pair of such dice, the sum of ten shillings."[31] Such target items proved misplaced for British authorities. Many tavern-goers were lower-class folks, and the gambling tax did not sit well with them. Indeed, such malcontents often formed mobs who rallied against the act.

RIGHT:
Angry Bostonians burn copies of the Stamp Act in 1765.

A Patriot in Deed

Yet even among the membership of one of the most virulently radical Patriot organizations in the thirteen colonies, a traitor to the unfolding cause of revolution stalked their ranks. One among them was a spy. Evidence is scant, but indications are that Dr. Benjamin Church, a longstanding leader among the Sons of Liberty, first turned traitor against the Patriot cause—and thus became an agent for the British—sometime during 1774, before the famed shots of Lexington and Concord had even been fired.

Dr. Church was at the center of leadership within the Sons of Liberty and beyond. Rubbing shoulders with the likes of John Hancock, John Adams, and Adams's cousin, Sam, Church was appointed to the Massachusetts Provincial Congress, as well as the Massachusetts Committee of Safety. First established in Boston on November 2, 1772, this committee's purpose was to provide a frontline defense against British military power by authorizing itself to call out militia units. Eventually the group also helped coordinate the stockpiling of Patriot weapons and ammunition for a potential conflict with the British troops who occupied the colony. Dr. Church was among the organization's twenty-one charter members, alongside such other Patriot luminaries as Dr. Joseph Warren and Josiah Quincy.

But Church's support for the Patriot cause also put him on the front lines. In mid-December 1773, in protest against the Tea Act—which was designed to force Americans to purchase tea from a single supplier, the British East India Company, to shore up the bankrupt firm's bottom line—Patriots engaged in a restrained form of protest soon dubbed "The Boston Tea Party." As a large crowd of Bostonians looked on, several dozen protesters, who had thinly disguised themselves as Mohawk Indians, boarded three East India tea ships and quietly tossed 342 chests and half chests of tea overboard into the dark waters of Boston Harbor. Dr. Benjamin Church was one of the group's leaders. No additional damage was done to the ships, but the ire raised in England was swift and harsh and bent on retribution. A series of acts was passed—referred to in England as the Coercive Acts, and in Boston as the Intolerable Acts. In addition, the port of Boston, the trade lifeline for the city, was closed; the Massachusetts Assembly, a duly elected representative body, was dissolved; and a new royal governor was appointed.

British general Thomas Gage would be the first to fill the new governor's shoes in 1774. His was a dual role, as he was also the commander-in-chief of all British forces in America. His governorship established de facto military rule over Massachusetts. (When he arrived in Boston that May during a dreary, cold spring rain, he saw Bostonians wearing black armbands in protest. As the weeks passed, Boston church bells tolled as if in mourning. He could not have missed the symbolic significance.) Gage was not new to America. He had fought alongside George Washington during the disastrous Battle of the Monongahela in the summer of 1755, when British general Edwin Braddock so famously lost to the French, only mere miles from where the young Washington had trekked through southwestern Pennsylvania and encountered the French at Jumonville Glen. Gage liked America so much that he stayed on after the war and even married an American woman. Now he was the royal governor of Massachusetts, and the colony, especially Boston, was under virtual occupation.

By this point, the rift between Patriot colonists and the British government had reached a crisis point. The political gulf between the two sides was wider than the three thousand miles separating England and America. With Gage wielding extraordinary power over Massachusetts, colonists chose a Provincial Congress, one meeting in Salem rather than the political hotbed of Boston.

A Second Tea Party

Although the Boston Tea Party protest of December 1773 stands today among the seminal events signaling the widening animosity between Great Britain and the American Patriots, the nighttime raid on East India tea ships was not unique. Alexander McDougall had organized a Sons of Liberty chapter in New York City during the late 1760s. A few months after the Boston Tea Party, McDougall and his Sons of Liberty boarded a tea ship in New York Harbor, similarly dressed as Mohawks, and dumped its cargo of tea.

A Change in Allegiance

In time, through his high profile roles as a Patriot leader, spokesman, and pamphleteer, Church gained yet another important position. He became a member of an organization known as the Mechanics, one serving a different role than any other in the Sons of Liberty network. The Mechanics was a spy network. Its purpose was to gather actionable intelligence against the British military stationed in Massachusetts.

The Mechanics' original members included Church, Samuel Adams, John Hancock, and Dr. Joseph Warren. One of its earliest covert operatives was Boston silversmith Paul Revere, whose name would become synonymous with a late-night ride through the Massachusetts countryside to warn the Patriots that the British were marching out of Boston toward the sleepy country towns of Lexington and Concord. At its core, the mission of the Mechanics was to collect information about British troops—where they were stationed, what orders were being issued to various units, when they went seeking Patriot weapons caches. To facilitate their mission, the Mechanics developed a system of spies, street informants who made contact with the British, either directly or indirectly. (The Mechanics and their field operations will be discussed in more detail in Chapter Three.)

From its earliest days, the Sons of Liberty had functioned, in terms of modern-day political structures, as a united front, representing a combined political and social organization. During the twentieth century, Communist movements in such places as Russia, China, and even smaller states like Cuba and Vietnam, gained direction and ultimately succeeded in their revolutions through their united front structures. The Sons of Liberty's united front was no less effective in standing up to British political and military power during the 1760s and 1770s. The Mechanics simply extended that front to clandestine intelligence activities.

But even as Dr. Church reached his apex of influence, position, and power within the ranks of the Mechanics, the Sons of Liberty, and its auxiliary organization, the Committee of Safety (The Committee of Safety in Massachusetts would, by 1774, serve as the de facto Patriot government), the good doctor appears to have had a change in allegiance. As stated previously, the exact date that Church took up his intelligence activities—in effect, his spying—against the Patriot cause is not clear. Some historians

suggest his turncoat actions may have begun as early as 1772 during the tenure of the royal governor of Massachusetts, Thomas Hutchinson, a constant target of Sam Adams and the Sons.

But an even earlier date is also a possibility. Dr. Church first roused suspicions among the ranks of the Sons of Liberty as early as the late 1760s. He was often seen in the company of a retired British officer still on half-pay from the army, one Captain Arthur Price, as well as a Loyalist customs agent named John Robinson. Church was questioned about these companionships but he pushed aside the queries, assuring his fellow Patriots that he was only pumping them for information regarding their views on the new taxes the British government was levying on the colonies. In fact, Church may have been routing intelligence reports through one or both of these men as early as 1768.

One important factor that likely motivated an otherwise loyal Patriot like Church to spy for General Gage was, simply, money. Although relatively successful in his medical practice, Dr. Church spent more than he took in. He had a large waterfront summer home built in 1768 outside Boston. Three years later, he bought another home, this time in Boston proper on the north side of Marlborough Street, a ritzy neighborhood where the homes were large, stylish, and expensive. Church made these significant purchases at a time when he was known for being shy of an adequate cash flow. (He also had a mistress with expensive tastes.)

Historians point to an intriguing letter penned by Governor Hutchinson in January 1772 in which he alluded clearly to Dr. Church: "The faction seems to be breaking, the Doctor Church who wrote the Times is now a writer on the side of Government."[32] It seems the doctor was writing something for the British government, but what exactly is not known. Spy reports are a possibility. But he may have just been writing essays for a Loyalist newspaper, the *Boston Censor*.

What is clear, however, is that Church was in the employ of General Gage by late 1774 or early 1775, a couple of months before the war's first shots were fired. Church was paid several hundred British guineas for his services. What he may have done to receive the money is not known, but Hutchinson, making reference to Church and the payment, labeled his report, dated February 24, 1775, with one word: "intelligence."

Suspicion eventually fell on Dr. Church's shoulders.

Church's Spying: Did His Treachery Really Matter?

The mystery of when Church began spying for the British remains unsolved even today. Some experts suggest that he may have spied for Royal Governor Thomas Hutchinson even prior to 1770, a full five years before the Revolutionary War even started. It is almost certain that he was up to his spying tricks by 1772. Once the war opened, Royal Governor General Thomas Gage relied on Church and his intelligence reports, one of which led him to dispatch Redcoats to Lexington and Concord to destroy military supplies. Sending those British soldiers to Concord led to, in fact, the opening shots of the war at Lexington on April 19, 1775. In this, Dr. Church had a role in determining when the "shots heard round the world" were fired.

REPORTS TO GAGE

Once the war began in the otherwise quiet, rural Massachusetts town of Lexington, Church was sending intelligence to General Gage with regularity. It was a continuation of what he had been doing even before the fighting began that spring. Sometimes, he met directly with Gage in Boston, meetings that required singular cautions on his part. On other occasions, he delivered his intelligence reports through third parties, including women he could trust.

Such a courier is known today in the intelligence community as a *cutout*. A cutout is typically an individual who is tapped to pass information between a field intelligence agent and an intelligence officer. Cutouts often know full well that they are handling sensitive intelligence, but sometimes they do so unaware of either the content of the correspondence or the nature of the information. Usually, cutouts have to blend into the environments they are sent into and often have convincing cover stories that justify being in a certain place at a certain time. Repeatedly, whether directly or through a cutout, Church sent Gage valuable intelligence reports.

Prior to the battles at Lexington and Concord, Church had kept Gage abreast of actions being taken by the Committee of Safety, including the number of Minutemen available for immediate action against British

Redcoats, as well as the number and location of cannon held by Patriot groups at locations in and around Boston, including Concord. He reported that the whole of Patriot-held gunpowder, approximately one hundred barrels, was sitting in storage in Concord. Because Church and his fellow Sons of Liberty comrade Dr. Joseph Warren were tapped to appropriate such potential war materiel as medical supplies, provisions, and other items, Gage also received important intelligence on these matters, which could help him assess the immediate threat represented by Patriots in eastern Massachusetts.

Church's reports to Gage were sometimes extremely specific and might have been what motivated the general to dispatch hundreds of Redcoats to Concord in April 1775, a march that led them through Lexington. He told Gage about four brass cannon and two mortars hidden in a "Mr. B——['s]" cellar. He added: "Two pieces of iron ordinance . . . are mounted (on carriages said to be very indifferent) in the court house. . . . Eight more pieces of Iron ordinance were this day conveyed to C—— [Concord] and L—— [Lexington] where they had been deposited a few days preceding their last removal."[33] Church also provided specific information about roads leading from Boston to Concord.

In an early May 1775 report Church expressed his concerns about being detected as a spy for the British: "Caution on my part is doubly necessary as instant death would be my portion should a discovery be made . . . Secrecy respecting me on the part of the General is indispensable to my rendering him any services and be the event what it may is necessary to the preservation of my life."[34] In this same letter, Church also reminds Gage that he was due a payment for his services within a few weeks.

On May 13, the doctor routed a report to the general informing him that the Patriots were gearing up to fortify the heights around Boston, including Bunker Hill to the north and Dorchester to the south, intent on pinning Gage and his forces down in Boston. Ironically, Gage took no action based on Church's specific intelligence, giving the Patriots the opportunities they needed. In the same report, Church informed Gage of actions being taken by the Massachusetts and Connecticut colonial governments in support of the unfolding revolution.

By late May, the Massachusetts Provincial Congress sent Church to Philadelphia to present a request to the Continental Congress to include

General Thomas Gage,
painted by John Singleton
Copley around 1768.

thousands of Massachusetts militia and lesser-trained Patriots in the Continental Army. Church wrote a note to Gage lamenting that he would be unreachable while in Pennsylvania and unable to send reports during his absence. In this same missive, Church is saddened to inform Gage that "a body of troops from Connecticut have taken [Fort] Ticonderoga with 120 iron cannon." He provided additional information about the expanding numbers of Patriot troops. Before ending his intelligence report, Church made his allegiance clear: "There is a general revolt of all the colonies and sorry I am to say that a temper of submission and accommodation under the present claims of Britain is nowhere to be found . . . may I never see the day when I shall not dare to call myself a British American."[35]

&ぷ ※ ぺ

The Misplaced Mary Wenwood

Through a series of missteps, Church's days as a turncoat came to a halt in the summer of 1775. By then, the war had opened, the skirmishes at Lexington and Concord were already the stuff of Patriot legend, and New England militia and Minutemen surrounded Boston. Gage and thousands of Redcoats were stranded in a city under virtual lockdown. Church had been traveling in and out of the city and, on at least one occasion, was seen in the presence of General Gage at his home. Word of the meeting made its way to members of the Mechanics, and Church was summoned to appear before them to explain himself. He claimed, plausibly enough, that British soldiers had arrested him when he tried to enter Boston to get intelligence information for Patriot units outside the city. He had been taken directly to Gage to explain his actions and had managed to satisfy the general that he was simply an innocent civilian. The Mechanics were skeptical, though. Paul Revere knew he had a leak in his organization—a mole, in modern spy parlance—and already suspected Church. But he had never uncovered any real proof, no "smoking gun" evidence that the doctor, and a fellow Mechanic to boot, had gone over to the British and their Loyalist allies.

Then, Church made a serious mistake. For reasons that remain unclear, he altered his normal system of delivering messages to Gage. Sometimes,

in the intelligence business, operatives who have worked covertly for years are finally exposed because they change their routine. This is the mistake Church made, and the reason why may never be known.

He decided to change couriers and chose his mistress, Mary Wenwood, who was pregnant. Little is known of Ms. Wenwood, but her reputation among some was as a prostitute. Dr. Warren, one of the most important Patriot leaders in Boston, thought she was little more than a trollop, writing to John Adams: "The Doctor [Church] having formed an infamous connection, with an infamous hussey to the disgrace of his own reputation, and probable ruin of his family."[36] When she was given responsibility for delivering a simple coded message to General Gage, she managed to bungle her way along until things went completely awry.

Church's instructions to her were straightforward. A three-page letter was to be delivered to a "Major Cane" in Boston, but it was to be done so in a roundabout way. Instead of going to Boston, she was to travel to Newport, Rhode Island, to deliver the letter to James Wallace, the captain of the British warship HMS *Rose*. According to the story, Mary Wenwood first carried the sealed envelope to Newport sometime in late July. (To keep the letter out of sight, it was said she tucked it away in one leg of her stockings.) She soon arrived at Godfrey Wenwood's bakery and bread shop, located on Bannister's Wharf. Wenwood was Mary's former husband and was apparently a baker of renown who supplied baked goods to Royal Navy crews docked at Newport.

She asked Wenwood to do her a favor—to arrange a meeting with Captain Wallace, then docked at Bannister's Wharf. Since Wenwood made regular visits to the dock and British ships, his boarding the *Rose* would not raise suspicions. Ultimately, the female courier wanted to make contact with Charles Dudley, the royal collector of customs, or a local Tory merchant named George Rome, who was coordinating with Captain Wallace to supply British troops in Boston with food and other necessities. Church had hoped Wallace could serve as the go-between to contact either of these officials directly. Rome was an intelligence agent, similar to Church, who delivered information and messages to General Gage directly.

Wenwood must have thought her relationship with her ex-husband would be incentive enough to convince him to help her out in her mission, but it seems she knew nothing about his politics. He was, in fact, a strong Patriot and a respectable businessman, who hobnobbed with the town's upper crust. As one frequenter of his bakery noted: "In the rooms above [Wenwood's bakery was in a basement] he often had as guests the best society of the town, whom he entertained with a princely hospitality."[37] Wenwood had since moved on to another woman, one he had plans to marry soon, "a young lady of great beauty and merit,"[38] so Church's former spouse—with her unwholesome reputation—was at best an unwanted caller. And yet, despite his politics and his concern for his own standing in the community, he agreed to take the sealed envelope and do the deed.

Wenwood delivered the letter—but not to the British and General Gage. After vacillating for weeks over whom to deliver it to, if anyone, he finally settled on a plan. He consulted a friend, a Patriot teacher named Adam Maxwell, who ran a school close to the bakery; he suggested they open the mysterious letter together.

The two men looked over the three pages of text and realized they were staring at an encrypted message. Although they had no idea what they were reading, they knew what it represented. Based on Mary's plea, they deduced that the message was a piece of intelligence meant for General Gage's eyes only. Yet Wenwood held onto the letter, uncertain which way to turn and to whom.

As for Church, his pro-British intelligence gathering had been facilitated because he was working in the Continental Army's Hospital Department, which put him in close contact with the army and its officers, including General Washington. Though, as summer moved into fall, Church began to be concerned about the status of his letter. With two months having passed since he had tasked Mary Wenwood to deliver his coded message, he panicked, believing the letter had been intercepted.

Church tried to resign from the army on September 20, having cooked up some excuse about a family emergency (with his mistress increasingly pregnant, perhaps this claim was not a genuine stretch). He didn't wait for an answer, but took a furlough instead. Church made for home, likely intent on destroying any incriminating evidence. Washington, however, refused to accept his resignation, though he extended the furlough. Meanwhile, Church questioned Mary Wenwood about the letter, and she told him she had left it with Godfrey. Highly concerned, Church gave her immediate instructions to pen her own letter to the baker to inform him she was aware the letter she had left with him had not yet been delivered. Wenwood responded by finally taking action and delivering the mysterious envelope to Henry Ward, the Patriot secretary for Rhode Island. Perusing the coded message, Ward sent Wenwood up the chain of command to General Nathaniel Greene, one of Washington's top officers, then commanding forces from Rhode Island in Cambridge, outside Boston.

What About Dr. Church's Family?

Among those hurt by Dr. Church's actions were members of his own family, including his wife and their three children. Prior to being arrested by Washington, Church had left them and taken up with Mary Wenwood, who was pregnant when she tried to deliver Church's letter to General Gage. While Church was jailed, his wife, Sarah, claimed an angry mob "broke open his house pillaged and destroyed every thing it contain'd," leaving her nothing, not even "a change of cloaths, nor even a bed for her and her children to lie on."[39] By the summer of 1777, Sarah Church had had enough. Her fate unalterably attached to her husband's, she made plans to leave for England. (Despite her claims of having nothing, she had retained the family silver, which she sold to purchase passage to Europe.)

The family sailed in July, and their ship was soon captured by an American war vessel, *Flora*, and directed to Rhode Island. After weeks of delay, Sarah and her children reached England, landing first in France. Over the following years, she applied several times to the British government for a pension, claiming her husband had lost everything due to his spying for the British. During the proceedings, several individuals confirmed, under oath, that Dr. Church had acted as an agent for the British, including one William Warden, who testified he had received intelligence reports from Church on several occasions, including drops made at Salem and Marblehead, both towns in Massachusetts.

A grateful British government agreed to Sarah's application and elected her an annual pension of £150, which, for reasons unknown, was reduced to £100 yearly in June 1782. Mrs. Church died six years later.

COLLAPSE OF COVER

Once he had seen the letter, General Greene made haste and delivered it and Wenwood straight to General Washington. In a private meeting, Greene instructed Wenwood to tell Washington his entire story. Washington knew the letter meant that he had a traitor in his midst. Wenwood was then sent back to meet with Mary to try and elicit further information from her, especially the name of the agent who had sent her to Newport. But she refused to implicate Church. When Wenwood returned to Washington's headquarters, the general would not accept the collaborating woman's refusal to cooperate. He ordered her arrested and delivered to him. Another of Washington's officers, Major General Israel Putnam, a bulldog of a Massachusetts Patriot, was sent to retrieve her.

When he returned, on an evening in late September, Washington burst into a rare show of laughter. According to tradition, "Washington was in his chamber at head-quarters, when he beheld from his window, General Putnam approaching on horseback, with a stout woman *en croupe* behind him.[40] The scene presented by the old general and his prize overpowered even Washington's gravity."[41] There was the portly General Putnam with Mary Wenwood riding pillion directly behind him, this known "loose" woman clinging to the embarrassed officer. The scene was more than Washington could bear, despite the seriousness of the situation.

As Mary Wenwood was ushered into Washington's headquarters, a private house that had been offered for his use, he waited for her at the top of a long staircase. Looking sternly down to a frightened Mary on the landing below, Washington sought to intimidate her into telling all, as he "assured her in a severe tone . . . that, unless she confessed everything before the next morning, a halter would be in readiness for her."[42] After all, she was complicit in an act of possible treason, and there would be consequences.

No official record of Washington's interrogation of Mary Wenwood is known. Washington had served back in Virginia, before the war, as an examining magistrate, so he was likely accustomed to asking questions of reluctant individuals. At first, Church's mistress stood firm;

Washington later wrote how "for a long time she was proof against every threat and persuasion to discover the author."[43] At last, Mary couldn't take Washington's questions or his unflinching stare any more. Noted Washington: "However, at length of about four hours she was brought to a confession." [44] She named Church as the man at the other end of the letter's long and interrupted journey.

Washington was stunned at the news: Dr. Benjamin Church, physician to countless Continental soldiers in the army's makeshift hospitals around Boston. Washington did not have to go far to retrieve the traitor.

~ ※ ~

BREAKING THE CODE

It is surprising the traitorous doctor succeeded in collecting intelligence against the Patriot army for as long as he did. He was not typically circumspect and even displayed a devil-may-care attitude, as is evidenced by his reliance on an untested woman to deliver sensitive intelligence. He had worked for Gage for many months, perhaps several years, was paid well for his services, and yet had gone ultimately undetected. In fact, the extent of what Church did for Gage would not be discovered for another 150 years. But for now, his time as a traitor had come to an end.

All Washington would come to know was what Church had done over the previous couple of months. Church was delivered to Washington under guard. He came quietly, even confidently, to the general's house, and he seemed to have an answer for every one of Washington's questions. In the style of a well-trained intelligence field operative, Church refused to let his commander in chief see him crack under pressure. When asked if he had written and dispatched the letter in question, he casually admitted he had, seemingly with no more concern than if he were asked what he had eaten that morning for breakfast. After all, Patriots sent letters between the lines to Tory friends all the time, didn't they? Hadn't General Charles Lee, an officer under Washington's command, sent several letters under a truce flag to his old companion in arms, General John Burgoyne, of the king's forces, in an attempt to convince the British commander that pursuing the Patriots would ultimately fail?

Indeed, Washington was aware of Lee's letters to Burgoyne. But that was the point: Lee had sent his missives out in the open, with Washington's full knowledge and blessing. Why had Church sent his letter secretly, through several couriers, in code? That Church's message was coded was not an indisputable piece of evidence; some people in that era often sent coded letters. Envelopes were not common, and a letter's content might be sensitive or even simply personal. (Thomas Jefferson, one Founding Father who wrote many letters, penned more in code than not.) But it is here that Church's parallel with Charles Lee broke down. Washington ordered Church to produce the key to the cipher. Church remained tight-lipped and refused. Washington peppered him with more questions: If you're an innocent man, why not decode the message? Why send the letter through Newport? Church insisted he had not intended to be clandestine, only discreet. The interrogation had reached an impasse. What Washington needed was the key to the code that disguised the letter's message from him. For the time being, Church would remain under arrest, a guard at his side at all times.

Washington sent out word that he needed someone to decode a letter. A team of three men was soon assembled, including a Continental Army chaplain, Reverend Samuel West, from Dartmouth, Massachusetts; Elbridge Gerry, who worked with the Committee of Safety, and who had some experience with codes and deciphering; and, at Gerry's suggestion, Colonel Elisha Porter, who served with a Massachusetts militia unit.

Given that the code was simplistic, a basic system of letter-for-letter transfer, the decoding did not require a significant amount of time. Today, cryptographers, using English, know that such codes may be broken by looking at letter frequency. Two basic patterns are usually utilized: ETOANIRSHDL (based on frequency) or ETOANRISHDL. It seems the three designated cryptanalysts, to use the modern term, knew this rule of thumb. By simply counting the frequency of each word substitute, they had the code broken in short order. (In fact, the three men did not work side by side; West worked singularly, while Gerry and Porter collaborated.) By October 3, the two decryptions were finished. When General Washington compared them, they matched word for word. At last, Church's words could be read and his guilt determined.

His words spoke of treason. Church had recently paid a call to the Continental Congress meeting in Philadelphia, and he filled in General Gage concerning the details, including the revolutionary spirit of the political leadership, referring to the Congress as "united, determined in opposition."[45] But much of the letter's content told a story of military intelligence gathering. Throughout his missive were snapshots of such vital statistics as numbers of cannon and ammunition; the exact number of artillery pieces in Kingsbridge, New York, and their sizes, which he had seen firsthand; how well the Continental Army was supplied with food; and the level of recruitment into the Patriot army. Church also supplied troop numbers stationed in Philadelphia.

The deciphered spy correspondence also made it clear that Church had not worked alone, but had relied on a courier—someone other than his mistress—to deliver several pieces of intelligence on previous occasions, including one during which the courier was detained by officials. Church's message was not detected, though, as the messenger had sewn the correspondence into the waistband of his pants. By the time he was released after several days of captivity, his captors had still not found the incriminating document. As Church noted in the damning letter, his agent had paid off someone for his release: "A little art and a little cash settled the matter."[46]

～ ※ ～

STEPS TO BE TAKEN

As Washington read of Church's subterfuge, he took immediate steps to respond to the treasonous actions of a man who had stood, publicly, as a stalwart supporter of the Patriot cause. He called a council with his generals, convened a court-martial, and showed them the documents. Church was soon delivered, the decryptions placed before him, and the doctor began to explain his actions, although not to Washington's satisfaction.

Church's Overly Simple Cipher

When the Patriots gained possession of the coded message Church had sent through his mistress to Gage in the summer of 1775, it did not take long to crack it. Church was using one of the simplistic codes imaginable. Called a *monoalphabetic substitution code*, this cipher relies on substituting one letter or character for another. Such codes, especially if long enough, can be broken if the decoder knows anything about the frequency with which specific letters are used in common English. The most frequently utilized is the letter "e," the second most common is "t," and so on. Otherwise a decoder looks for context clues such as "th" or the placement of vowels. While multiple types of codes were in use during the American Revolutionary War, some quite complicated, Church might not have even bothered with such a simple cipher at all. After all, the fact that the message was written in code signaled immediately to the Patriots that Church was likely involved in espionage for the British.

Clearly cornered, Dr. Church admitted that the translations were correct, so the content of the letter was no longer a question. But things were not as they seemed, he explained. He was not a spy for the enemy, but had instead written the letter—with all its details concerning cannon, troop numbers, and recruitment statistics—to scare the British, to convince them that the Continental Army represented a stronger force than Gage and his subordinates might have thought. He even claimed to have padded his numbers to create a Potemkin village image of the Patriots and the threat they posed.

On this point, Church was correct: he had indeed overstated some figures. Washington and his generals certainly knew that. Why he did so remains a question. Perhaps Gage and Church had agreed to "encode" such numbers to provide the spy with an explanation of his actions in case he were ever captured. For example, if Church had listed a certain number of enemy cannon, with Gage knowing that the actual figure was, say, a third less than what he provided, then Gage could calculate the real number, while Church would be able to claim under interrogation exactly what he claimed to Washington—"I did it to deter the enemy, not aid him."

But no evidence existed at the time, and none has been discovered since to point to such an arrangement between spy and general. Likely,

Church just guessed at some of his figures and hoped he was close enough. Such mistakes were common in the spy business that took place during the American Revolutionary War, and they are still common today. (Just one of the more infamous examples include President George W. Bush using faulty intelligence about the supposed presence of so-called "weapons of mass destruction" to justify the 2003 invasion of Iraq.) It makes sense that Church overestimated his military figures, since he never had access to military reports issued from Washington's headquarters. The doctor had collected his information, generally, by firsthand observance, but in doing so, likely never gained a full picture of the presence and strength of Washington's boots on the ground. When Church was finished with his defense, his accusers—Washington and his officer staff—remained unconvinced. There was simply too much to explain away. The doctor was put in a cell under guard.

An Accused Church and the Articles of War

Once General Washington had Dr. Church arrested, a court-martial was convened to determine the alleged spy's guilt and punishment. But there was a hitch. No adequate punishment was possible.

Just two months after the Revolutionary War opened, the Continental Congress passed a series of sixty-nine Articles of War, designed to govern how the military would operate, including how it could punish its troops. According to Article XXVIII: "Whosoever belonging to the continental army, shall be convicted of holding correspondence with, or of giving intelligence to, the enemy, either directly or indirectly, shall suffer punishment as by a general court-martial shall be ordered." However, Article LI limited the punishments a court-martial could issue, stating: "That no persons shall be sentenced by a court-martial to suffer death, except in the cases expressly mentioned in the foregoing articles; nor shall any punishment be inflicted at the discretion of a court-martial, other than degrading [this refers to a drop in rank], cashiering, drumming out of the army, whipping not exceeding thirty-nine lashes, fine not exceeding two months' pay of the offender, imprisonment not exceeding one month."[47]

To Washington and to the men of his general staff, as well to as many Patriot officials, these punishments did not match the severity of Church's crime of espionage, which many European governments of that day punished through execution.

INADEQUATE PUNISHMENT

Next Washington had to decide what, exactly, to do with a man who was clearly an enemy intelligence operative. It is here that the situation became awkward at best. (Today, someone convicted of espionage or treason against the United States is liable to receive a significant prison sentence. By law, he might even face the death penalty.) Earlier in June of that same year, the Continental Congress had established in Article XXVIII that a person caught communicating with the enemy was to be turned over to court-martial. In certain cases, a court-martial could result in the execution, by hanging, of the convicted. However, under Article LI, the Congress had limited the punishment meted out by a court-martial as, at best, a combination of two punishments—either thirty-nine lashes on the bare back or a fine of two months' army pay, and discharge from the army. Clearly the Continental Congress had failed to imagine that actions, such as those in which Dr. Church had involved himself, would ever take place.

This left Washington in a quandary. It appeared he might have no option but to order Church simply flogged, then released. Even cashiering wasn't an option, as army regulations stipulated that only army officers could be dealt this punishment. (Thanks to the Church case, Congress acknowledged its short-sightedness and altered the regulations just a month later, on November 7, providing for the death penalty in cases of captured and convicted spies. However, the new policy could not be applied retroactively to Dr. Church.)

To discuss the Church case, General Washington called a meeting at his headquarters in Cambridge for October 18, and sessions continued until October 22. Those attending included various revolutionary officials from Rhode Island, Massachusetts, and Connecticut, as well as Benjamin Harrison and Thomas Lynch, both members of the Continental Congress. Taking up Church's situation, including what to do to punish the spy in their midst, the group decided to refer Church to the General Court of Massachusetts Bay for trial and sentencing. But they also decided to put off any such action until possible directives were issued from the Continental Congress. Four days later, Church was removed from his confinement by High Sheriff William Howe, who was accompanied by Adjutant General Horatio Gates, one of Washington's generals, and a detachment of soldiers; he was to appear before the Massachusetts Provincial House, of which Church had been a member until his resignation under suspicion of spying.

Following a prolonged proceeding in front of his former colleagues, the House issued a report on November 11. One of its conclusions was that the Articles of War did not provide an adequate punishment for Church's crime if he appeared before a court-martial. In the words of the House committee: "The Counsel of this Colony be, and they hereby are desired to take suitable measures for causing the said Benjamin Church, in case of his being liberated from his present confinement, to be apprehended and secured, that such further measures, with respect to him, may be pursued, as the security of this People loudly demands, and the laws of this Colony will justify."[48] The Massachusetts House of Representatives was taking no chances. If it appeared that Dr. Church and his crimes were going to go inadequately unpunished, the House would take its own measures.

The Church spy case sent ripples throughout New England and beyond. For such an influential member of the Sons of Liberty and a Massachusetts political figure to have turned traitor was unfathomable to many. In a letter written to his wife, Abigail, Patriot leader and fellow Massachusetts man John Adams lamented:

> *The Fall of Dr. Church, has given me many disagreeable reflections, as it places human nature itself in a point of bad light, but the virtue, the sincerity, the honor, of Boston and Massachusetts Patriots in a worse.— What shall we say of a Country, which produces such characters as [Royal Governor Thomas] Hutchinson and Church?*[49]

~ ※ ~

Removing One of Their Own

When Dr. Benjamin Church's guilt became obvious in the fall of 1775, the fallout extended in several directions. Church was, after all, a member of the Massachusetts Provincial Congress. His fellow congressmen, those who had known him for years as a stalwart Patriot, suddenly realized that they, among others, had been duped. They could not contend with a spy in their midst. Some action seemed necessary.

Church did them a favor by taking the first step. Once he was convicted, he took it upon himself to resign from the Massachusetts assembly on October 23, 1775. But his former legislative comrades were not content. Intent on making a statement, the assembly voted to remove him from their membership—in official words, they "utterly expelled" Church.[50] In doing so, the members of the Massachusetts Provincial Congress made their position on Church clear.

Church may have resigned for pragmatic reasons as well. By doing so, he believed he would not have to appear before his colleagues to account for his actions. But Washington made certain otherwise. Following his appearance before Washington's war council, Church was delivered to the Massachusetts House to explain himself.

OUT OF SIGHT, OUT OF MIND

In November, the Continental Congress intervened in the Church case and sent him to jail in Norwich, Connecticut. This action by the Congress appears to have been beyond the law, but its members felt justified in considering Dr. Church a threat to the revolution. In addition, Connecticut governor Jonathan Trumbull did not raise a finger in support of Church. Because of the nature of his crime, he was denied any access to pen, paper, and ink. The Congress also ordered "that no person be allowed to converse with him except in the presence and hearing of a magistrate of the town or sheriff of the county where he shall be confined, and in the English language, until further orders from this or a future Congress."[51] So severe was Church's incarceration that the windows in his cell were boarded up.

After a fashion, Church found himself in a legal limbo. There was no legal recourse by which his case could be adjudicated. Perhaps his situation was comparable to that of detainees held at the American military facility in Guantanamo Bay. As enemy combatants, the detainees were denied a legal trial, thus necessitating their open-ended incarceration.

Given Church's asthma, the sentence proved even harsher than intended and prompted the doctor to diagnose himself and ask for some leniency. He was permitted, in this instance, to write an appeal to the Continental Congress asking for "clear, elastic air."[52] Congress showed mercy and ordered him removed to another prison, even allowing him outside movement while under guard. But officials in Connecticut delayed long enough that Church made a second request, this time accompanied by signatures from three doctors claiming that the convicted spy's health was at risk. Finally, Congress allowed him to leave jail after he put up a surety of £1,000 and swore to two stipulations: he would have no contact with British officials, and he would not leave Massachusetts.

Even though liberated from prison, Church was not exactly free. When word spread that Church was out of jail on his own recognizance, local Patriots threatened to hang him themselves. For his own protection, Church was then placed in the jail in Waltham, Massachusetts, which was soon attacked by an angry mob; the doctor barely escaped with his life.

Church seemed to have few options. No legal process was pushing his case forward, and Patriot officials seemed satisfied to have basically placed him in prison and symbolically thrown away the key. Then, in 1777, there was a break for Church. General Gage, Church's former spymaster, was no longer the military governor of Massachusetts, having grown tired of his responsibilities in America. He was replaced by General Sir William Howe, who took an interest in Church's case. The governor decided to make an offer to the Patriots. Would the rebels consider a prisoner exchange—Dr. Church for another American surgeon who had been captured? A swap was arranged, and the British dispatched a ship in July to pick up Church. But when word of the exchange hit the streets, so did angry Patriots, a second mob demanding Church be returned to jail.

~ ✖ ~

A Hopeful Father

Although Dr. Benjamin Church's guilt as a spy was without question, one person remained hopeful that he might, indeed, be innocent—his father.

While Church was jailed for his crimes, awaiting his uncertain fate, his father paid his expenses. He argued with anyone who would listen in support of his son, claiming, just as the doctor himself claimed, that he had carried out his actions to discourage the British, not to encourage them. But he also realized the difficult position in which his son had placed himself, noting: "But alas! For him, & me! He was improvident—and thereby expos'd himself to ye resentment of his Country."[53]

Even when Church's ship bound for exile on the island of Martinique disappeared, his father still hoped his son might be alive somewhere, eluding capture, preparing to return home someday. In his will, he left Dr. Church five pounds and all of his personal books. He expressed his anguished feelings in his will, as well, stating, "for alas; he is now absent—being cruelly banish'd [from] his country—and whether living or dead God only knows."[54]

CHANGES IN LATITUDE

Given the public outcry, officials reconsidered their decision to release Church as part of an exchange. Some thought he might still provide valuable information to the British that could prove "greatly Detrimental to the United States at this Juncture of our Publick Affairs," wrote General William Heath.[55] During the summer of 1777, a large British army under the command of General John Burgoyne was marching south from Canada through the lakes region of eastern New York, intent on forcing a military wedge that might split New England off from the remainder of the colonies. Military pressures were simply too strong for any brokered deals concerning Church beyond what jail to transfer him to next. Even after two years, Church was still a thorn in the side of those supporting the Revolution.

Church remained jailed until the following year. By then, he was no longer considered much of a threat. The Patriots and their Continental Army had not yet gained independence from Britain, but the future looked promising. The French government had signed an alliance with the Americans to provide military and financial support to their cause. Three years had passed, and any intelligence he had failed to pass off to the British would have been woefully out-of-date and useless. Despite these developments, few thought he should simply be released. Instead, Congress took a decidedly novel next step—they banished him.

Dr. Benjamin Church was ordered "exiled to some Island in the West Indies, and threatened with death in case he shod [should] ever return."[56] On January 9, 1778, the Massachusetts legislature passed a resolution to this effect, declaring that "Doctor Benjamin Church be and he hereby is permitted to take passage on board the Sloop *Welcome* Captain James Smithwick, Master, bound for the Island of Martinico [Martinique]."[57] To make certain Church's spying days were over, the legislature also ordered the sheriff of Suffolk County "to search his person and baggage to prevent his carrying any letters or other papers that may be to the detriment of the American States."[58]

Free at last, Dr. Church likely believed his ordeal was behind him and that one day, should he choose, he would return to America or perhaps to Great Britain. He had, after all, stated in the spring of 1775: "May I never see the day when I shall not dare to call myself a British American."[59] But that opportunity never came. Not only did he not return to American soil, he didn't reach his destination, either. The sloop carrying Church set sail in mid-February 1778, but never arrived in Martinique and was considered lost at sea.

Since Church's exact fate was unknown following the departure of the *Welcome* from Rhode Island, Massachusetts passed an act designed to keep him from returning. In 1778, the legislature created a list of "undesirables," individuals who were not welcome to return to the state. It was an extensive list, mostly of Tories who supported the British but had left Massachusetts, and Dr. Benjamin Church's name was included. Massachusetts authorities had had enough of the wayward doctor and did not intend to allow him to show his face in their state any time in the future.

≈ ✄ ≈

CHAPTER THREE

The Mechanics:
The Paul Revere Gang

A New Spy Organization

s rifts widened between dissatisfied Americans and the British authorities, suspicions on both sides led each to develop spy networks to inform them of the other's plans, deployments, and potentially hostile movements. The British were much better at such activities, as their secret service had a long history of espionage. The Americans, on the other hand, needed to organize their efforts from scratch. Despite its amateur status, Patriot intelligence and counterintelligence was successful in its own right.

As early as the fall of 1774, a group of Americans organized a spy network that would remain active in Boston until the British military evacuated in March 1776. This homegrown intelligence organization was created by civilians—volunteers, essentially. In a sense, it was a form of resistance group, similar in some respects to those that formed across Europe during World War II; such groups spied on the Nazis, performed acts of sabotage, and distributed propaganda under cover of darkness.

This first American spy ring called itself "the Mechanics." Its members included approximately thirty Patriots, along with their leader, Boston silversmith Paul Revere, best remembered today for his famed "Midnight Ride," on the night of April 18–19, 1775, during which he warned local militiamen of the approach of the king's troops. Revere saw his organization's purpose as decidedly straightforward and critical, including "watching the movements of the British soldiers, and gaining every intelligence of the movements of the Tories."[60] Sometimes his amateur spies simply took to the streets of their city, often in pairs, trolling for intelligence. Their nighttime movements appear to have hardly raised any suspicions on the part of British officials, and as citizens of Boston, they did not need any elaborate cover. All that was required was an observant eye and a cool head. The Mechanics knew the city—Boston in the 1770s was a small urban setting, home to perhaps fifteen thousand citizens— and its streets, byways, and back alleys. If they needed to give some British night patrol the slip, they could easily thread their way through familiar back streets and take refuge in the homes of friends.

The Mechanics thrived on secrecy, but they did not follow the cardinal rule of nearly all professional spy organizations—members must not be familiar with one another. The more independently each agent operates from another the better. If one is discovered by the enemy, he or she is in no position to reveal the names of other agents. Revere's gang of street spies, by contrast, met together publicly at Boston's Green Dragon Tavern. Believing in one another's loyalty, they swore an oath to keep each other's identities secret and to make their work known only to the leaders of the Sons of Liberty, including the likes of John Hancock, Sam Adams, Dr. Joseph Warren, and, unfortunately, Dr. Benjamin Church![61]

Today, the intelligence community uses a specific term for the sort of secrecy the Revere gang chose not to employ. Called *compartmentation*, it involves limiting information concerning any intelligence activity to those who are on a "need-to-know" basis. Each agent is made aware of only the information he needs to carry out his mission or assignment. For whatever reason, Revere chose not to keep the identities of his men secret from one another. Instead, the members relied on the honor of their fellow spies, each man taking his turn at every meeting to swear on a Bible that he would keep all Mechanics business a secret from enemy ears and eyes. Obviously, Dr. Church did not take his Bible-sworn oaths as sacred.

A Bit of Patriot Disinformation

Espionage commonly uses the practice of disinformation, the purposeful planting of false information, sometimes through a double agent, to misdirect or disrupt the enemy. One of the grandest uses of disinformation by the Patriots was in 1775, during the opening months of the Revolutionary War. It would become an example of how much a little intelligence gathering could shift the course of the Revolutionary War in favor of the rebels.

James Wright was destined to become the last of the royal governors of Georgia. As hostilities opened in the spring of 1775, Wright was alarmed at the strength of the Patriots in his colony and sent a letter to General Gage's naval commander, Admiral Thomas Graves, informing him that Georgia was highly vulnerable, that he was certain his cache of gunpowder would soon be seized, and that he was in need of "immediate assistance" in the form of a naval presence, such as "a sloop of war of some sort."[62]

But Wright's missive never reached its intended destination. Instead, Patriots intercepted it and replaced it with one they wanted General Gage to read. In the new version, Governor Wright informed the general that all was well in Georgia and few rebels were present. In his words, "No danger is to be apprehended." He further assured Gage the same was true for his neighboring colony, South Carolina. Revolution has not erupted "in the proceedings or designs of our neighbors of South Carolina."[63] To add icing on the cake, Wright's altered letter stated emphatically: "I now have not any occasion for any vessel of war."[64] The letter Gage received could not have failed to convince him of its authenticity. The Patriot conspirators even managed to include nearly perfect versions of the Georgia governor's royal seal. Wright himself would not become aware of the forgery until January 1776.

INTELLIGENCE AND SABOTAGE

During the eighteen months or so that Revere's Mechanics operated as Boston's chief Patriot intelligence-gathering organization, it appears they did so right under General Gage's nose. Revere seems to have drawn Gage's attention from time to time, but not for spying. In one report to Gage, dated August 14, 1775, a British agent operating in Concord spotted Revere, just days before the opening of hostilities at Lexington:

"Last Saturday the 7th of April P——— R——— toward evening arrived at Concord carrying a letter that was said to be from Mr. W———," a reference to Patriot leader Dr. Joseph Warren.[65] But such references cite Revere as a courier, a horse-bound letter carrier, *not* as the leader of a Boston spy ring.

How exactly Revere and his Mechanics delivered their spy reports to the leaders of the Sons of Liberty is not fully known. Historians are not even certain to whom such reports were distributed. Dr. Warren was a likely connection, as several members of the ring, including Revere, kept close ties with him. A militia colonel named William Conant, who lived across the river from Boston, in Charlestown, was another Revere contact. Both Sam and John Adams may have also been links in the chain of reports delivered by the Mechanics. But there are more mysteries than facts concerning the delivery of information by the Mechanics.

One of the most successful efforts carried out by Revere's spy ring was sabotage. Gun positions around Boston were constant targets and the Mechanics damaged or stole cannon right under the noses of the British. Over in Charlestown, agents made off with every piece of British artillery that had been deployed for a coastal battery, the guns whisked away into the Massachusetts rural countryside. The British North Battery, located in Boston proper, was a target in September 1774, resulting in every one of the battery's guns being spiked. The raiding party even took the lighter artillery pieces and dumped them in nearby Mill Pond.

Such acts of sabotage were likely difficult to accomplish, implying a significant amount of planning and possibly the bribing of British soldiers. Hauling away heavy cannon would have required horse-drawn wagons, and spiking guns would have meant metal banging on metal, a sound difficult to muffle. But British artillery pieces disappeared with frustrating frequency. When a pair of brass cannon vanished one night from an artillery unit commanded by Major Adino Paddock, the major stationed guards over his two remaining cannon. But soon, they, too, were carried off into the night by Revere's spies.

One particular raid—the record is unclear, but it may have been the one perpetrated on Major Paddock's battery—involved six agents, including William Dawes, who, like Revere, would serve as a rider on the night of April 18–19, 1775. The British had stored several brass cannon in a gun shed, secured them under lock and key, and posted an overnight sentry. Dawes and his associates approached the rear of the storage facility, removed the boards, and sneaked off with the cannon barrels without alerting the guard. One of the Patriot raiders, a schoolmaster named Abraham Holbrook, offered to hide the gun barrels in his schoolhouse located nearby, where they were placed in a long wooden crate. All such cannon collected through night raids wound up in the hands of Patriot groups, including militia and Minutemen. In this atmosphere of general uncertainty, military conflict was assumed possible or even inevitable. The Patriots wanted to be ready with arms of their own.

British cannon were not the only targets of Revere's raiders. Hay—fodder for all the king's horses—disappeared or was set ablaze. Boats vanished or had holes punched in their hulls. Building supplies to be used to construct perimeter fortifications were stolen or the boats carrying such materials were sunk. Civilian spies-turned-saboteurs drove the British to distraction with their constant nighttime raids.

Revere's agents managed other victories against their perceived British enemies. In December 1774, as Gage prepared to dispatch two Redcoat regiments to protect a cache of military supplies in Portsmouth, New Hampshire, the Mechanics caught wind of the action. Revere sent agents in advance on a large river craft called a gundalow (see "A Gundalow," following page). They reached the munitions first, and, after subduing the small number of British troops stationed at the site, loaded up a hundred barrels of gunpowder and sailed away to safety. Tradition says that some of the powder was used in the Battle of Bunker Hill six months later.

~◈~

A Gundalow

Patriots managed to pull off a deft act in December 1774 by stealing a large cache of gunpowder from a British post in Portsmouth, New Hampshire—just one more example of how the rebels were able to effectively sabotage the British prior to the first shots at Lexington and Concord.

The team of saboteurs sailed a gundalow to their rendezvous with the British. A gundalow was a common type of flat-bottomed river vessel used in New England. Some were up to seventy feet in length. They featured a single sail, usually lateen in trim. Gundalows were deployed during the Revolutionary War, with cannon mounted to provide firepower. During the battle of Valcour Island on October 11, 1776, the gundalow USS *Philadelphia* was sunk in Lake Champlain, New York. In 1935, the ship was raised and is today preserved by the Smithsonian Institution.

OUR MAN IN CONCORD

While Gage may have appeared to miss some obvious cues regarding the Patriots' espionage efforts, he was not without his own spy network. As we have seen, it is without question that Benjamin Church provided Gage with significant intelligence; many of his reports are still available today. (He was, incidentally, the only agent of Gage's whom the Americans ever detected and captured.) But the British general had additional, equally skilled agents, including one who operated out of Concord, a cloak-and-dagger figure whose identity is still unknown today, but one who seems to have rubbed shoulders with several Patriots. He may have been a Tory named John Howe operating under the alias "John Hall." Whoever this shadowy agent was, he provided Gage with important information concerning Patriot actions in and around Concord during March and April of 1775, the weeks leading up to start of the war.

Many of this agent's reports were written in French, which is inexplicable, since his French grammar and syntax were quite poor. Gage did speak French, so using the language could have served as a limited "code," protecting the intelligence from anyone who did not know French. If Gage's Concord agent was actually John Howe (or Hall), he might have picked up the language when serving the British military in Canada.

Otherwise, the choice of French is baffling. It is known today that, as late as the opening months of 1775, General Gage was not using any official code system with his field agents, a remarkable situation indeed. Apparently he was unversed in such cipher systems and had no officer handy to create one for him. This may explain why Dr. Church relied on such a simplistic substitution cipher in his fateful correspondence.

Questions concerning bad French aside, Gage's embedded Concord agent filled his reports with gems of intelligence gathering, including information about rebel artillery, as well as the locations of caches of Patriot stores, such as muskets, powder, and shot, and even food (stockpiles of dried peas, flour, and lard). He also provided possible routes for any British unit dispatched from Boston to the Massachusetts countryside in search of Patriot materiel. There are details related to roads, back lanes, and the tangle of footpaths that crisscrossed the handful of miles separating Boston and Concord. When Gage finally did order more than one thousand Redcoats to Concord to capture rebel leaders and confiscate Patriot supplies, the road they followed led them straight to their destination.

Gage's Concord spy even knew details about Patriot movements in and around Charlestown, north of Boston. He knew, for example, where arms were stored. He was also aware of Patriot efforts to encourage British "defection," stating:

> Spies and messengers are continually in the city to lure away the soldiers and there is a boat which, as an ordinary thing, carried them from behind the city to the other side of Cambridge Bay [a reference to the mouth of the Charles River]—landing at Philipps's Point. This information is confirmed by a deserter, who recently gave information to the priest at Concord (named Emerson[66], a very bad subject), to whom he stated that he escaped by the route.[67]

How could Gage's spy have known such details concerning a British deserter and the name of the person who helped him desert? While no answers are known, every logic suggests that the spy was likely comfortable

FOLLOWING:
The Battle of Lexington, 19th April, 1775 *by William Barnes Wollen, 1910, shows Massachusetts militiamen taking casualties while facing ordered ranks of British Redcoats.*

The "Loyalty" of Mrs. Gage

By the mid-1770s, the colonies' population was roughly split between Patriots and Loyalists. Sometimes these political differences even divided families, including husbands and wives. Questions lingered about General Gage and his own wife, for he married an American woman in 1758 while serving during the French and Indian War. Writing long after the Revolutionary War, clergyman William Gordon from Roxbury, Massachusetts, made the claim that Revere received intelligence on the night of the British march to Concord from "a daughter of liberty unequally yoked in point of politics."[68] Was this a reference to Mrs. Gage?

Some historians have pointed to Margaret Kemble Gage as the alleged "daughter of liberty." Patriots undoubtedly knew Gage's every step toward Concord in advance, and matters concerning Margaret became suspicious when Gage admitted he had only told his wife of his plans before he informed his officers. Gordon would later claim that Mrs. Gage told Dr. Warren the exact nature of Gage's plan to march to Concord, arrest Hancock and Adams, and capture rebel military stores.

But no real evidence exists today to indicate that she was ever an informant to Revere or even that she ever revealed any information concerning British military plans to any Patriot source. She did not relish the British action against the colonists, but nothing has been found to link her to any Patriot spy or intelligence source.

Still, with suspicion circling over her, Margaret Kemble Gage was sent to England following the opening of hostilities and never returned to America. When Gage left for England a year later and was reunited with his wife, they found themselves emotionally detached from one another and their marriage declined.

RIGHT:
John Singleton Copley's portrait of Margaret Kemble Gage, c. 1771.

in Patriot circles and trusted among Concord's rebel leaders, just as Dr. Church himself was.

Information from Gage's capable agent in Concord continued to reach his desk until the opening shots at Lexington on April 19. He reported other Redcoat desertions, including a member of an artillery company in Boston who had been recruited to drill Minutemen in Worcester, another rural Massachusetts town near Concord. In early April, a report indicated four brass cannon and a collection of mortars, all stolen from British posts in Boston, were in Concord, safely ensconced in the farmhouse of rebel militiaman Colonel James Barrett.

～ ※ ～

REPORTING ON THE REBELS

Looking ahead to the bloody encounters at Lexington and Concord, a spy report dated April 3 informed Gage of a recent meeting of the Massachusetts Provincial Congress during which members discussed how Patriots should respond in case British troops were sent out to capture their supplies. The legislators decided "that should any body of troops with Artillery, and Baggage, march out of Boston, the Country should be instantly alarmed, and called together to oppose their March, to the last extremity."[69]

General Gage had other agents at his disposal, including some in high places. One was Joseph Galloway, a member of the Pennsylvania delegation to the Continental Congress. He was a known Tory, as well as a longstanding friend of Benjamin Franklin; both had lived in Philadelphia. Galloway is known to have given Gage detailed reports of the congressional sessions and even information on the particular political leanings of members. He continued these activities until he left the Congress in 1775.

One of General Gage's primary goals during the months before the war was to determine how much resistance his troops might face in Boston and the surrounding areas. To do so, he gathered intelligence from several sources, including Major General William Brattle, who commanded the Massachusetts Royal Militia. Brattle collected official militia information and forwarded reports to Gage, especially concerning activities in

Cambridge. (Cambridge would become Washington's headquarters by the summer of 1775.)

While tens of thousands of Massachusetts residents had turned Patriot by early 1775, many others had not. The villages and farmsteads surrounding Boston were home to Tories as well, some of whom offered information concerning rebel activities in such communities as Worcester, Taunton, Plymouth, and Concord. Perhaps one of the most unique was a dyed-in-the-wool Loyalist named Henry Pelham, a young Boston painter and engraver. (Pelham was the half brother of John Singleton Copley, one of the colonies' most well-known and successful painters.) Pelham used his artistic skills as a cover for his clandestine activities. He roamed around the perimeter of British-held Boston, "innocently" sketching the country-side, all the while producing scaled drawings of rebel fortifications and encampments, including those on Bunker Hill. He left Boston along with other Loyalists by August 1776. The following year, an aquatint derived from his sketches, called *Plan of Boston*, was engraved and sold in London.

Another of Gage's spies was Benjamin Thompson, a major of the New Hampshire militia. Ironically, one of Thompson's first overt Loyalist activities was to deliver British deserters, not to Patriot authorities, but to General Gage directly. Once local patriots were informed, Thompson left New Hampshire for his own safety and settled in Woburn, Massachusetts, where he had grown up. In some respects, Thompson was less of a spy and more of an informant, a loyal Tory who gave information to Gage on several occasions. He did employ a bit of spy craft, however, penning his missives to Gage with invisible ink, a chemical process referred to at the time as a "sympathetic stain." Thompson was arrested in March 1775 and stood trial for his clandestine activities, but inadequate evidence ensured he was found not guilty. Under a cloud of suspicion, Thompson left Woburn, but continued providing Gage with information on the Continental Congress's efforts to recruit men into the army during the summer of 1775. He also reported on troop movements in and around Boston. After muskets were fired in anger at Lexington and Concord, Thompson managed to find a new informant, a "Field officer in the Rebel Army," adding in one report, "if that mass of confusion may be called an Army."[70]

Thompson remained an active agent of Gage's until November 1775, when Sir William Howe took command in Boston. He then reported to

Howe until the British were forced out of the city on March 17, 1776, the cannon having arrived from Fort Ticonderoga, allowing the rebels to ring Boston with artillery. After that, Thompson soon returned to England, but he did not take along his wife or young daughter, nor did he inform them he was leaving them behind. Oddly, he changed his name to Count Rumford, eventually settled in continental Europe, and became a well-known scientist.

FOLLOWING:
This map of Boston was drawn in October 1775 to show the location of British and rebel forces.

~ ※ ~

A PAIR OF UNDERCOVER OPERATIVES

Patriot activities continued as the early months of 1775 passed from winter to spring. Despite Gage's spies and various informants, Patriots managed to keep the British in the dark, moving supplies from one town to another beyond Boston. Dozens of wagons carried rebel flour from Marblehead to Worcester. Patriots even stored some supplies in Charlestown, across the river north of Boston. Carpenters were building gun carriages in the town, practically right under Gage's nose.

As a result, General Gage began ordering units of his Redcoats to search for stashes of weapons and other rebel supplies outside Boston. But before doing so, he needed adequate information regarding the appropriate roads to travel, available Tory contacts, and other useful intelligence.

In late February 1775, Gage sent out his first spies. They were British soldiers, including an officer and an enlisted man. Captain William Brown held rank in the 52nd Regiment of Foot. His comrade was Ensign Henry De Berniere, who belonged to the 10th. Their mission was to carry out reconnaissance and collect specific intelligence. As Gage wrote in his instructions: "You will go through the counties of Suffolk and Worcester, taking a sketch of the country as you pass; it is not expected you should make out regular plans and surveys, but mark out the roads and distances from town to town, as also the situation and nature of the country; all passes must be particularly laid down, noticing the length and breadth of them, the entrance in and going out of town, and whether to be avoided by taking other routes."[71]

Obviously, Gage's spies could not wear their scarlet uniforms in rural Massachusetts. Patriots throughout the region anticipated such

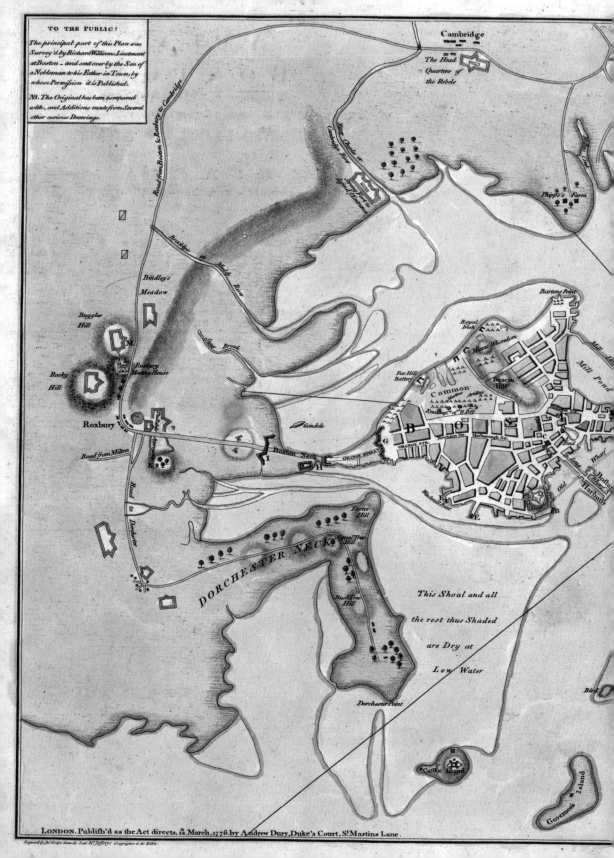

LONDON, Publifh'd as the Act directs, 1ſt March, 1776, by Andrew Dury, Duke's Court, Sᵗ Martins Lane.

A PLAN of BOSTON,

and its ENVIRONS.

shewing the true SITUATION of

HIS MAJESTY'S ARMY.

AND ALSO THOSE OF THE

REBELS.

Drawn by an Engineer at Boston. Oct.ʳ 1775.

REFERENCE.

A. { Corps Hill, a Battery of 8 Pieces of Cannon, Mortars, &c. &c. Erected to favour the Troops Landing on 17ᵗʰ June &, to set Fire to Charles Town......

B. { North & South Batteries, built by the Province, for the defence of ỹ Harbour, they are in a ruinous State..........

C. Town Hall..........

D. Fanuil Hall..........

E. Two Batteries Erected on Wharfs against Dorchester Neck..........

F. Fort Hill, a proper Place for constructing a Citadel..........

G. Fortification now constructing for the immediate defence of the Town..........

H. A Block House & 2 Strong Batteries pointing on part of Dorchester Neck..........

I. Lines to defend the Boston Neck..........

K. { A Hill from whence the Enemy annoy ỹ Centries & Officers with small Arms, but seldom do any Execution..........

L. { Roxbury Meeting House, upon a Hill from whence ỹ Enemy often Fire Cannon into the Lines..........

M. { A Strong Post of the Enemy, Fortified in appearance with great Judgment, & much Elevated, from whence with a 24 Pounder they can just reach the Lines..........

EXPLANATION.

The Works shaded Green shew those constructed by His Majestys Troops..........

The Works shaded Yellow shew those thrown up by the Rebels, as they appear from Boston..........

Hill

Plough'd Hill

Winter Hill

Mistick River

Penny Ferry

Charles Town Neck

Lines & Redoubts thrown up by our Troops after ỹ Victory on 9.¹ 17 June 1775.

Gondoles

Gen.ˡ Howe's Camp

Artillery

H.ⁱ L L

KR.S

Route taken from ỹ Rebels by Gen.ˡ Howe

Dragoons

A Pond

Marines

Troops Landed 17 June under General Howe

Charlestown Point

Road to Marble Head & Salem

Winnisimmet Ferry

NODDLES ISLAND

Williams's House burnt by ỹ Rebels.

H O G I S L A N D

Yards or Half a Mile

intelligence-gathering missions by the British and were ready to respond. A group over in Worcester had already set aside a large quantity of tar and feathers and intended to use it on any such agent, as well as any local Tory collaborator they might also catch. Thus, to protect themselves, the two British soldiers dressed as local Massachusetts men (as best they could determine), donning "brown cloaths and reddish handkerchiefs round our necks."[72] No detail was to be overlooked. Gage needed information on roads, local waterways, defendable positions, possible sites for troop bivouac, sources of food, and fodder for horses.

Gage gave Brown and De Berniere their instructions on February 22 (George Washington's birthday), and even suggested a possible cover for the two—they could pretend to be surveyors. As they set out, one of Brown's servants, an enlisted man named John, accompanied them. Departing on February 23, they could not know how important to their mission John would prove.

The clandestine scouting party took the ferry at Charlestown, passed Breed's and Bunker Hills, reached Cambridge, then Watertown, where they stopped at an inn called Brewer's Tavern. The choice was underinformed, for the landlord, Jonathan Brewer, was a Patriot and a fiery one at that. During the French and Indian War, Brewer had served in a ranger company under General James Wolfe, the hero of the 1759 Battle of Quebec. But those days had long been forgotten. The British were now the oppressors. And the strangers only raised suspicions because the Patriots of Watertown were anticipating spies. When they sent John into the kitchen to eat with the servants, the suspicions seemed warranted. Brown and De Berniere laid out maps on their table to provide evidence of their "surveying" cover. As their food arrived, they commented to the tavern maid, a black woman, how fine the country through which they were passing was. Her own Patriot leanings were soon apparent, as she warned: "So it is, and we have got brave fellows to defend it, and if you go up any higher you will find it so."[73] Dinner over, the two decided they had best move on and not risk spending the night.

But they did not know how much trouble they were in until John joined them outside the tavern. He informed his companions that the tavern maid had told him that she recognized Brown as a British officer she had seen in Boston five years earlier. She recognized John as well. Even though John pushed her assertion aside, she knew she was right and added, "She knew our errand was to take a plan of the country; that she had seen the river and road through Charlestown on the paper; she also advised him to tell us not to go any higher, for if we did we should meet with very bad usage."[74] Their stop at the tavern revealed how unprepared these spies of Gage's were and that the locals they were going to encounter were no naive country bumpkins.

The unmasked spies now wondered whether to proceed or abandon their reconnaissance mission. Since they were more afraid of how Gage would respond to their coming back empty-handed than what abuses they might face from the Patriots, they continued on their way. After traveling several more miles—including hitching a ride in a farm wagon—they arrived at another tavern, this one a bit friendlier to their cause. As they ordered coffee from the landlord, a man named Isaac Jones, he responded by offering "what we pleased, either tea or coffee."[75] The word "tea" was a code among Loyalists, since all Patriots had elected, due to the Tea Tax, to boycott the stuff. In the hands of a friend, Brown and De Berniere received much-needed information, including which taverns to stop at when they arrived up the road at either Framingham or Worcester.

~ ※ ~

TROUBLE AT EVERY TURN

Progress was slow the following day, as the weather was rainy, but the roads they traveled were fairly empty, so few asked questions. Hungry by midday, they stopped at yet another tavern, one not suggested to them the night before by Jones. Unfortunately, they again chose poorly. The landlord, Joseph Buckminster, kept to himself but eyed the men warily. He was a member of the local Committee of Correspondence, so he was on the lookout for strangers. The next morning, February 25, a Saturday, the party of spies took to the road, headed straight for Worcester, located thirty miles away. Along the way, they succeeded in sketching some of the local land. That evening, they reached Worcester and stayed at a tavern, operated by another Isaac Jones (a relative of the first Jones), who proved as Loyalist as his relation.

The following day was Sunday and nearly everyone in the region was expected to attend church. To avoid questions, the spies remained in their room. Once services were over, they ventured out, sketching some sites they thought might serve well as places for Redcoat units to encamp. That evening, Jones informed them some men had come by to tell him they knew the visitors he harbored were British soldiers in disguise. Brown and De Berniere decided they had risked enough. They would start back toward Boston at dawn.

The spies wisely took a different road as they trudged back to the east, one that took them through Shrewsbury, rather than Grafton. Just beyond Shrewsbury, they were stopped by a farmer riding a wagon. He said nothing, but stared at them intently, then snapped the reins and headed in a rush down the road in the opposite direction. The concerned spies switched roads again, this time heading toward Framingham and Buckminster's Tavern. They could not have known the significance of their detour at that moment, but it was fortunate. The man in the wagon was Timothy Bigelow, a Worcester blacksmith, Minuteman captain, and member of the Provincial Congress. He had driven his wagon to Marlborough and told the local Patriots that a trio of disguised British soldiers was headed their way.

A new discomfort awaited the spies when they arrived back at Buckminster's Tavern, for a local militia unit was drilling near the inn. De Berniere later wrote: "We did not feel very easy at seeing such a number so very near us," but, as things turned out, the citizen-soldiers paid them little attention.[76] After an uneventful night, they continued the next day back to Weston. The weather had turned pleasant and they became a bit more confident, having spent practically a week doing reconnaissance without harm or capture. Against their better discretion, they decided to examine the main road between Boston and Worcester, which they had avoided on their way west the previous week. To make certain that the information they had already collected and sketched reached General Gage, they sent John on his way back to Boston.

✧ ※ ✧

A DISINTEGRATING COVER

As Brown and De Berniere split off from John, they soon found trouble again. The weather turned foul, and snow began to fall, accumulating at an alarming rate. "We found the roads very bad, every step up to our ankles,"[77] but they continued on slowly toward Marlborough, which lay sixteen miles away. Eventually, when they were three miles from their destination, they were approached by yet another curious colonial, a man on horseback, who stopped and began to ask probing questions, including whether they were British soldiers. Convinced of their true identities, the rider spurred toward Marlborough to signal the approach of disguised Lobsterbacks, yet another Patriot name for the Redcoats.

When they reached town, the pair searched for a local Tory, Henry Barnes, an applejack distiller and merchant. He informed them their cover was blown, and everyone in the village knew who they were. Barnes told them they were not safe, as the community was a hotbed of Patriot supporters. Barnes also informed them of the arrival of a British deserter, a drummer. This could not have been more unfortunate, since the man, whose name was Swain, was in Brown's own company. Once again, they were running the risk of being identified by someone who had known them back in Boston. Asking Barnes what might happen to them if they were identified and captured, their host was reluctant to say, but indicated "we might expect the worst of treatment from them."[78] When a local member of the Sons of Liberty soon knocked on Barnes's door, even though he had not spoken to Barnes in two years, the spies knew they needed to get out of town fast.

Barnes successfully put his Patriot visitor off, and Brown and De Berniere thought they might be able to rest a few hours, before sneaking out of town around midnight. But when a servant of Barnes warned them that a party of local Patriots was headed their way, they rushed out their host's back door and hightailed it down a back lane toward the Sudbury Road. They had only been under Barnes's roof for approximately twenty minutes.

Following an arduous trek through snow, and having failed to eat, the pair finally reached Weston and a safe tavern. The next day, March 2, they arrived in Boston, where General Gage and his staff barely recognized them. After eight harrowing days, Brown and De Berniere were dirty, mud-spattered, hungry, and worn to a frazzle. They reported their findings, and showed Gage their sketches, which pleased him enough that he sent them out less than three weeks later on a similar reconnaissance to Concord. This time, they reached their destination—traveling through Roxbury, Brookline, and Weston without serious incident.

Once in Concord, they took refuge at the home of a local Tory, Daniel Bliss, having been guided to his house by an unsuspecting local woman. No sooner had they reached Bliss's home, than a woman arrived at the door, wailing that local Patriots had threatened her for aiding Tories. Bliss, who had been gathering intelligence about Patriot cannon and stores of Minutemen provisions around Concord, feared for his life and begged to accompany Brown and De Berniere back to Boston. They agreed, as Bliss led them down another road, one that passed through Lexington and back to Gage's headquarters. Again, the pair of disguised British soldiers had accomplished their mission.

～ ※ ～

THE EXPLOITS OF
AGENT JOHN HOWE

Over the course of February and March 1775, Captain Brown and Ensign De Berniere's mission had managed to provide some actionable intelligence for General Gage. The general then wasted no time launching another pair of spies into the Massachusetts countryside to gain even more information. Just two weeks before the shots were fired at Lexington, Gage sent out Lieutenant Colonel Francis Smith of the 10th Foot and an assistant, John Howe. Both went in disguise and, like their predecessors, headed to Worcester.

This time the disguise featured "leather breeches, gray coats, blue mixed stockings, and handkerchiefs knotted about their throats,"[79] plus an added touch—both men carried a bundle hung from a stick, a poor man's suitcase of sorts.

No sooner had Smith and Howe set out than they met their match. Only six miles from Boston, the agents stopped at a tavern in Watertown.

LEFT:
*Portrait of John Howe
by William Valentine,
c. 1820.*

Sitting down for breakfast, they found themselves face-to-face with the very same black tavern maid who had identified Brown and De Berniere as British spies.

An unsuspecting Smith played his role, asking the girl if she was aware of any local employment, to which she responded, even stating his name: "Smith, you will find employment enough for you and all General Gage's men in a few months."[80]

Hastily finishing their meal, the British agents spoke to the landlord about the "saucy wench" he employed. He explained that she was from Boston "and had got acquainted with a great many British officers and soldiers."[81] Smith's cover was completely blown, so he had no choice but to head back to Boston, leaving Howe on his own. With a promise of an officer's commission if he continued the mission unescorted, Howe pressed on.

As Howe met people along the way, he explained he was an out-of-work gunsmith, a clever ploy that helped him gain valuable information. He was told the locals might be in need of a skilled gunsmith soon. As one explained: "[The Patriots] were in want of guns, for they meant to be ready for them," referring to the British Redcoats.[82] Over several days, the adroit Howe met with various Tories, who provided him with assessments of Patriot numbers, strength, and munitions. He had several close calls, including the arrival of a large number of local Patriots who had heard of a stranger in the area asking awkward questions. Howe barely escaped with his life out of an upstairs window, falling and skidding off the roof into six inches of snow.

Ultimately, Howe managed to convince the right locals that he was a Patriot himself and a gunsmith to boot, so he was led straight into Concord and introduced to Major John Buttrick of the local Minutemen. Buttrick took Howe into a shop where he placed several broken muskets in front of him—likely a test to determine whether Howe's "cover" was for real. Indeed, Howe was trained in the smithing arts and the busted muskets were soon "repaired with neatness and dispatch, considering the tools I had to work with."[83] It was all Buttrick needed to see. Before the day was over, Howe had been taken to see the Concord magazine, a veritable Patriot munitions paradise. Howe had gained what all spies long for—access to secret information known only to the enemy, while operating undercover. With his mission accomplished, Howe made his way back to Boston (with the aid of additional helpful local Tories), and he reported his findings to his superiors. His reward was immediate, including fifty guineas. (His promised officer's commission would be forthcoming.) Meeting with officers, including Francis Smith, Howe debriefed the group, and perhaps inadvertently exaggerated Patriot strength, stating emphatically that ten thousand Redcoats would not be enough to reach Worcester, much less Concord.

Possibly intent on redeeming himself, Smith spoke up: "Howe has been scared by the old women." To which a fellow officer, Major John Pitcairn of the Royal Marines (who would die in the battle of Bunker Hill), chided: "Not by a black wench, John."[84]

The Boston of 1775

Today, the city of Boston is one of the largest urban centers in the United States. The same was true during the colonial era. At that time, it was home to perhaps fifteen to twenty thousand inhabitants and ranked, population-wise, in the top three cities in the colonies, along with New York and Philadelphia.

The Boston of 1775, though, was a much smaller place than its modern-day counterpart. Then, the city proper was centered on a peninsula of land, sometimes thought to resemble a partially inflated balloon, with the only land connection situated at the south end, an area called Dorchester Heights. The city's Back Bay, unlike today, was water and had not yet been filled in.

When General Gage prepared to dispatch troops to Concord in April, everyone knew there were only two possible routes for the Redcoats to take. They would either march south along Dorchester Neck, or ferry across the Charles River to Charlestown and catch the main road heading west to Concord. Thus, the famous "one if by land, and two if by sea" phrase (see "One if by Land, and Two if by Sea," page 92).

So, on April 15, as the British unloaded a large number of boats into the Charles River, their purpose was clear—Gage was dispatching significant forces across the river, and they were likely bound for Concord to intercept a cache of hidden Patriot military supplies.

A MOVE TOWARD CONCORD

As General Gage made his decision to send troops to capture rebel supplies in Concord, he did so based, in part, on the reports of his spies. One report said that Paul Revere was riding to Concord to deliver a letter from Dr. Warren. Revere was there to warn local Patriots of an imminent British plan to attack, though he was uncertain of the exact date. A second report on April 18 informed Gage that the Patriots in Concord were in the process of moving their stored munitions, but that it would take some time before the task would be complete. This spurred Gage into immediate action.

Even as Gage prepared to dispatch troops across the Charles River and toward Concord on the night of the 18th—with the aim of capturing

Place IV. A View of the South Part of Lexington

Patriot leaders Sam Adams and John Hancock—he did not seem to take seriously the possibility of Patriot spies alerting colonials of the Redcoats' approach. As early as three days before, Revere's men spotted a plethora of boats being lowered into the Charles from larger transport vessels. While the boats were off-loaded under cover of darkness on the night of April 15, they were perfectly visible as they bobbed in the water the morning of April 16 and for the next few days. Only the most clueless of spies could have failed to grasp their meaning and Gage's intentions. Beyond Charlestown, the road led straight to Concord, where a large cache of military supplies was stored.

Gage made a half-hearted effort to disguise the reason that so many boats had been moved into the Charles River. He engaged in a small bit of deception, spreading a rumor the boats were part of a special training exercise. Few Bostonians could possibly have been convinced.

The Mechanics adroitly determined that Gage was intent on marching Redcoats to Concord where Hancock and Adams were allegedly hiding out. In fact, they were actually in Lexington, as Revere knew, and the Boston silversmith-spymaster rode out to the small town to warn them. He caught up with both men in the home of one of Hancock's cousins. In addition, Patriots in Concord were alerted concerning British intentions and they swung into action.

Meanwhile, Revere made his way quietly back to Boston, as his Mechanics took steps to counter Gage's intended march out of the city. A signal system was devised involving the now-famed lanterns in the steeple of Christ Church (today known to many as the Old North Church). If the British chose to leave Boston to the north, across the Charles River, two lanterns would be placed in the steeple; if to the south through Dorchester Neck, one lantern light would be the signal. Revere's fear was that his alarm riders might not be able to leave the city when the time came because the British patrols were thick on the streets of the city.

Gage knew his men were being watched, and he took counterintelligence measures of his own that night. In addition to the patrols in the city and along the roads leading to Concord, he also positioned a British naval vessel, the HMS *Somerset*, her decks bristling with sixty-four guns, at the mouth of the Charles River. But his efforts and even his own men ultimately failed. As British officers instructed their grooms to prepare their horses for the march, they inadvertently said too much, indicating to the local horsemen that something big was going to happen. One even told his groom that there would be "hell to pay tomorrow."[85] Informers came to Revere's home to with these little pieces of intelligence.

So many Patriots hid in the shadows of Boston along the banks of the Charles River that one of Gage's commanders, Lord Percy, who was to command the second of the two units scheduled to embark for Concord that night, accidentally crossed paths with one in the darkness. Following a final meeting at Gage's headquarters at the Province House, Percy went out to check on the situation with his troops. Although he wore his uniform, it was covered with a great cloak. From the shadows, he heard a voice: "The

British troops have marched, but will miss their aim." A surprised Percy responded to the unseen informant: "What aim?"

"Why, the cannon at Concord." Then the mysterious Patriot vanished, not knowing he had been speaking to one of Gage's high-ranking officers.[86]

It was clear the British mission of search-and-capture had been compromised.

"One if by Land, and Two if by Sea"

Many recall the phrase "One if by land, and two if by sea" from Henry Wadsworth Longfellow's poem "Paul Revere's Ride." It was intended as the signal for alarm riders and others regarding the route the British might take out of the city of Boston on the night of April 18, 1775. But Longfellow did not exactly get his facts straight.

Published in 1860, Longfellow included the following stanza:

> *He said to his friend, "If the British march*
> *By land or sea from the town to-night,*
> *Hang a lantern aloft in the belfry arch*
> *Of the North Church tower as a signal light,—*
> *One if by land, and two if by sea;*
> *And I on the opposite shore will be,*
> *Ready to ride and spread the alarm*
> *Through every Middlesex village and farm,*
> *For the country folk to be up and to arm."*[87]

That the British might head out from Boston that night "by sea" is a bit misleading. There was no "sea" to span, only the Charles River that flowed between Boston and Charlestown. Yes, crossing the river was about crossing water, but the fact is that Longfellow used poetic license, needing a rhyme for his following line: "And I on the opposite shore will be." Actually, that line has its own problems. When the British did embark across the Charles and then take up the march along the road leading out of Charlestown, Revere was still in Boston, not "on the opposite shore" in Charlestown.

A Fine Prize Denied the British

When General Gage dispatched hundreds of Redcoats to Concord on April 18, 1775, one of their goals was to capture a large supply of military materiel.

The supplies at Concord were considerable, including everything from food to firepower. The inventory represented what would have been a fine prize for the British: twenty thousand pounds of musket balls and cartridges, fifty reams of cartridge paper, three hundred and eighteen barrels of flour, seventeen thousand pounds of salt fish, and thirty-five thousand pounds of rice.[88]

A Lantern in the Old North

Once the Patriots launched into action, it seemed everything followed in rapid order. Lanterns were displayed in the belfry of the Old North Church, alerting a Patriot agent over in Charlestown. The church sexton, Robert Newman, barely escaped before Redcoats, having spotted the signal, broke in in search of those responsible. Although Newman was later arrested at his mother's house, he was soon released, claiming he had loaned his church keys to Captain John Pulling. By the time the British knew to look for Pulling, he had already skipped town.

Just blocks away, Revere was at home, trying to prepare to leave the city and warn Adams and Hancock of the approach of the British. With troops in the streets near his house, he had to sneak out, leaving his spurs behind in case he was caught. Spurs (which would have suggested a fast ride out of the city) might have been difficult to explain so late at night, especially for the spymaster the British knew him to be. Soon, he rendezvoused with two agents who rowed him in a small boat across the Charles. To muffle the sound of the oars, Revere slid over to the corner of North and North Centre Streets, where he signaled to a young female acquaintance of his. In seconds, she tossed a petticoat out of her window; Revere would later claim it was still warm.

Revere and his party floated quietly past the *Somerset*'s great hulk. Fortunately, no one spotted them, and he soon found his way to Colonel Conant's house. With the British headed to Concord, he wasted little time, mounting a horse he borrowed from a wealthy Patriot in Charlestown. Through the night, in what would become the stuff of legend, he rode through the Massachusetts countryside, trumpeting the approach of regular British soldiers and managing to rouse thousands of Minutemen and Patriot militiamen before dawn on the 19th. By then, the shots on Lexington Green had been fired. But the mission of Revere and the Mechanics had been successful.

An organization credited today by the Central Intelligence Agency as the first American intelligence network had managed to keep tabs on British movements in and around Boston for months, and had successfully delivered intelligence to Patriot leaders. Adams and Hancock had escaped the grasp of General Gage, and Patriot weapons, ammunition, and food-stuffs remained in their hands. They would soon be badly needed. No longer were the British and their colonial subjects going to debate taxes, customs duties, and arbitrary rule. The war was on, and America's future hung in the balance.

~ ※ ~

LEFT:
Boston's Old North Church, whose belfry served as one of the central signaling points for the Patriots to pass along information.

CHAPTER FOUR

Nathan Hale:
A Lamb to Slaughter

A WAR UNDERWAY

PREVIOUS:
Last Words of Nathan
Hale *by Alexander Hay
Ritchie, 1858, illustrates
Hale's September 22,
1776, execution in
Manhattan by hanging
after being charged with
being a spy.*

he war was finally on. A handful—approximately seventy souls—had met the British regulars on the Lexington Green in the early hours of April 19. Eight Patriots had fallen, with no loss of life for the British. The Mechanics' spymaster and, on that particular morning, alarm rider, was still in the neighborhood when the opening salvos of war and rebellion rang out. No one knew then or now which side fired the first shot.

Armed conflict erupted later that day in Concord. The rebels managed to meet the enemy full square on Concord's North Bridge. The defeated Redcoats' ragged march back to Boston took the remainder of the day and much of the night, and it exacted a serious toll on their forces. Thousands of Patriot militia and plain old private citizens—armed with any musket, squirrel gun, or shotgun they could shoulder—rallied in the aftermath of the day, giving the retreating British hell to pay along the twenty miles to Boston. Dozens of British soldiers were killed and hundreds wounded along the route remembered later as "The Bloody Chute." War had arrived in earnest.

Some Patriot Psychological Warfare

One advantage Washington and his men had during the months of 1775 and early 1776, when the British occupied Boston, was control of the countryside surrounding this most important of New England's cities. This meant the British, at least several thousand Redcoats and their supporters, could be kept to one place. Although the British controlled the open sea and, thus, Boston Harbor, they were not able to gain access to adequate supplies at every turn. The shortages created a crisis of confidence among British soldiers.

The Continental Army and its citizen allies understood the difficulties the British faced in obtaining regular supplies, and they exploited them. They produced pieces of propaganda, such as flyers and leaflets, as well as word-of-mouth rumors, that any British soldier who was not being provided adequate food, access to doctors, and even personal liberties should defect to the Patriot side, where such necessities were readily accessible. Even as the Americans lured some Redcoats to their side, the desertion rate among British soldiers stationed in occupied Boston remained low.

At first glance, the American propaganda campaign seems to have been a failure. But a closer look reveals a factor that is difficult to quantify: its effect on morale. Such claims of a better world outside Boston often demoralized both the Redcoat enlisted men and many of their officers.

WASHINGTON TAKES COMMAND

During the weeks that followed, the Continental Congress convened a Continental Army and selected a commander in chief, one with as much military experience as the colonies could boast. A member of the Congress's Virginia delegation, George Washington had not donned a uniform in nearly twenty years. But when tapped to lead the various militia units already in the field, as well as the thousands of Patriots volunteering for duty on a daily basis, he could not refuse. (In a sense, he even campaigned for the job, wearing a new uniform he had designed to congressional meetings.)

The new commander set out from Mount Vernon, his beloved Virginia plantation, and arrived in Massachusetts several weeks later (too late for the Battle of Bunker Hill). He found an army in chaos: undisciplined, inexperienced, underfed, and ill-prepared. In short, the men were hardly an army and stood short of every necessity. But Washington worked hard to transform his ragtag force into men who could match the British Redcoats, one of the most disciplined and highly trained armies in the world.

Among the many missing resources was good intelligence. While the British had a reasonably skilled spy network in place in 1775, Washington did not. The Mechanics could no longer be relied on. Many of its members, especially Paul Revere himself, were well known as Patriot agents already, thus limiting—if not eliminating—their effectiveness as spies. Revere, in fact, had already left the city, certain the British would target him for capture. (With Revere in hiding outside of the city, his wife, Rachel, became concerned for his safety and livelihood and sent a personal letter to him, along with £125. She used Dr. Church as the courier, without realizing he was a double agent. True to his habits, Church never delivered the letter or the money—it was eventually discovered among General Gage's papers years later.) Another Mechanics leader, Dr. Joseph Warren, was killed during the Battle of Bunker Hill.

But, even if Revere's Mechanics were no longer able to function as a whole, there were still a few members who remained in the field as independent agents. One was James Lovell, a schoolmaster-turned-spy, who continued to engage in rebel espionage after the war opened. But events

John Trumbull's 1785 painting The Death of General Warren at the Battle of Bunker Hill, June 17, 1775. *This was the first Revolutionary War painting finished by Trumbull, who served in the Continental Army from 1775 to 1777.*

soon caught up with him. Following Dr. Warren's death at Bunker Hill, British soldiers rifled through Warren's clothing and found documents leading back to Lovell. By late June, British authorities arrested him and delivered him to a prison in Halifax, Canada. Eventually he was released as part of a prisoner exchange and ended up working for Congress as an expert in codes and cipher programs.

Revere's fellow alarm rider, William Dawes, remained above suspicion, and he managed to move in and out of Boston without notice. Dawes—and perhaps some of the other agents—managed to trundle engraving equipment out of Paul Revere's shop in Boston to print Continental and Massachusetts paper money.

Another agent at this time was Boston merchant John Carnes. His handler was Colonel Loammi Baldwin, one of Washington's officers. (Washington had assigned Colonel Baldwin as one of his intelligence organizers in July 1775.) Carnes passed information to Baldwin indirectly, through a pair of cutouts (individuals who deliver intelligence on behalf of another agent). Carnes reported to a nameless "waterman" who ferried across the Charles River. In turn, he handed the intelligence to a third man named Dewksbury, who lived down the road from Loammi's headquarters in Chelsea, and could deliver the correspondence. The lack of direct contact between the first source and final recipient maintained the veil of secrecy between agents.

Actionable intelligence came to Washington in frustrating dribs and drabs, and he often received either inadequate, incorrect, or conflicting reports. It was strictly amateur, even if well intentioned. Since the British were occupying Boston, they had to deal regularly with the local citizens: they did business with them, lived in their houses, purchased their food, frequented their brothels. A local farmer selling his pumpkins to a Redcoat commissary officer might hear a few tidbits, just as an eavesdropping fish wife might overhear a random conversation between British officers in a tavern. But these were only scraps of information, not a systematic intelligence effort. Washington's army did establish observation posts surrounding the city, from which they could monitor British troop movements and other military activities, but such posts did not tell him what he desperately needed to know: What were the British planning, and what move would they make next?

Because of the occupation, access to adequate food was a continual problem, so Gage's naval commander, Admiral Thomas Graves, allowed local fishermen to continue to ply their trade—which also conveniently delivered fresh fish to British army tables. This loophole allowed some rebel spies an easy cover. While Gage's practice was to issue passes to fishermen to make them "official," it became fairly commonplace for a fishing party of four or five men to include at least one who was functioning in a second role—that of spy. One pair of spy-fishermen were agents known as Goodwin and Hopkins, whose espionage and intelligence gathering began as early as May 1775. They were described "as bad Rebels as any,"[89] and they regularly smuggled informants out of Boston, whom they sometimes provided disguises.

Another such amateur intelligence agent was George Robert Twelves Hewes. He possessed a fishing pass, and for more than two months, sold fish to the British while collecting also military information for the

Americans. Finally, loaded with intelligence, he made his way to General Washington's headquarters. Telling his biographer the tale many years later, Hewes said that Washington, after he had received the Boston fisherman's information, "didn't *laugh* to be sure, but *looked amazing good natured.*"[90] Hewes related how he and his boatmates were invited to dine with Washington and his wife, Martha, who "waited upon them at table all dinner-time and was remarkably social."[91]

Washington desperately needed a system by which to spy on the British. To that end, he began organizing a small-scale spy network of his own. According to a July 15 ledger entry, the new commander in chief was willing to pay for intelligence. One line reads: "333.3 Dollars given to to enduce him to go into the Town of Boston, to establish a secret correspondence for the purpose of movements and designs." At the end of this page in his account book, Washington added: "The names of Persons who are employed within the Enemy's lines, or who may fall within their power cannot be inserted—"[92] Whomever Washington had employed, his efforts seemed to have paid off, whether directly or indirectly. In less than a week, Thomas Machin, a British soldier from the 23rd Regiment, deserted and provided Washington with information on British fortifications within the city.

As for British spying efforts, they already had a system in place and utilized it to the fullest. Gage's secret service was led by his brother-in-law, Lieutenant Colonel Kemble. Since the rebels held every access point in and out of the city, it was nearly impossible to repeat forays such as what Brown and De Berniere or even John Howe had carried out. Instead, like Washington, Kemble had to rely on local citizens to do the spying.

Some of these amateur spies were able to produce valuable intelligence. As early as May 1775, a Tory spy from Boston reached the town of Roxbury. There he managed to observe troops drilling, as well as artillery movements; he then slid deftly over to Cambridge, where he counted fewer than twenty Continental tents in a single camp and watched the passing of artillery units through the area. During a regularly scheduled prayer session within the encampment, he hurriedly counted heads and pegged the number at three thousand. On his return to Boston, he observed troops stationed at Roxbury, also at their prayers, and counted about four hundred men. On the final leg of his successful reconnaissance, he spotted nearly a dozen four-pounder cannon outside a Roxbury

church. One day's spying by one amateur resulted in an enviable report for General Gage.

For far longer than they should have, British spies in Boston had easy access to the ferry that operated between Boston's Winnisimet neighborhood (today's Chelsea) and Cambridge, where Washington's headquarters was located. One of Gage's agents—known only by his codename, "the Deponent"—traveled back and forth on the ferryboat and made contact with a decidedly Tory butcher who served in a rebel artillery unit. From the butcher's intelligence alone, the Deponent gained valuable military information regarding artillery placement and numbers; locations of stored ammunition; specs on fortifications; numbers of floating batteries and whaleboats; as well as the total numbers serving under Washington's direct command. He managed significant elicitation, sharing meals with one American captain, and he even sat down with General Israel Putnam, a New England commander known for his rigid expectations. The mysterious agent also had other contacts in Cambridge who provided information and intelligence. Unfortunately, Washington did not express a concern about the ferry being used by enemy agents until March 1776 and by then the British were evacuating Boston.

Gage and his intelligence network even reached into other colonies. One volunteer traveled to Connecticut and Rhode Island and reported to the general on troop movements there. Another agent—named in reports as "W. C."—observed deployments in parts of New York. However, he was discovered and captured by local Patriots who threatened to whip him and coat him with tar and feathers. Only after W. C. toasted the death of the British prime minister, Lord North, were such threats neutralized. In another instance, when rebels hatched a plot to kidnap the Tory governor of New York, an unknown agent informed Gage, and the plot was thwarted.

As the members of the Continental Congress met in Philadelphia, several of Gage's agents were there operating on his behalf. Within the ranks of the Congress was Joseph Galloway, who provided information regarding congressional sessions. He also informed Gage of Benjamin Franklin's return from England. The general managed to convince the captain of Franklin's ship to examine any letters sent to Franklin from England, and vice versa. If any contained "some intelligence of the Rebels here," the captain was to turn the incriminating letters over to the general.[93]

For a time, a pair of Tory agents operated out of Philadelphia, collecting intelligence for Gage. Dr. John Kearsley, a Pennsylvania horse doctor and creator of an animal medicine called "Kearsley's Pills," elicited any and all information regarding the rebels and routed the intelligence to London through Gage. The second agent, John Brooks, ran an intelligence line between Philadelphia and Albany, New York. By October 1775, both men were exposed, arrested, and clapped away in jail in Lancaster, Pennsylvania. Although Brooks managed to escape in 1777, Kearsley died the day following his release in 1778.

With the rebels outside Boston and Gage and his thousands of Redcoats bottled up inside, Gage determined the situation was untenable. He knew he could not remain in the city indefinitely. And, in fact, he didn't. He left both Boston and America in October 1775 and was replaced by General William Howe. In December, Howe confirmed Gage's determination of the British position, although the actual evacuation did not take place until spring. By March 17, 1776, the last of the British Redcoats in Boston were gone. Washington and his men entered the city in cautious triumph. Spyglass views of the city's streets revealed British sentries still on duty. Only after they entered Boston did the Continentals realize the trick—the British had set up straw dummies in red coats. But the city was now in the hands of the Americans. A siege, not a battle, had finally knocked the British out of Boston.

Washington did not remain in the city for long. Knowing the strategic importance of New York City—this second largest city in the colonies boasted a busy port and a thriving merchant class—the very next day he ordered his riflemen and five regiments of infantry to occupy New York. Even as Washington split his men, he was concerned about a British response. And he continued to worry about being spied on, writing: "The enemy have the best knack at puzzling people I ever met with in my life. . . . There is one evil that I dread, and that is, their spies."[94] He then ordered a dozen of his own amateur agents to seek out information between Boston and his army on the move. They came back loaded with intelligence. The last of the British ships out of Boston had set out to sea, headed to Halifax, Canada. Boston was safe, and Washington could concentrate on New York. He arrived in the city by mid-April and established his headquarters on the lower end of Manhattan, the city center.

If Boston had been a hotbed of radicalism for more than ten years, the same could hardly be said of New York City, which was home to many Loyalists. In fact, it had one of the highest percentages of Loyalists of any city in the colonies, and Washington knew he would have intelligence issues. As Gage had been to Boston and the rebels, so would Washington be to New York and its Tories. In fact, Washington had more to worry

A Pair of French Agents

Although the British and Americans spied on one another with regularity both prior to and during the Revolutionary War, other nations sometimes delivered their own espionage operatives into the conflict as well. Before the battles of Lexington and Concord, the French government, interested in the events in the mid-1770s, sent two undercover operatives to check out the unfolding revolution in America.

The two were Achard de Bonvouloir and the Chevalier d'Amboise. They had entered New England by sailing up from the Caribbean, and they moved about the colonies, gathering information on the developing political split as well as the American and British military presence. Bonvouloir was directly in the employ of the French embassy in London. They were both in Lexington on the morning of April 19 and watched the beginning of the conflict. With the war underway, they moved back to Boston and were soon in Washington's encampment in and around Cambridge, observing the troops, assessing their capacity to face the British. What they saw did not impress them; they considered the early Continental Army to be amateurish at best and undisciplined otherwise, even if their mission intended to support the Americans over the British.

Once they had their findings, Bonvouloir and Amboise left for London where they reported to the French embassy. Almost immediately the French government sent them back to America to continue their work. But British intelligence had already ferreted out these French connections. One British secret service agent reported on their comings and goings as soon as August 6, 1775. (At one point, the agent had even shared a conversation and a bottle of champagne with Bonvouloir, hoping the alcohol would put the French agent off his guard, but the Frenchman refused to take the bait. He spent the conversation criticizing the American military but kept his own counsel concerning British forces.) By September, Bonvouloir was back in America, his cover disguise that of a Dutch merchant. Soon, he was working closely with one of the Committees of Correspondence, gathering further intelligence, which was used later to aid the French government in making its decision to support the American cause with troops, money, and supplies.

about than just being spied on. He was soon the target of various Tory groups, who wanted to kidnap or assassinate him.

New York was buzzing with tales of such intrigue. One story claimed that Washington had sat down to dinner in a local tavern and, for some reason, had chosen not to eat a plate of peas served to him, even though peas were one of his favorite foods. When the plate was removed and the peas thrown outside for the chickens to feed on, the poor fowl died. Whether this was an actual assassination attempt, no one can be certain.

∽ ✖ ∾

WOULD-BE ASSASSINS

Then another plot was thwarted. A petty criminal named Isaac Ketcham was serving time in a local New York jail. While on the inside, he overheard a conversation concerning a plot to kidnap General Washington. Ironically, the two men were Sergeant Thomas Hickey and Private Michael Lynch, both Washington's own bodyguards. Both Hickey and Lynch had been caught trying to pass counterfeit Continental currency. Within earshot of Ketcham, Hickey informed Lynch of his involvement in the assassination plot. After eliciting more information from both Hickey and Lynch, an opportunistic Ketcham sent word to the Provincial Congress, offering what he had picked up in exchange for release.

Ketcham soon confirmed what New York officials were just learning on the streets. A New York businessman, William Leary, had revealed a conversation he had shared with a former employee, James Mason, who told him he was on the payroll of the British as an informant. Mason was arrested, and Hickey was soon implicated in the plot to kidnap Washington. Other arrests—more than twenty people in all—were made as the group of co-conspirators was rounded up. Details soon emerged. One scenario had Hickey plotting to kill Washington by stabbing him. Another suggested that poisoning had been considered. (Hickey may have actually been the one who, through an accomplice, had delivered the poisoned peas to Washington's plate.)

As a sergeant in the Continental Army, Hickey soon faced a general court-martial. He was charged with "exciting and joining in a mutiny and sedition, and of treacherously corresponding with, inlisting among, and receiving pay from the enemies of the United American Colonies."[95] Interestingly, none of the charges against Hickey addressed kidnapping or assassination. With several eyewitnesses testifying against him, Hickey could not avoid conviction.

The verdict against him was unanimous: "That the prisoner Thomas Hickey, suffer death for said crimes by being hanged by the neck till he is dead."[96] As he was removed from the court and taken back to his cell, Hickey was asked if he wanted to speak to a chaplain, to which he snapped: "they were all cut-throats."[97]

The end came swiftly for Hickey. His execution took place within thirty-six hours of his conviction, upon a hastily constructed gallows. As four brigades of his comrades stood by, his executioners blindfolded him, and he was hanged at 11 a.m. on June 28, 1776. Washington's orders that day allude directly to Hickey's execution: "The unhappy fate of *Thomas Hickey*, executed this day for mutiny, sedition, and treachery, the General hopes will be a warning to every soldier in the Army to avoid those crimes, and all others, so disgraceful to the character of a soldier, and pernicious to his country, whose pay he receives and bread he eats."[98]

Washington had dodged the bullet, the plots against him having been foiled by informants who happened to be in the right place at the right time.

~ ※ ~

The Young Nathan Hale

Washington and his men had little time to contemplate the fate of the conspirator Thomas Hickey. Just two days later, British troops began to occupy Staten Island, in New York Bay. With the British across the bay from his headquarters, Washington needed to know what their next move might be and he required a special agent to go behind enemy lines to find out. He asked Lieutenant Colonel Thomas Knowlton, the commanding officer of a unit known as "Knowlton's Rangers," to appoint one of his men. Knowlton was a seasoned veteran of war. Like Washington, his service dated back to the French and Indian War. He had fought at Bunker Hill. His men were accustomed to danger, but when Knowlton approached Lieutenant James Sprague—also a veteran of the French and Indian conflict—with the assignment, he refused, stating: "I am willing to go & fight them, but as far as going among them & being taken & hung up like a dog, I will not do it."[99] Perhaps Sprague had witnessed Hickey's hanging and wanted no part of such activities. Still in need of a volunteer, Knowlton summoned his officers for a meeting in September, only to have their session interrupted by one of his rangers, a man named Nathan Hale, who announced: "I will undertake it."[100]

Perhaps few of the agents recruited to spy for General Washington were ever as unlikely as Nathan Hale. Born in Coventry, Connecticut, on June 6, 1755, the twenty-one-year-old volunteer came from a family whose roots in America extended back into the seventeenth century. (John Hale, Nathan's great-great-grandfather had participated in the Salem witchcraft trials in 1692.) Nathan had attended Yale before the war and had studied religion and the classics. His classmates considered him an "intelligent, religious, athletic individual with a gentle and kind nature."[101] By late 1774, he had become a teacher and was serving as the master of the Union School in New London, Connecticut. When the war opened, Hale received a letter from one of his former classmates, Benjamin Tallmadge, encouraging him to join the Continental Army, his words heavy with patriotic appeal: "Was I in your condition . . . I think the most extensive Service would be my choice. Our holy Religion, the honour of our God, a glorious country, & a happy constitution is what we have to defend."[102] His friend convinced him to enlist. (As for Tallmadge, he was destined to play a significant role in Washington's espionage circles. Washington later appointed him to serve as the senior handler—or case officer—for the Culper Ring, one of the most successful American spy networks of the war.)

From the outset, there were doubts expressed about young Nathan Hale and his volunteer spy mission. He innocently informed a fellow officer, Captain William Hull, yet another classmate from his Yale days, about his mission. (This action alone was a poor move on Hale's part, since it potentially compromised the security of his mission. Hale's mission was also generally known among his fellow Rangers. There is no evidence that any of the members of his band of brothers knowingly or unknowingly passed on information to anyone else about his mission, but the mere knowledge of it was a security lapse.) Hull had doubts about Hale's abilities as a spy, writing later that it was "not in his character: his nature was too frank and open to deceit and disguise, and he was incapable of acting a part equally foreign to his feelings and habits."[103] If Hull's assessment of his friend was correct, then Hale was not the man for the job that Washington had in mind. He would need to lie convincingly, which Hull thought him incapable of doing.

Hale was launched into his mission with almost no training. After Washington approved him, the young yet eager spy was delivered by ferry from Stamford, Connecticut, to Long Island. His cover was a natural one, in a way. He would pose as a Dutch schoolmaster in search of a teaching or tutoring position, even carrying his Yale diploma to prove his identity and academic credentials. Even if he could convince others of his cover, posing as a schoolteacher made little sense. An out-of-work schoolmaster would have little reason to interact with British soldiers.

There were other potential issues with Hale's appointment as a spy. He stood out in a crowd, since he was taller than most men, and, more significantly, he bore a noticeable and easily remembered powder burn on his right cheek, one he had received during a musket accident. Another potential problem was that Hale was not new to New York; his unit had been stationed in the city for months prior to the Army's evacuation to New Jersey. The cards seemed decidedly stacked against his spy mission.

Hale unfortunately was not adept at spy craft. Tasked with collecting information about troop numbers and fortification positions and such, Hale needed to write his data down. A good strategy would have been to carry books and other materials common to an itinerant schoolteacher for him to jot down his intelligence information in invisible ink, which was readily available at the time. Rather, Hale chose to keep his documents in his shoes, one of the first places anyone stopping him for inspection would have looked. And this is exactly what happened.

So much worked against Hale's success as a spy. No sooner had he landed on Long Island, but the British moved against Washington, landing on the southern tip of Manhattan on September 15. He simply had no time to accumulate any actionable intelligence. With the attack, Hale's mission had lost its primary objective—find out ahead of time what the British were preparing and with what resources.

Washington had much occupying his mind and his time during Hale's first week undercover, but he did worry about the young spy's safety. Once the week passed and no word had reached him, the Continental commander thought Hale might have succeeded. At least he hoped Hale's cover was still intact, even if the mission had fundamentally changed. Those hopes were soon dashed.

Piecing together the exact trail of Hale's movements on Long Island is tricky, but the following explanation seems close. With British operations on Manhattan underway, Hale likely understood his changed mission. He seems to have decided to head for Brooklyn, which would have placed him closer to American units in the field. But, according to reports, Hale does not seem to have fooled anyone with his Dutch schoolmaster cover and, unfortunately, one Loyalist in particular took note of him—Robert Rogers.

～ ⚒ ～

ROGERS' RANGERS

The name Robert Rogers was well established across New England even before the opening of the Revolutionary War. His legend extended back to the French and Indian War, during which he formed an elite unit of special fighters—they would come to be named "rangers"—whose purpose was to move behind enemy lines as scouts to collect intelligence and, if the situation arose, engage the enemy. A New Hampshire regiment, Rogers' Rangers became known for their brutality in the field. These rough-hewn special forces—armed with muskets and rifles, razor-sharp tomahawks and large knives—participated in bloody raids against both military and civilian targets. The Rangers even carried out missions in the dead of winter, bundled in heavy coats and furs, and wearing snowshoes. If moving along a frozen lake front, such as Lake George, Rogers and his men donned ice skates.

Following the French and Indian War, Rogers struggled, finding himself out of the element in which he had thrived. He married, failed several times at business, moved to London for a while, failed again in business, and ended up in debtor's prison. Once released, he became keenly aware of the developing strife unfolding in the American colonies and decided to return, uncertain which side he might take. He was prepared to offer his services to the highest bidder. However, both generals Gage and Washington had known Rogers from the earlier war, and neither was fond of the aging ranger. But, by late 1775, with Gage out and Howe in, Rogers convinced the new British commander to give him a shot. (Rogers had played Howe, convincing him that the Americans were interested in him as well, which was not the case.) When Rogers had shown up to meet with Washington, the general was suspicious, knowing Rogers had already been in contact with Howe.

Washington ordered Rogers's arrest, but the wily special forces veteran escaped his guards and, by midsummer, found refuge on a British naval vessel docked in New York. On August 6, General Howe offered Rogers a commission to raise a battalion of rangers to fight for the British. Even though the unit's official name was the Queen's American Rangers, the force was essentially Rogers's private army, known, just like his earlier unit, as Rogers' Rangers. During the intervening weeks, the paths of the war-hardened and world-weary Robert Rogers and the neophyte young spy, Nathan Hale, crossed, with dire consequences for the disguised Dutch schoolmaster.

Hale was in Huntington, Long Island, on September 16. Rogers and his men were in the same vicinity, their mission being to observe the movements of the Americans in Connecticut and Long Island and to keep a wary eye out for anyone who could be a spy. Rogers had ample resources at his disposal, including a sixteen-gun brig, the HMS *Halifax*. He also was already in the process of forming a network of reliable informants. The captain of the *Halifax*, William Quarme, received intelligence on the evening of September 16 that a pair of small rebel ships had landed off the coast the previous day. A local Tory witnessed two men disembark from one of the ships, the four-gun sloop *Schuyler*. When the rebel ship departed, only one of the men had returned onboard. Perhaps the remaining mystery man was a spy. He was certainly suspicious. At least Rogers thought so, and he decided to be on the lookout for anyone out of place.

It is no wonder Hale would draw his attention. By September 18, Rogers was at Sands Point, where he almost immediately heard from local informants of a stranger in the neighborhood, one who seemed to be asking far too many questions for an unemployed schoolteacher. Two days later, Rogers caught up with Hale, but managed to keep his distance, choosing to shadow the American agent throughout the day. He became certain of Hale's identity as a spy when he noticed Hale stopping along his route to jot down some notes whenever he saw the passing of a unit of Redcoats or when he spotted a

British post, sentry, or barracks. Come sundown, Hale reached a local tavern and sought a room and a meal. It was a Friday evening. Rogers was a much savvier agent than Hale, and he used his skills to draw out the young agent. Asking to join him at his table, Rogers was soon engaged in elicitation. He prepared to entrap Hale in conversation, and the unwitting amateur agent was little more than a Connecticut Yankee in Robert Rogers's court.

The talk began as convivial, even innocuous, but Rogers soon turned the conversation his way. He identified himself as a soldier in Washington's army who now found himself behind enemy lines, given the recent Redcoat deployment into New York City. Now, he complained to the younger Hale, he was "detained on an island where the inhabitants sided with the British against the American Colonies."[104] Hale seems to have been wary of Rogers initially, but was soon pulled into his dinner partner's confidence. When Rogers told Hale "that he himself was upon the business of spying out the inclination of the people and motion of the British troops," he had Hale convinced.[105] Here was a fellow spy, it likely seemed to even the skeptical Hale. Soon, the two men, sharing a meal in a Long Island tavern deep in Loyalist country, lifted their wine glasses and exchanged toasts to the Continental Congress, with Hale's confession as a chaser. The disguised schoolmaster spilled his story out almost without thinking; for if he had given his actions any thought, he might have cut his admissions to a total stranger off short. Rogers now knew, without a doubt, that he was in the company of an agent of General Washington.

But only Rogers knew what Hale was about and for whom he was working. He needed additional corroborating witnesses. And he knew just what to do. He invited Hale to join him for a second meal the following evening, and Hale was more than happy to oblige. He thought he had found a friend, a confidant, a fellow

RIGHT:

This 1868 map shows the then-current street grid of Manhattan laid over the geography of where the Battle of Harlem Heights took place.

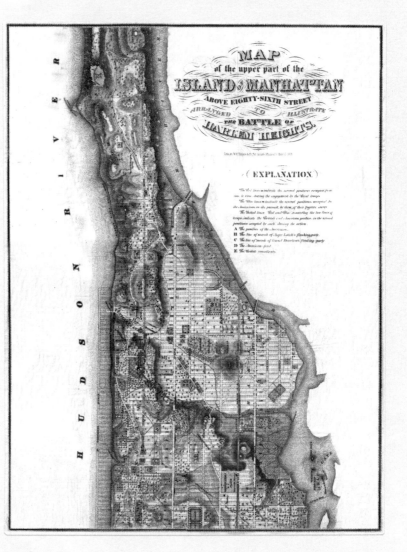

MAP
of the upper part of the
ISLAND of MANHATTAN
ABOVE EIGHTY-SIXTH STREET
ARRANGED TO ILLUSTRATE
THE BATTLE OF
HARLEM HEIGHTS.

(EXPLANATION)

spy. Saturday night approached, and the two men met again at yet another tavern; only this time, Rogers was not alone. Hale found himself being introduced to three or four other alleged supporters of the rebel cause, yet each was one of Rogers' Rangers in disguise. Rogers ordered a round of ales, and the talk soon centered on the war and the righteousness of the rebellion against Great Britain. Even as the men shared conversation, food, and drink, the rest of Rogers's men were gathering outside the tavern, covering all the entrances and exits. At last, Rogers sprang up and an astonished Hale was clapped in irons, accused of spying against the Crown. Hale did his best to lie and claim he was no such thing, but Rogers had him trumped from every direction. Outside the tavern, several individuals were presented, each of whom stated they knew the accused as a member of the Hale family from Connecticut and as a supporter of the rebel cause.

In short order, Hale was taken aboard Rogers's sloop and, an hour later, he was standing face-to-face with General Howe in Manhattan. Howe, who was so distracted by issues involving his New York campaign, did not bother to convene a court-martial. Plus, Hale's guilt was evident—there were a host of witnesses, Rogers had his own version of the events, and they found the damning documents he kept in his shoes. As the hour was late that Saturday night when Rogers delivered Hale to Beekman Mansion, the general's head-quarters (it then stood at the corner of First Avenue and Fifty-First Street), Howe simply signed Hale's death warrant and went back to sleep.

Knowlton's Rangers

When Nathan Hale volunteered to spy for Washington, his unit, known as Knowlton's Rangers, was itself newly formed. Washington was behind its inception. He was in need of a ranger-style unit that could conduct tactical surveillance and reconnaissance on the British in the New York City area. This explains why Washington approached Knowlton for a spy volunteer. While the unit produced Nathan Hale, one of the best-remembered American spies of the war, Knowlton's Rangers did not last long.

During the days Hale was engaged in surveillance in New York, the Rangers were dispatched on a reconnaissance mission along British lines in the vicinity of Manhattan's Harlem Heights. On September 16, Knowlton and his men ran into the disciplined Black Watch, a hardcore Scottish regiment of the British army known for its tenacity in a fight. The encounter did not go well, and Knowlton was killed, along with many of his rangers. Many others were wounded. Cut to pieces, Knowlton's Rangers were effectively no more. Most of the survivors were captured two months later at Fort Washington, also in Manhattan, while serving in a rear guard action that allowed Washington's main force to evacuate the island and cross the Hudson River to safety in New Jersey.

Today, the U.S. Army considers Knowlton's Rangers to represent its first military intelligence organization. The modern army intelligence emblem includes the number "1776," which refers to the year the Rangers unit was established.

An Immediate Fate

Through the night, Hale was kept in the Beekman Mansion greenhouse under the watchful eye of a notorious guard of the provost marshal, the drunken William Cunningham, who would one day himself be tried for forgery. (When Cunningham went to the scaffold, he confessed to mistreating thousands of prisoners during the war, even poisoning some and selling their food for money.) The next morning Hale witnessed his last sunrise. He was delivered to an artillery park, situated a mile from Howe's headquarters.

Hale's hands were tied behind his back and a black-trimmed, white execution gown was placed over his disguise. A line of Redcoats stood at attention, their muskets at their sides, with fixed bayonets. Hale climbed a ladder, the noose was placed around his neck, and the ladder was kicked out from under him. A grave had been dug close by.

Today, Nathan Hale is remembered more often for his alleged last words than for what he did that led to his arrest and conviction: "I only regret that I have but one life to lose for my country." But this has become a part of the myth of American history. A witness to Hale's hanging was Captain Frederick MacKenzie, who, following the execution, wrote of Hale's final moments: "He behaved with great composure and resolution, saying he thought it the duty of every good officer, to obey any orders given him by his commander in chief; and desired the spectators to be at all times prepared to meet death in whatever shape it might appear."[106] A rather detached account was made later that day by one of General Howe's aides in an orderly book: "A spy from the enemy (by his own full confession) apprehended last night, was this day executed at 11 oClock in front of the Artillery Park."[107] Hale's body remained suspended for several days before it was removed, placed in a simple oak coffin, and buried without ceremony. Next to his hanging corpse, a group of Redcoats had hung a board painted to look like a Continental soldier and written the name "George Washington."

The news of Hale's hanging reached Washington's headquarters officially on September 22, just a week after his initial arrival on Long Island. One of Howe's aides-de-camp, Captain John Montressor, approached the rebel encampment under a white flag to deliver a letter from Howe regarding possible prisoner exchanges in the future. Hale's fate was mentioned only as an afterthought.

Despite the martyr's status Nathan Hale has today, little was done at the time to elevate his actions to those of a tragic hero. Washington did not allow the news to be broadcast to his troops, thinking it would adversely affect morale. Engaging in a bit of disinformation, he ordered Hale's death listed among other members of the 19th Regiment's casualties as "Nathan Hale—Capt—killed—22 September."[108] Even Hale's family was not informed of the nature of his death. But word eventually filtered out. Hale's brother, Enoch, a minister, received more accurate details before the end of the month. He wrote in his diary: "Heard a rumor that Capt. Hale belonging to the east side Connecticut River, near Colchester, who was educated at college, was sentenced to hang in the enemy's lines at New York, being taken as a spy, or reconnoitering their camp. Hope it is without foundation. Something troubled at it. Sleep not very well."[109] A month later, Enoch came to Washington's headquarters and spoke with his brother's comrades in the 19th Regiment, and his fears that Nathan had been hanged as an intelligence agent were confirmed.

Today, statues dot the American landscape in honor of Nathan Hale. There are even schools named for him. The young man from Connecticut had volunteered for service in the Continental Army, then, out of a sense of duty, accepted an assignment for which he had no discernible skill set. Hale was thrust into the unyielding world of wartime espionage and barely managed to scribble down a few details regarding Redcoat numbers and the locations of barracks before his cover was blown by a seasoned officer of the Crown. He had moved into a world that he did not understand, one for which he was woefully under-prepared, and his inexperience cost him his life. Washington may have had his regrets about the ordeal, but he never expressed them that history has recorded. However, Hale's death did accomplish one thing: Washington emerged from the experience resolute and determined to create a spy network that would function professionally, clandestinely, and successfully.

CHAPTER FIVE

Agents of the General

John Jay's Spy Network

PREVIOUS:
A map of the Battle of Trenton made by Hessian soldiers taken prisoner by the Continental Army.

By the late fall of 1776, the Americans had already surmounted several significant hurdles on the road to separation from Great Britain. None stood taller than the decision by the Continental Congress to officially severe the political connection between the British government and the colonies. The early days of July in Philadelphia were heady with decisions and declarations, including the drafting of one of the most cherished and potent documents in all of American history—the Declaration of Independence. No longer were the colonies to suffer under the arbitrary and sometimes punitive rule of King George III. No longer would the proclamations of Parliament carry any weight from Boston to Savannah. At this point, however, such political moves were little more than paper pronouncements, political theater on a shaky stage. As the end of the year loomed, General Washington was concerned.

His army had experienced a humiliating rout out of New York City, a series of defeats from August to October that ended with the British solidly in control of the city and the Continental troops in New Jersey. Hale's mission had been brutal and short, a singular failure with a sober ending. The rebel cause needed an effective, organized intelligence network and, fortunately, a few hearty agents were already in the field.

A counterintelligence ring was in the making that autumn season of 1776, under the leadership of a Patriot who would one day serve as the first chief justice of the United States Supreme Court—John Jay. Unlike many of the Founding Fathers, Jay was not British by birth. He was a native New Yorker with French and Dutch roots. Jay was born in 1745 into wealth; his family included merchants, shippers, and government officials. His father traded in such New World commodities as timber, wheat, and furs. A lawyer by profession, Jay joined the Patriot movement, becoming a member of New York's Committee of Correspondence in 1774. At first he was a moderate who thought the colonies and the mother country might be able to reconcile and patch up their differences. Later he hardened into a hardcore Patriot, supporting independence. A member of the New York delegation to the Second Continental Congress, he was not present when the Congress voted on independence, as his local congressional responsibilities hindered him from being in Philadelphia in early July 1776.

Jay's spy organization was not born out of Washington's efforts, but those of the new state government of New York. Its name explained its purpose—the Committee and First Commission for Detecting Conspiracies—and its reach was fairly limited. Agents were deployed to ferret out any Tory spies functioning up and down the Hudson River. Officially, the group was assigned with "inquiring into, detecting, and defeating conspiracies . . . against the liberties of America, . . . to send for persons and papers, to call out detachments of the militia in different counties for suppressing insurrections, to apprehend, secure or remove persons whom they might judge dangerous to the safety of the State." Since their activities might often be clandestine in nature, they were also "to enjoin secrecy upon their members and the persons they employed."[110]

Such efforts could be fraught with difficulty on a practical level. The civilian population was significantly divided among the rebels who supported separation from Great Britain; the Tories or Loyalists who longed for reconciliation and a return to the English fold; and those who refused to take sides—those for whom neutrality meant more than nationalism. Thus, any counterintelligence organization always found itself with the sometimes confusing task of separating friend from foe.

Jay's network included nearly a dozen field agents. Along with his close associate and fellow spy handler, Nathaniel Sackett, Jay met with four of his agents on a regular basis—Enoch Crosby, Martin Cornwill (his name also shows up as Cornell), Nicholas Brower, and John Haines. Another half-dozen agents were used less frequently and included Benjamin Pitcher, William Denney, Henry Wooden, Joseph Bennett, Elijah Frost, and Samuel Hopkins. A few shadowy others also provided intelligence. The organization sometimes relied on various militia units to carry out arrests and raids on British-held positions.

Jay's organization began its counterespionage work in the summer of 1776. Agents soon delivered intelligence reports regarding an alleged plot by New York Tories to take control of New York City. Two names surfaced as the primary suspects—William Tryon, the royal governor of New York, and David Matthews, the New York City mayor. British officials, including King George III, were aware of the conspiracy, which included Tory sabotage of rebel military targets in and around the city, as

well as the recruitment of some of the city's Tories to act as spies. It also called for the assassination or kidnapping of General Washington. (This plot, which included Washington's own bodyguard, Thomas Hickey, was explored in Chapter Four.) Through Jay's intelligence agents, several of the conspirators were exposed and arrested. As has been previously mentioned, Thomas Hickey was executed following a court-martial. Governor Tryon managed to slip through the cracks, taking refuge on a British warship docked in New York Harbor. Matthews was arrested and held under house arrest for a time until he managed to escape. It was following this successful counterintelligence operation that New York officials tapped Jay to lead their state-sanctioned organization, which became official on September 26, 1776. (Initially, Jay had served as the organization's secretary, then chairman.)

Guiding much of Jay's intelligence work was his expectation that Tories would be sought out through proper procedures, not through frenzied mob action. (He had seen too much of that activity during the years leading up to the Revolutionary War.) He was opposed to any vigilante actions by New York citizens, whose suspicions regarding who might be a Tory were not always on point. Pursuit of alleged Tories had to follow what Jay referred to as "rigid impartiality," an approach based on the collection of evidence through systematic processes that followed as straight a legal path as possible. For the future Supreme Court chief justice, the rights of the accused had to be recognized and upheld.[111]

Tasked to uncover Tories along the Hudson Valley, Jay and his organization had relative freedom to pursue their investigations. They followed up hundreds of reports and typically handled each by questioning those singled out and requesting they sign an oath of support for the rebel cause. Sometimes the accused were even friends of Jay, but it did not stop him from asking the hard questions regarding their loyalty.

OPPOSITE:
Stuart Gilbert's portrait of John Jay was begun in 1784 and later completed by John Trumbull, 1818.

IDENTIFY, PENETRATE, AND NEUTRALIZE

Jay's organization also pursued undercover operations to identify supporters of the Crown. His agents would infiltrate Tory groups, taking on aliases and other covers. A typical approach was to pose as a Tory, gain the suspect individual's or group's trust, join their ranks, then collect intelligence. Arrests might be made, sometimes during underground meetings whose time and place had been reported by the agent operative. At the heart of the organization's mission was the expectation to identify, penetrate, and neutralize the Tory threat.

Without question, the most adept agent within Jay's ring was Enoch Crosby. Unlike many who operated secretly during the Revolutionary War years and remained unknown even after the war ended, Crosby's exploits were well documented and made public by the nineteenth century (see "James Fenimore Cooper's Spy," page 126). These undercover operations put him several times directly in harm's way.

Born in 1750 in Harwich, Massachusetts, Crosby grew up in New York and became a professional shoemaker. In 1775, he participated in the American invasion of Canada, which was led by Benedict Arnold. That mission failed miserably, and Crosby left the military, his health suffering from the rigors of the winter march through the frosty back reaches of Maine. When the war opened, he was living in Danbury, Connecticut. By August of 1776, he reenlisted. Though only in his late twenties, he proved a skillful infiltrating agent. But his work as a spy began unintentionally, through an accident that put him in the right place at the right time.

In late August 1776, Crosby was on the road between Carmel and Kingsbridge, New York, headed to a rebel encampment. In Westchester, he met up with a local Tory named Bunker who mistook him as a friend of the king. Not to miss the opportunity, the would-be spy played along and soon convinced Bunker of his own Tory leanings. Bunker then introduced Crosby to a larger group of Tories, and, in conversation, he discovered that a Tory militia unit was being formed locally, intending to join the British in New York City. Crosby used his elicitation skills so well that he even gained the names of the force's officers. Needing to deliver this important bit of information, Crosby bade the group good-bye. He returned to the road and, once out of sight, doubled back to the home of Squire Young, a local member of the New York Committee of Safety. Young followed up the intelligence and was so impressed by Crosby, he sent him to Jay's headquarters in White Plains. Jay soon recruited Crosby into his circle of agents and informed Crosby's commanding officer of his new assignment.

To provide Crosby a cover for returning to his Tory "friends" and joining up with the pro-British group, a simple plan was concocted. Crosby was delivered to a unit of American rangers who "arrested" him and held him under guard. Crosby then "escaped"—he took off when he went outside to relieve himself—with the Rangers firing their muskets to provide authenticity. By the time Crosby caught up with the Tory militia, he had a believable story to tell, one that included leaping over a fence and thrashing his way through a cornfield with rangers in hot pursuit.

Crosby had infiltrated the group and was functioning as an undercover spy. He spent several days with the new Tory militia unit and, as they prepared to march south to the city, he suddenly disappeared, returned to Young, then linked up with the same American ranger officer who had held him as "prisoner." He went back once again to the Tory unit, where he was among those rounded up in a rangers' dragnet. To continue the ruse, he was held for a while as one of the Tory prisoners, only to be ultimately placed under guard separate from his Tory "colleagues" and released, his mission accomplished. Crosby had proven himself to have the skill set for an undercover spy.

～ ※ ～

BAYONETS AND HAYSTACKS

Crosby was soon handed another undercover assignment. This time he disguised himself as an itinerant shoemaker, an obvious choice given his previous profession. In no time, he had gained the trust of a Tory family from whom he collected intelligence about yet another new militia unit. Crosby feigned interest in joining, but hesitated as a ruse, stating he wanted to first check the roster to see if any of his acquaintances had already joined up. Before he was done working the militia unit's commander, Crosby had

James Fenimore Cooper's Spy

Enoch Crosby's exploits as an agent operating under John Jay's New York counterintelligence organization became the stuff of legend. So well-known were Crosby's adventures that one of America's successful early writers, novelist James Fenimore Cooper, adapted them into an espionage novel he titled *The Spy*. In Cooper's book, the agent is named Harvey Birch, but many who read it knew who they were really reading about—Enoch Crosby.

ABOVE:

Charles Kennedy Burt's illustration from James Fenimore Cooper's The Spy *shows George Washington (seated at far left with book) and "the spy Harvey Birch" (standing at right, holding cloth).*

been shown a second muster roll, one kept hidden beneath a rock, as well as a fake haystack that was hollowed out to provide a secret hiding place for new militia recruits. That very night, he sneaked away and reported to a Patriot organization in White Plains, making it back to the Tory house he was staying in before dawn. Before the next sunset, American rangers had surrounded the house and captured the entire newly formed Tory militia. Once again, Crosby, who hid in a closet, was arrested along with everyone else to maintain his cover. In time, he "escaped," once more in a hail of gunfire, but not before being spotted by a former schoolmaster, who was stunned his pupil had gone the way of the Tory faction. The teacher contacted Crosby's family and delivered the bad news.

The difficulty for Crosby soon became obvious. Given the limited region in which he was operating as a spy, how many times could he manage to infiltrate Tory ranks, be arrested along with British sympathizers, then pull off yet another escape?

But Crosby returned to his cover again, this time heading off to Marlboro, New York, situated on the west side of the Hudson, near Newburgh, where Washington's army would later encamp during the final months of the war. Using the unlikely codename of "John Smith," he again joined another new Tory regiment. He remained undercover for a week or so, then, in early November 1776, as the unit was being deployed, he sent a report through a local Committee of Safety member:

> *I hasten this express to request you to order Captain Townsend's company of Rangers, to repair immediately to the barn, situated on the west side of Butter-Hill, and there to secrete themselves until we arrive, which will be to-morrow evening, probably about eleven o'clock; where, with about thirty tories, they may find,*
>
> *Your obedient servant,*
>
> *JOHN SMITH*[112]

That night, Crosby met with his Tory comrades as they prepared for the march to Butter Hill, outside Cornwall, New York. From out of the darkness, Crosby heard a cough, which he immediately recognized as that of Colonel William Duer, leader of the local Committee of Safety. In code response, Crosby answered with his own cough. Soon, a unit of American Rangers sprang from the woods, ready to arrest every Tory in sight. Once again, Crosby played his part, running off and hiding in a haystack. For security purposes, Crosby's handlers did not typically inform the Ranger officers they utilized in such raids of the field agent's identity. This meant he was treated as though he were an actual Tory, since the Rangers could not have known he was not a true believer among the ranks of the Loyalists.

Crosby surrendered his hiding place when "fifty bayonets were instantly plunged into as many different sections of the haymow."[113] He was, once again under arrest, clapped in irons and tossed in a secure room in John Jay's own house!

With Jay out of town at that time, no one could vouch for Crosby or lend help in an escape. But Crosby proved himself an agent with sex appeal, convincing a servant girl in the house to dope his guards with brandy laced with drugs, then unlock the door of his room. (Jay may actually have made arrangements with his maid to aid Crosby by drugging the guards just in case Crosby was brought to his house while the spymaster was away.) Having been in Jay's house on several occasions, he knew the layout and made his way out into the night. Unfortunately, he was caught again by a pair of alert Patriots, forcing Crosby to play his final card. The agent produced a slip of paper sewn into his vest, one that identified him as a Patriot recruit of John Jay's. But the frustrated Crosby was not yet home free. On the road, he was stopped by a Tory who accused him of being a Patriot and prepared to capture him. But the wily Crosby convinced his accuser that he was wrong, that he was, indeed, a Loyalist. (After all, he had become adept at playing one when it was necessary.) Finally, the weary agent reached Duer, who gave him directions to a safe house in Dutchess County.

With Crosby's face becoming too well known in New York, Jay decided to send his best agent off to Connecticut to scout out Tories there, but it was not long before Crosby was back in New York, up to his old spying tricks of deceit and infiltration. Yet another Tory militia was the target. This time, Crosby had a new handler, Nathaniel Sackett, a member of

Jay's intelligence committee. Once Crosby had gained enough information on the targeted Tory regiment, Sackett dispatched American forces, under the command of Captain Peter van Gaasbeck, to capture them. His orders to the captain made specific reference this time to Crosby: "I had almost forgot to give you directions to Give our friend an opportunity of making his Escape Upon our plan you will Take him prisoner with this party you are now wateing his name is Enoch Crosbey Alias John Brown I could wish that he may escape before you bring him Two miles on your way to Committee. . . . By no means neglect this friend of ours."[114] The raid went off as planned, another gang of Tories was arrested and jailed, and Enoch Crosby managed to slip away, with another spying adventure to his credit.

This was the last time Jay utilized the amazing talents of Enoch Crosby. His repeated missions had simply overexposed him up and down the Hudson Valley. One random sighting by the wrong person would not end pleasantly. For a short stint, Jay's most successful field agent was tied to a desk, assigned administrative duties within the spy organization. But it didn't suit him. He soon asked for a leave that turned out to be permanent. But for nine months, Enoch Crosby had carried out repeated missions, gained intelligence on Tories, and thwarted the efforts of multiple militias, even as he had been shot at, nearly bayoneted, and imprisoned with irons on multiple occasions.

The Restless Enoch Crosby

Enoch Crosby proved to be one of John Jay's most capable field agents and for most of a year carried out mission after mission at increasing risk to his life. He seemed to thrive on the clandestine nature of the spy business, adapting to every situation with an aplomb that seems to have come to him naturally.

Even after he was taken out of service, his duty to the rebel cause assumedly complete, Crosby was restless. He returned to his family and made a go of living with his brother as a civilian up in the highlands of the Hudson River Valley. But it would not do for the man who loved adventure and espionage. Although he had already served in the Continental Army before his spying days, Crosby joined the Army once again and remained in uniform until the end of the Revolutionary War.

BUTCHER, WEAVER, SOLDIER, SPY

Perhaps the grandest American intelligence coup of 1776 came during the final weeks of the year. Hessian troops, mercenaries fighting for George III, had taken up positions in Trenton, New Jersey. By December Washington was intent on attacking them. But he needed intelligence before taking such an audacious gamble, which would require a surprise attack, possibly during poor winter weather.

He found his man in John Honeyman, a New Jersey weaver and butcher. The general had been introduced to Honeyman in Philadelphia near the war's opening, when Washington was representing Virginia in the Continental Congress. Like Washington, Honeyman had served in the French and Indian War and had a clear-eyed concept of the type of military intelligence Washington might want someone like him to collect. Washington next bumped into him as his forces were retreating across New Jersey in late 1776. Washington likely recruited him

Washington's Note to Mrs. Honeyman

With John Honeyman operating undercover as a Tory who supplied meat to the British, the New Jersey butcher was a wanted man. On one occasion, local Patriots, intent on locating him, found out where he lived. An eighteen-year-old local named Abraham Baird led the group to the Honeyman house only to find he was not at home. After searching the house, they then began to threaten Mrs. Honeyman.

Fortunately, General Washington had prepared for this possibility. Mrs. Honeyman produced a letter, which she showed to the men who were intent on capturing her husband: "It is hereby ordered that the wife and children of John Honeyman, of Griggstown, the notorious Tory, now within the British lines, and probably acting the part of a spy, shall be and hereby are protected from all harm and annoyance from any quarter until further orders. This furnishes no protection to Honeyman himself."[115]

The note was ingenious. By writing the letter, Washington had protected the wife of one of his spies, while maintaining that operative's cover as a double agent. Mrs. Honeyman was no longer harassed.

around mid-December, and his cover was as simple as it was calculated. Honeyman was to pronounce himself publicly to be a Tory, then to leave his home in Griggstown, as he would no longer be safe among the locals. Orders were even issued for his arrest. But these called only for his capture because Washington wanted him alive. The American commander in chief led all outside his circle to understand that he intended to hang Honeyman himself, if given the opportunity. The ruse was complete.

Once in Trenton, Honeyman made himself available to the Hessians stationed locally, offering to sell them meat. As he made contact with the German troops, he was spying for Washington, collecting as much intelligence as he could. In fact, Honeyman was still observing the Germans just hours before the Christmas Eve attack that became legendary for Washington and his men, the march including the now-famed "crossing the Delaware." Honeyman had regular contact with the Hessian commander. Colonel Johann Rall, who continually expressed a hard-nosed contempt and disregard for the Americans encamped on the Pennsylvania side of the Delaware River.

Then, a complication arose. Prior to the raid on Trenton, Honeyman was caught by rebels who identified him as a local Tory who did business with the British and the Hessians. On December 22, a patrol of American soldiers hauled him at gunpoint to Washington's headquarters. (Actually, Honeyman spotted the patrol and then made certain he was caught, taking pains to steal a cow from a local field, one he then noisily led down a local road, cracking a whip all the way.) A grave-faced Washington thanked his men for delivering the wanted Tory and dismissed them, assuring the patrol that, if Honeyman tried to escape, he was to be shot on sight.

Alone in Washington's presence, the New Jersey butcher debriefed the general. Within forty-eight hours, the commander in chief and his men were on their way to Trenton. His report complete, Honeyman was allowed to "escape" the next day, a torched haystack providing the needed distraction.

Soon Honeyman was back in Trenton, reporting to Rall and informing him the Americans were suffering from exposure and a lack of food. He assured the German officer he had little to worry about. His undercover mission accomplished, Honeyman then bade a farewell to Rall and headed to New Brunswick. He did not want to be anywhere near the action that would soon be unfolding, an attack that completely surprised

FOLLOWING:
Emanuel Leutze's painting Washington Crossing the Delaware *is one of the most famous artistic representations of the Revolutionary War. Acquired by the Bremen Kunsthalle, it was destroyed by an Allied bombing raid in 1942.*

Doubts About Honeyman's Spying

Today, John Honeyman's story has its detractors. Generally, historians through the nineteenth century believed the story of his intelligence work for Washington to be true, but some more modern scholars are less than certain. Historian David Hackett Fischer, in his book, *Washington's Crossing*, states the story lacks documentation.[116] Alexander Rose, author of the bestseller *Washington's Spies*, says emphatically, "John Honeyman was no spy."[117] But author Kenneth A. Daigler takes issue with those who doubt Honeyman's spying on the Hessians. As a retired senior case officer in the Clandestine Service of the CIA, he is more prone to accept the Honeyman story. In his book, *Spies, Patriots, and Traitors*, Daigler explains "why an intelligence officer would put more faith in the story, even without full documentation, than someone outside the profession."[118] Those who doubt the Honeyman version of events base their criticisms on a lack of evidence to corroborate the claims made by members of his family many years after the Revolutionary War. But Daigler argues that the story matches up with the approach General Washington was utilizing at the time to spy on the British.

In the end, historians may just have to agree to disagree concerning the veracity of the Honeyman story of Hessians, Trenton, and his spying.

the Hessians, killing more than one hundred—including Rall himself—and capturing nearly one thousand, who were then marched through the streets of Philadelphia. In addition, Trenton was no longer in enemy hands. Honeyman's intelligence work helped provide Washington with a victory on Christmas Day that would rally his men through the cold winter of 1776–77.

～ ✕ ～

CATCHING BRITISH AGENTS

Agents such as Enoch Crosby may represent the best that Jay's New York organization had to offer, and his success in ferreting out Tory supporters scattered along the Hudson River Valley is beyond question. But the New York operation only lasted a mere matter of months, shutting down by the early spring of 1777. In the meantime, the Continental Army was able to achieve a few successes of its own, including the capture of a pair of pro-British spies—Edmund Palmer and Daniel Taylor. (Taylor will always be remembered for a small bit of spy craft he utilized in his intelligence gathering: a hollow silver bullet.)

Edmund Palmer hailed from Yorktown, in Westchester County, New York, where he served as a lieutenant in a Tory regiment as early as 1775. By the spring of 1777, British officials tapped him for a special mission in his hometown. His assignment meant returning to Westchester to engage in spying and, possibly, to participate in an assassination plot against the rebel general Israel Putnam, who had commanded New England forces in early 1775 before Congress appointed Washington as commander in chief. Putnam and his command were stationed in Westchester.

Little is known concerning the months Palmer served as a British intelligence agent in the field. But he was finally captured in early July 1777. The exact date is unknown, but likely during the week of July 8–15, Palmer and a fellow agent kidnapped American captain Henry Strang of the 3rd Westchester Militia. The two men found Strang in a blacksmith shop, where they subdued him, stabbed him with a bayonet, and tied him up, all in the middle of the day. Then they force-marched their prisoner out into a local woods. For several hours, Palmer tried to elicit information from Strang, repeatedly pricking him with his bayonet "and Occasion[ing] him to bleed in many spots."[119] Strang was searched, presumably for incriminating documents, but none were found.

Although several versions of the story were later told, around eleven o'clock that night, Strang managed to escape his captors. During the days or weeks that followed, American militiamen scoured the region in search of his kidnappers. On July 18, a trio of militiamen located Palmer, arrested him, and delivered him to General Israel Putnam's headquarters. They found several papers on him that connected Palmer with the Tory governor of Connecticut, William Tryon. With Palmer's spying revealed, he was handed over for court-martial, under charges of "Robing the Inhabitence & Leving war Against his Country." By late July the court-martial met in Peekskill, and, by then, the charges had been expanded to "Plundering, Robbing, and carrying off the Cattle, Goods &c. from the well-effected Inhabitants and for being a Spy from the Enemy."[120] The evidence clear, the court found Palmer guilty and he was ordered to be hanged on August 1.

A Spy and His Family

The Tory spy Edmund Palmer was eventually captured, court-martialed, sentenced, and hanged. But before he was executed, he tried to do right by the family he would soon leave behind, even as they tried to stave off his execution.

After Palmer's sentence was delivered, the condemned spy's wife visited General Putnam's headquarters. Carrying her young child with her, she appealed to the general for mercy, desperate that her husband should be saved. Putnam refused to relent, and Palmer's distraught spouse nearly collapsed and had to be carried away.

As for Palmer, his final thoughts were for his wife and son. Awaiting his sentence, he wrote out a list of his personal property, knowing it would all likely be confiscated by the rebels. His hope was that an appeal might be made on his behalf to British officials in London to compensate his family for their assumed losses, which Palmer tallied at £600.

Eventually, the British government did recognize Palmer's service and paid his son a death benefit of £200, only one-third of the figure Palmer had requested.

But before the sentence was carried out, the British became aware of Palmer's situation and and made a serious attempt to intervene on his behalf. A British warship, HMS *Mercury*, arrived at a nearby port on the Hudson River, and an officer approached General Putnam's headquarters at Peekskill carrying a white flag, signifying he wanted to parley with the general. When the two men sat down together, the British officer delivered a stern warning to Putnam, suggesting that, if Palmer's hanging went on as planned, there would be grave consequences for the general and any rebels in the region.

ur being in possession of Ticonderoga, which is a great Event carried without Loss. I have rec. your two Letters Viz. from
discover'd in a double wooden Canteen, you will know if it was of any consequence; nothing of it has transpir'd to us. I will observe I u
I learn, to Albany.—My Intention is for Pensilvania where I expect to meet Washington, but if he goes to the Northw. contrary to my

be yours; but my wishes are that the Enemy be drove out of this Province before any Operation takes place in Conecticut. S. Wm. Clinton
ours & W How.

Putnam, hard-boiled bulldog that he was, was not intimidated. Although several versions of his response would be told later, the best has him sending a curt, no-nonsense missive back to Governor Tryon. It read:

ABOVE:
Quill letters, like the ones shown here, were used during the Revolutionary War by spies who wrote out messages on thin strips of paper that they then rolled up and hid inside the shafts of their quill pens.

SIR—

Nathan Palmer, a lieutenant in your King's service, was taken in my camp as a Spy—he was tried as a Spy—he was condemned as a Spy—and you may rest assured, Sir, he shall be hanged as a Spy.

I have the honour to be, &c.

ISRAEL PUTNAM

His Excellency Governor Tryon

P.S. Afternoon. He is hanged.[121]

(Despite Putnam's unflinching reply to the British, he got Palmer's first name wrong.)

The general had pursued Palmer's court-martial and conviction, in part, to serve as a warning to other British and Tory agents operating in and around Peekskill. While Putnam might have appeared unrelenting in his decision to execute Palmer, at least he offered the accused spy a military trial. When another British agent, Daniel Curwen, was captured in the region, he was executed without benefit of any trial. Once he "confessed he was sent out from N York by Colonel Robertson to make Discoveries of our Condition and Carry him Intelligence," another American general, Lord Stirling, issued an immediate order—Curwen was to be "immediately hung up before his Door."[122]

Just a couple of months following Palmer's hanging, another British agent was detected by the Americans. At that time, the British were on the move, marching from Canada through the backcountry lakes region of northeastern New York, headed to Albany. Led by General John Burgoyne, the plan was for British forces to slice through the region and geopolitically separate New England—the most recalcitrant of the American colonies—from all the others, a form of divide and conquer. For Burgoyne's field army to remain in communication with British headquarters in New York City, messengers were sent through American lines. They were typically soldiers dressed in plainclothes, which technically turned them into spies. Several of them were captured en route. One, a Henry Williams, carrying a message to Burgoyne, simply panicked in mid-trip and sought out a Patriot group to just turn over his message.

To provide better security for some of these spy-messengers, the British took pains to conceal the communications they carried. Various tricks were utilized, such as placing rolled slips of paper into hollow writing quills. Another means of concealing messages was to utilize a special bit of spy craft, a form of coding called a *mask* (see "The Cardano Mask System"). In effect, this allowed a message to be concealed in plain sight. On a sheet of paper, a message was written, one that, when read, would present nothing unusual, suspect, or clandestine. The recipient would then take a cutout shape, a mask, and place it over the longer block of text. Within the cutout shape, the true message was revealed. On the following page is an actual example of a "masked" communication between General Henry Clinton in New York City and General Burgoyne in the field, dated August 10, 1777. With this example, the recipient of the message holds a dumbbell or hourglass "mask" over the delivered text, which filters out all the extraneous wording, exposing a separate communication, in effect, the true hidden and intended message:

While both messages have a specific context, the hidden message can be delivered without fear. Even if such a letter were intercepted, the unintended reader fails to grasp the letter's true meaning.[123]

General Clinton utilized yet another form of spy craft during 1777. Just days before General Burgoyne finally surrendered to American forces following the Battle of Saratoga, a spy-courier arrived at General Clinton's headquarters carrying a message from Burgoyne, dated August 28.

The Cardano Mask System

When General Clinton sent secret messages to General Burgoyne during the fall of 1777, he was utilizing a special system, one that relied on a "mask" or a "grille" to reveal the message.

The technique was known as the Cardano System and was named after an Italian named Girolamo Cardano, who lived in the 1500s. The system was incredibly simple in design. It comprised a message within a message—no coded cipher system here. By utilizing a lay-over cutout, only the words of the secret message would be revealed.

But, as simple as the system was in design, it still required someone to write in a way that allowed the larger paragraph to read correctly and make sense while grouping some the larger text's words to convey the real message. Putting such a text together likely called for someone with more than common composing skills.

ABOVE AND RIGHT:
Examples of the Cardano cryptology system utilized by Washington's intelligence operatives.

RIGHT:
An example of how the secret message (highlighted here in red letters) contained in the Clinton Burgoyne letter would appear after the mask paper is placed over it.

You will have heard, Dr Sir I doubt not long before this

Can have reached you that Sir W. Howe is gone from hence. The

Rebels imagine that he is gone to the eastward. By this time

However he has filled Chesapeak bay with surprise and terror.

Washington marched the greater part of the Rebels to Philadelphia

In order to oppose Sir Wm's. army. I hear he is now returned upon

Finding none of our troops landed but am not sure of this, great part

Of his troops are returned for certain. I am sure this countermarching

must be ruin to them. I am left to command here, half of my force may

I am sure defend everything here with much safety. I shall therefore send

Sir W. 4 or 5 Bat[talio]ns. I have too small a force to invade the New England

provinces; they are too weak to make any effectual efforts against me and

You do not want any diversion in your favour. I can, therefore very well

Spare him 1500 men. I shall try something certainly towards the close

Of the year, not till then at any rate. It may be of use to inform you that

report says all yields to you. I own to you that I think the business will

quickly be over now. Sr. W's move just at this time has been capital.

Washingtons have been the worst he could take in every respect.

Sincerely give you much joy on your success and am with

great Sincerity your [ ] / HC

The missive focused on Burgoyne's deteriorating field position and asked whether he should stand or retreat. In a response dated October 8, 1777, Clinton had a message written out on a thin line of silk rather than paper. The message—in which Clinton refused to advise Burgoyne on his situation—was then rolled up and placed inside a small silver capsule about the size of a bullet.[124] The ball could be unscrewed into two parts to reveal its contents. Clinton handed the special ball and its hidden message to Daniel

Taylor, a young British officer. His instructions were simple: if he was captured, he was simply to swallow the silver capsule, so its contents would be irretrievable.

Clinton sent Taylor off on his mission on October 8, bound for General Burgoyne. In the no-man's-land between New York City and Burgoyne, rebel supporters were thick as flies, and Taylor was running a gauntlet lined with misadventure. Within twenty-four hours, he was captured by an American patrol. (He got lost and needed to ask directions, and the Patriots fooled him by dressing as British Redcoats.) The Patriots discovered on Taylor's person no fewer than seven damning personal letters from British officers and Loyalists to their comrades in Burgoyne's ranks. To compound his predicament, he forgot to ingest the silver ball, which was hidden away in a pocket. Taylor was soon dragged before the American general George Clinton to account for himself. The silver ball still undetected, Taylor finally pulled it out and thrust it in his mouth, swallowing it whole. Several of his captors leapt forward and tried to retrieve it, but were too late.

General Clinton was not prepared to accept defeat. He called for his physician, Dr. James Thacher, and ordered him to administer a counter-intelligence measure in the form of "a very strong emetic, calculated to operate in either way."[125] Once Taylor was forced to swallow the medicine, he almost immediately vomited up the capsule. But the British agent quickly grabbed the silver ball and swallowed it a second time. Now, an otherwise patient Clinton "demanded the ball on pain of being hung up instantly and cut open to search [for] it. This brought it forth."[126] With the silk message inside the silver ball now in Clinton's hands, Taylor's fate was all but sealed.

Within a week, the alleged British spy was brought before a court-martial and charged with spying. He entered a not-guilty plea based on his accusation that the Americans who had captured him had worn British uniforms, thus deceiving him. But this mattered little as the American officers convicted him, condemning him to death by hanging. Just days later, a rope was thrown over a ragged branch of an apple tree, Taylor climbed a ladder, and a noose was tightened around his neck. Just as the ladder was removed, a rider galloped into General Clinton's encampment, carrying a message from General Horatio

Taylor's Silver Bullet Today

British spy Daniel Taylor will always be remembered for the strange bit of spy craft symbolized by the hollow "silver bullet," which he unsuccessfully tried to swallow following his capture by the Americans.

Taylor was tried in Fort Ticonderoga, a massive star-shaped masonry fort captured by Benedict Arnold and Ethan Allen in 1775. The "Spy House" located inside is the exact location of Taylor's trial. Also, the silver bullet is housed at the fort, a timeless reminder of Taylor's failure and the nature of some of the spying that took place during the American Revolutionary War.

Gates, whose forces had been engaged with Burgoyne's off and on for several weeks. Burgoyne had surrendered. But the news did nothing to turn the fate of Taylor.

~ ※ ~

A TRIO OF AGENTS

With the defeat of General Johnny Burgoyne's forces in New York—a series of battles that unfolded during the fall of 1777, during which American general and future traitor Benedict Arnold dramatically distinguished himself on the battlefield—the pieces on the Revolutionary War chessboard shifted. One cause for the failure of the Burgoyne campaign, which was intended to cut off New England from the remainder of the colonies, was the lack of support from General Howe in New York City. Burgoyne's plan had called for Howe to sail his men up the Hudson and join with Burgoyne in the field. Howe had other plans. In late July, a British army was ferried by ship from New York City to Sandy Hook, New Jersey, its destination unknown to Washington. While he rightly suspected Howe's target to be Philadelphia, where the American Congress was based, he needed intelligence to confirm his suspicions.

That need became even more apparent by mid-September when Washington engaged Howe's army near Chadds Ford, Pennsylvania. Called the Battle of Brandywine (named for a local creek), this September 11 conflict revealed how little Washington knew not only of Howe's deployments, but also of the geography of the region. Even his maps were misleading. Brandywine was a hard defeat and, in his after-battle report to Congress, the commander in chief cited one significant cause for losing the fight—a lack of actionable intelligence.

Within two weeks, Howe occupied Philadelphia, sending congressmen scurrying into rural Pennsylvania. But just as Washington had developed a relatively effective network of spies in New York, so too did he manage to piece together a similar system in Philadelphia. Like New York, Philadelphia was home to plenty of supporters of the British cause. But the City of Brotherly Love also boasted a plethora of civilians who were willing to feed Washington information about the Redcoats now occupying their city. In addition, his Excellency was already grooming three capable agents, all majors in the Continental Army—Benjamin Tallmadge, John Clark, and Allen McLane. Clark and McLane managed several agents operating between Philadelphia and Washington's headquarters, outside of the city. Tallmadge, who had already done some intelligence work for Washington, maintained his ties to spies in New York City. (In fact, Tallmadge and Clark had both overseen a limited spy operation earlier in 1777 in New York, Long Island, and Connecticut.) Over the next few years, these men served as Washington's eyes and ears in the intelligence-gathering business.

In Philadelphia, Clark operated a ring of civilian spies who either lived in the city or moved in and out of town on legitimate business (providing them the usual cover for any intelligence gathering). His was a multiple-level operation that included farmers peddling their wares to British commissary officers and others who bought and sold to the British, including those in the city's many shops and storefronts. Some of his connections were among Philadelphia's social elites who rubbed shoulders with Tories and British officers (and their wives) alike. Several of Clark's spies were women. Additionally and perhaps surprisingly he relied on several Quakers. As Quakers were pacifists, the British did not think they would support the war effort. In operating his ring, Clark was extremely circumspect about the identities of his agents, the information limited to a small circle. By maintaining the rings of his spy circle separate from one another, each agent's risk of exposure was limited.

Clark relied on the usual spy methods of the day, with many of his spies operating as double agents, offering their services to Howe and his officers, all while gathering intelligence for Washington. One such agent approached General Howe directly, offering to "risqué my all in procuring him intelligence."[127] Wanting proof of the individual's veracity, Howe asked what information the would-be agent might have to offer. The double agent handed the British general several papers, some in Washington's handwriting, one of which told a story of Washington ordering General Gates, the American victor over Burgoyne at Saratoga, to deliver eight thousand men to augment Washington's forces in an assault on Philadelphia. The information was false, but managed to convince Howe that the agent was the genuine article. Clark also worked closely with his commander in chief in crafting and planting this type of disinformation in order to mislead, misdirect, and confuse the British. (This was easy to accomplish, since Clark operated with double agents.) One of his coups was the interception of a pack of British passes, the kind issued by British authorities to individuals so they could pass between the lines to do business in the city or visit with friends or family. The passes that fell into rebel hands, and thus into Clark's, were unsigned, and ready for Clark to use at his discretion.

How much disinformation was fed to General Howe is unknown. But Washington gave Clark several examples of the kinds of deceptions he wanted to plant in the enemy's minds. Much of it was designed to increase Howe's concerns over New York City, which he fretted over anyway without any encouragement from the rebels. One line of disinformation presented New York City as constantly vulnerable, with rebel plans underway to retake it. Other lines suggested that General Horatio Gates was preparing to aid Washington's forces in of an attack on Philadelphia and, later, New York; that New York and New Jersey militias were being prepared to supplement the assault on Manhattan Island; and that Washington was preparing to attack Philadelphia.

One of the complications Clark and his field agents faced was one that Washington's spies had already experienced. Since agents operated, by necessity, undercover, local militia units were not aware of their identities. Thus, agents were sometimes stopped by rebels intent on catching British spies, not knowing they were in the employ of Washington. To overcome this possible

impediment Clark needed to provide plausible cover stories for those agents traveling between Philadelphia and Washington's headquarters.

While Clark's spies were never able to gain extensive advance information of General Howe's overall plans, they were able to gain more street-level information, including British casualty figures and data regarding supplies available to the British and their sources. They also discovered where troops were deployed in the city and in what numbers, where they were moving, and when reinforcements arrived, in addition to the general condition, including morale, of the Redcoats occupying the city. When Clark received information about a planned British assault on an American outpost, Fort Mercer on the Delaware River, the troops stationed there were warned ahead and withdrew in time.

During the months that Clark's spy ring was operational, some of his agents may have delivered their reports to a cutout, or go-between. One such contact may have been an elderly woman named "Old Mom" Rinker. According to stories, Mom Rinker passed on information in the most unusual of manners. Her family ran the local Buck's Tavern, and she is supposed to have set up a flax-bleaching operation at the top of a cliff rising over the Wissahickon Valley outside Germantown, which is today a suburb of Philadelphia. A local band of rebel guerrillas, the Green Boys, ranged in the area, where they made contact with her. "Old Mom" would occasionally drop a ball of yarn over the side of the cliff, in sight of the Green Boys, who would then scurry to retrieve it. Rinker would slip reports inside the "accidentally dropped" yarn; the boys would then deliver the information to Washington.

Early in 1778, Clark's work as a spy coordinator was over. He was struggling with health issues, which caused him to be sidelined. While some of his agents continued to provide intelligence as best they could through the winter of 1777–78 when Washington's forces were hunkered down and suffering at Valley Forge, the ring was without an effective head by spring. Others would have to step up their game and fill the breach.

One group of agents that continued to feed information to Washington included a female spy named Lydia Darragh. She lived in Philadelphia on Second Street, along with her husband, William, a local schoolmaster, and their two children. An Irish immigrant and member of the Quaker faith, the forty-eight-year-old Lydia was a midwife who even performed duties as an undertaker from time to time to supplement the family income. Despite her religion, Lydia supported the Patriot cause.

When the British occupied the city in September 1777, they soon commandeered private houses for their lodging, and the Darragh home was among them. One of General Howe's staff officers, John André (not only was André a spy for Howe, but he would also later be implicated directly in Benedict Arnold's treason) gave notice to the Darraghs they would need to evacuate their home. The forceful Lydia marched straight to General Howe's headquarters to protest, as the move would put her family of four in the streets. As fortune would have it, Lydia recognized one of her own second cousins among Howe's officers. He helped convince the British general to allow the Darraghs to remain in their home, while making their large parlor available for meetings involving Redcoat officers.

An opportunity had fallen into Lydia Darragh's lap. Not only could she collect intelligence in the streets for Washington, but she could also collect it from her very own front room, where the British officers would be meeting (on one occasion, she did just that). The possibilities seemed tremendous. The Darragh operation was soon a family affair, and the means of delivery was quite clever. Bits of information were written down on small pieces of paper, using a simple shorthand code. Lydia then placed the papers inside cloth buttons which she sewed on the coat of John Darragh, her teenaged son. Since John was only fourteen years old, he could pass between the British and American lines without notice. (He had an older brother, Lieutenant Charles Darragh, stationed at Whitemarsh, near Philadelphia.) Upon reaching Charles, John would cut off the special buttons, and his brother would "translate" the code. The messages were then delivered to Washington's intelligence officers. Little is known of the specifics, but deliveries were made on a regular basis.

Without question, this scattered pastiche of Philadelphia spies and couriers managed to accomplish significant intelligence coups on behalf of their spymaster, General Washington. Such agents as Sackett, Clark, Tallmadge, and McLane risked much. But for several of these men, their days as spies had only just begun. Especially for Benjamin Tallmadge and Allen McLane, their greatest adventures still lay in the future.

～ ※ ～

CHAPTER SIX

Silas Deane and Benjamin Franklin: Our Men in Paris

A French Agent in Philadelphia

n the early days of the war, anyone supporting the Patriot cause could only wonder where this long-delayed clash of arms might lead. It was certainly less than clear that it might ultimately result in American independence from Great Britain. But, as King George III himself had declared in a speech more than six months earlier, the die was now cast,[128] and only time would tell.

One question that loomed large in the minds of many of the men then serving in the Continental Congress focused not on the British, but on the French. Some congressmen suggested that any such rift between the Americans and the British Crown would have direct geopolitical ramifications in many European capitals, none, perhaps, more than Paris.

Twenty years earlier, as a result of the French and Indian War, the French had packed themselves up and left Canada to the British. North America had become England's grand reservoir of natural resources, offering everything from lumber to fur. If the rebellious colonists could manage to deliver any significant shift in the relationship with the mother country, France might gain some strategic advantage, especially if British trade laws and customs duties were forever abandoned.

As the Americans launched into military conflict, they would require access to necessities of war that only France might be able to provide— money, ships, guns, soldiers, and international support. King Louis XVI might not have been a lover of liberty, but some Americans believed he might have a significant interest in poking a sharp stick in an English eye or two—especially those of King George.

To that end, the Continental Congress reached out, establishing the American Commission in Paris, which included a trio of men whose goal was to work with the French and sign a treaty of support against England. But the diplomatic steps taken to bring about such a treaty were only part of the work the commission performed in the French capital. These men also engaged in espionage, carrying out covert actions to bolster support for the American military effort against the Crown. Their intelligence activities would be myriad, including sabotage, propaganda, clandestine military efforts, and support of privateering. They had their successes. But in time, the commission would be compromised, penetrated by a skilled and resourceful British agent operating in service to His Majesty.

Before the commission was dispatched, an important meeting took place in Philadelphia with one of Louis XVI's special agents in America. Julien-Alexandre Achard de Bonvouloir was an undercover operative, his cover that of a Flemish merchant. French foreign minister Charles Gravier, comte de Vergennes, had dispatched him to America in September 1775. In late December, he met with an old associate of his—none other than Benjamin Franklin. With the Philadelphia printer and world-wise statesman providing the introductions, Bonvouloir sat down with Congress's newly formed Committee of Secret Correspondence. On three cold, wintry nights between December 18 and 28, the parties gathered in a room in Carpenters' Hall. Although they could not have been certain in their assertion at the time, the committee members assured Bonvouloir that Congress would be declaring independence from Great Britain. Given that turn of events, they queried, might the French ally with the Americans against their common enemy? Most crucial was any promise of naval support the French might offer, since the Americans had almost none. Bonvouloir, while not making any promises, indicated the possibilities for French backing were good. Franklin and his colleagues were encouraged.

Beyond Bonvouloir, members of the committee were aware of another covert link already in place in Europe, who might also be able to help firm up the needed assistance. An American lawyer named Arthur Lee was in London where he had made a connection with a second French agent. On both sides of the Atlantic, the Americans were covertly pursuing a firm French commitment to their cause.

≈ ※ ≈

The Playwright Agent

Arthur Lee's French contact in London was hardly a man who simply worked behind the scenes in diplomatic circles. Pierre-Augustin Caron de Beaumarchais was actually a playwright of some renown, as well as a professional musician. He was the author of such masterful stage works as *The Barber of Seville* and *The Marriage of Figaro*, both of which had been worked into famous operas.

RIGHT:
A typically melodramatic scene from Beaumarchais' The Barber of Seville.

ALIAS, TOM JONES

With Bonvouloir dangling French support, the members of the committee chose an agent from their own ranks to join them in Paris—Silas Deane. A Connecticut delegate to the Continental Congress from 1774 to 1776, Deane seemed a solid choice. A Yale graduate, he was comfortable in crowds and a good conversationalist with a convincing smile and infectious laugh. Deane would move under the alias Thomas Jones, an American merchant dispatched to France to procure weapons, food, and other materiel for the rebel army. His cover was plausible. Deane's true mission, however, was to determine whether France was open to joining the American revolutionaries as allies.

The problem was that Deane had several marks against him. He was hardly a savvy sophisticate, having rarely left New England. Though a lawyer by education, he made his living as a merchant, which might have come in handy if his true mission to Paris had been to purchase war materials. To complicate matters further, Silas Deane did not speak French, a big disadvantage for an American in Paris.

Then, there was the problem of how to negotiate with the French on a practical level. Such diplomacy might be normal between two sovereign nations, but the colonies were hardly an independent country. They were still, officially, a part of the British Empire. The French could not exactly declare their support for the United States of America because that geopolitical designation did not yet exist. All talks, any negotiations, would need to be handled delicately, discreetly, sometimes even through unofficial channels and go-betweens.

ABOVE:
Silas Deane, c. 1781.

As Deane prepared to sail to Paris in the spring of 1776, Arthur Lee was already making headway in his own negotiations with the French. Lee's contact in London was Pierre-Augustin Caron de Beaumarchais, an undercover agent in direct service to King Louis XVI (see "The Playwright Agent," opposite). The two men had been in conversation since 1775 about French military support for the colonial conflict. By late spring of 1776, close to the time of Deane's arrival in Paris, Beaumarchais announced to Lee that the king was willing to provide £200,000 worth of military equipment to the Americans. The French were not yet, however, prepared to enter the war.

Upon arriving in Paris, Deane found himself swimming among sharks. He was a complete newcomer thrown into the complicated, secretive world of international negotiations and closed-door diplomacy. Historian Samuel Flagg Bemis describes the environment: "The capitals of Europe were full of international spies. The technique of deciphering intercepted dispatches attained a high degree of perfection. Corruption was the conventional instrument of diplomatic success. The art of dissimulation and deception was a necessary part of the equipment of any minister of foreign affairs . . . It was this cynical and brutal international world of the eighteenth century into which the United States of America was to be delivered."[129]

To help provide Deane with a network of contacts in Paris and other European countries, Benjamin Franklin and the members of the Committee of Secret Correspondence gave him a half-dozen names, including Arthur Lee in London. The others included a German living in Holland who had known Franklin for years; a French doctor named Barbeu-Dubourg; Jean-Baptiste Le Roy, another French friend of Franklin's; Charles-Jean Garnier, who was in France's diplomatic service in London; and Dr. Edward Bancroft, who also lived in London. According to the Committee's instructions to Deane:

You will endeavor to procure a meeting with Mr. Bancroft by writing a letter to him, under cover to Mr. Griffiths at Turnham Green, near London, and desiring him to come over to you, in France or Holland, on the score of old acquaintance. From him you may obtain a good deal of information of what is now going forward in England, and settle a mode of continuing a correspondence. It may well be to remit him a small bill to defray his expenses in coming to you, and avoid all political matters in your letter to him.[130]

Bancroft was the only one of the six with whom Deane was already familiar. Their friendship extended back fifteen years to when Deane had been Bancroft's tutor in Hartford, Connecticut. For Deane, Bancroft represented a friend and someone who was savvy about the European way of doing things. He was fluent in French. And he had connections of his own that might serve Deane well. But with Bancroft came controversy.

∿ ✖ ∾

SPYING FOR BOTH SIDES

Today, many historians believe that Dr. Edward Bancroft operated, at least during the months between July 1776 and March 1777, as an agent for the British, even as he did some intelligence work for the Americans, through such contacts as Franklin and Deane. The editors of Benjamin Franklin's papers have labeled Bancroft "one of the most successful double agents in the history of espionage."[131] Other historians suggest that Bancroft was a paid agent of the Continental Congress, but this remains uncertain.

Few question whether Bancroft delivered intelligence information to Silas Deane from London to Paris in 1776 and 1777. During this period, Bancroft also sent a report to British officials in August 1776 and was compensated for his efforts in February 1777. American ministers also paid Bancroft for all expenses he incurred while providing them information, although they never paid him a salary. Much of the controversy hinges on how official Bancroft was in his capacities as agent for either the British or the Americans. What is clear is that he was playing a double game.

To that end, what intelligence did he route to his old teacher, Silas Deane? It is known that he sent copies of British newspapers and recent pamphlets concerning the American Revolution and official doings in Parliament and Whitehall, all to keep Deane informed on the latest in politics. He also sent several letters, but not through the regular mail service, which would have allowed London postal officials to examine them. Instead, they were sent secretly through Garnier, the French *chargé d'affaires* in London. Garnier then placed them in his hands-off diplomatic pouch, which he delivered to Vergennes at Versailles, who finally handed them off to Deane.

The contents of these letters varied widely. Some were jam-packed with bits of intelligence, while others just recycled news available even to the average Parisian on the streets. One missive, sent on September 13, 1776, rings with information, including informing Deane of no news reported yet of Admiral Richard, Lord Howe, peace mission to America. (That year, Howe was authorized to negotiate with the Americans toward a peace settlement, but it came to nothing.) Bancroft writes of General Burgoyne's planned Canada–New York campaign, even as he expresses doubts that it would be launched that fall. He also informs Deane that the

London newspapers are full of gossip concerning Deane himself, including speculations regarding his work in Paris.

Bancroft also warns Deane that he is being spied on by a Dr. Hugh Williams, who had only recently arrived in Paris. Williams was already sending intelligence reports about Deane back to London, one of which stated that Deane and Bancroft were close friends. Bancroft advises the less-than-experienced Deane to operate with the "utmost circumspection." He then wraps up the letter with the following bit of concern about himself: "How long I may be safe & quiet here I really do not know; there are so many rascals to recommend themselves to Government by Tale bearing, that if they can get no intelligence, they may perhaps forge Lies, & throw me out of that State of security in which I had imagined myself to be."[132] Such a letter seems to strongly indicate that Dr. Edward Bancroft did, indeed, deliver intelligence to Silas Deane and that his interest in maintaining the secrecy between the two of them was a serious one.

But what of Bancroft's spying for the British? It, too, seems well-founded, although not without controversy. According to the commonly accepted version of events, Dr. Bancroft was in the employ of the British Secret Service long before Silas Deane's arrival in Paris. He was paid £500 for his services (an amount equal to nearly $40,000) and promised an additional £400 to £500 annually through the years of the American Revolutionary War, plus an after-war pension of £200 annually.

Once Deane was established in Paris, Bancroft had plenty of opportunities to spy on both him and the American Commission. He became Deane's translator during official, albeit clandestine, meetings with French representatives and agents. He eventually was even appointed secretary to the commission, which gave him access to "the progress of the treaty with France,"[133] as well as nearly all correspondence between the commissioners and Congress. Bancroft also would come to know the names of ships delivering communications between Deane, Franklin, and their connections in America.

Bancroft's British Secret Service handler was an American businessman, Paul Wentworth. Born in the West Indies in 1728, Wentworth came from a prominent New Hampshire family that owned coffee plantations in Surinam. By the late 1760s, he was living in London. He and Bancroft met for the first time in 1769, as Wentworth was aware that Bancroft had written a book about the natural history of Guiana, where some of his coffee works were located. Wentworth traveled extensively from one European capital to another, investing in stocks. Through the early 1770s, Wentworth was living off the profits made from his plantations, and he massaged friendships with influential British officials, including Lord Suffolk, who served as a secretary of state. In 1777, he met Beaumarchais, who later noted that Wentworth "spoke better French than he did."[134]

By the summer of 1776, Wentworth met with Bancroft in London, and Wentworth informed his associate that the British government was aware of his contact with Silas Deane. Knowing Bancroft was opposed to American independence, even if he was sympathetic to American grievances against the Crown, Wentworth managed to recruit him as an agent by mid-August. Bancroft was instructed on how to deliver reports clandestinely and what information he was to collect, including intelligence on efforts to seal an alliance between the Americans and the French; any covert French support for the Americans; and any other movements made by Franklin and Deane that might be of interest to the British Secret Service.

Some of Wentworth's instructions to Bancroft may be found in a letter Wentworth sent to William Eden, the undersecretary of state in the Northern Department of the British foreign ministry, dating from December 1776, in which he stated the following: "Dr. Edwards [Bancroft's code name] engages to correspond with Mr. Wentworth and to communicate to him, whatever may come to his knowledge on the following subjects. . . . Franklin and Deane's correspondence with Congress, and their agents; and the secret, as well as the ostensible letters from the Congress to them."[135] Bancroft proved a valuable agent to the British, so much so that, by 1780, the British Secret Service was paying him £1,000 annually.

By Dr. Bancroft's own admission, he served as a spy for the British service. In 1784, following the conclusion of the Revolutionary War—the British always referred to the conflict as "the American War"—Bancroft, then making application for a hearty pension, wrote a letter to the British secretary of state for foreign affairs, Lord Carmarthen, in which he described his activities as a spy:

I went to Paris and during the first year, resided in the same house with Dr. Franklin, Mr. Deane etc., and regularly informed his Government [the king] of every transaction of the American Commissioners . . . and when the Government of France at length determined openly to support the Revolted Colonies, I gave notice of this determination . . . and with unexampled dispatch, conveyed this intelligence to this City, and to the King's Ministers, within 42 hours, from the instant of their Signature [to the two Treaties of Alliance and Commerce].[136]

All deliveries of intelligence had to be made as secretly as possible, as the American Wentworth felt he had much to lose if he were discovered to be spying for the British. To maintain this secrecy, Bancroft was to write letters under the fictional names "Mr. Richardson" or "Mr. Edward Edwards." The missives were to appear to be nothing more than love letters to a woman. But, between the lines of the "love letter," Bancroft was to write his intelligence using an invisible ink the British provided him, which could then be revealed to the true recipient by using a chemical wash. Bancroft was to take such letters each Tuesday evening after 9:30 p.m. to a dead drop in the Jardin des Tuileries, one of Paris's famous parks. He was to place the report in a bottle and then place the bottle in a hole beneath a specific box-tree. A string was to be attached to it, so someone could see where it was buried. After Bancroft left the gardens, an agent would come to the location and remove the bottle, replacing it with another, along with any messages for the doctor-spy. Through this means, Bancroft managed to deliver hundreds of reports to Wentworth.

Unfortunately for Deane and Franklin, as well as the American cause, Dr. Edward Bancroft proved to be an excellent agent operating between both sides in a dangerous game of international espionage.

Dr. Bancroft's Later Years

Even after Silas Deane and Arthur Lee were pulled from active diplomatic and intelligence gathering and called back to the United States, Dr. Edward Bancroft continued his spying efforts. He remained the private secretary for the Paris Commission—reporting largely to Benjamin Franklin—until early 1783. By then, the war on the battlefield had ended (the last significant field fight was Yorktown in October 1781), and the Treaty of Paris was near signature.

After the war, Bancroft went to Great Britain and took up scientific work, studying chemistry. He died in 1821.

For the next sixty years, his legacy as double agent remained a secret, until an American historian, B. F. Stephens, discovered documents in British archives that clearly implicated Bancroft and his duplicity.

DEANE GETS TO WORK

By midsummer of 1776, just days after the men of the Continental Congress voted in support of American independence, Deane met with the French secretary of state for foreign affairs, Charles Gravier, comte de Vergennes. Gravier paved the way for him to sit down with Beaumarchais to hammer out details of a deal in which the French would exchange shipments of weapons and other materials of war for American farm produce. To keep some distance from the French government, the deal was done on the sly, through a false-front business called Roderigue Hortalez & Company. (In today's world of espionage, such a shell business is referred to as a "proprietary company.") From the outside, it had all the appearance of legitimacy. Beaumarchais—operating under the false name "M. Durand"—opened up its "headquarters" in a suite of rooms in a Parisian hotel.

Deane's efforts, as well as Arthur Lee's, were bearing fruit almost immediately. Soon, another American, Robert Morris, was added to the mix. Prior to Deane's mission, Morris, a prominent member of Congress, had been keeping the books for the rebel cause, seeking loans of both money and military equipment and supplies. He had not been particularly successful in courting the French. Now, with the new developments, Morris essentially became the American connection at home for Hortalez & Company. He maintained communications with Benjamin Franklin concerning Deane's mission and dispatched additional agents, most undercover as merchants for fictitious companies, to other destinations, including New Orleans and a foreign European port.

That summer, Beaumarchais routed one million livres to the Americans through Hortalez. By summer's end, another million had been sent from the Spanish. Yet another million came from a clandestine group of French merchants ready to receive inexpensive American produce. French connections negotiated with French munitions manufacturers for contracts, shipped the much-needed hardware and other supplies to the West Indies, then on through back-door shipments to American ports. French guns, powder, and ball were delivered in a triangular trade between Paris, the Caribbean, and the Atlantic seaboard while Americans shipped out tons of tobacco, rice, and indigo in exchange.

But, even though both the Americans and the French tried to maintain the secrecy of the firearms-for-food exchange, the amounts changing hands were so immense as to make continuous concealment difficult, if not impossible. To help provide cover, the French government explained that Louis XVI had ordered the modernization of his nation's military. To that end, old weapons were to be gathered up and sold off. Even if the ruse managed to convince the French public, the British knew the French were doing war business with the Americans.

Other glitches complicated the system. While the French were able to collect and dispatch military stores to the Americans worth five million livres by September 1777—an amount equivalent in today's money to half a billion dollars—the Americans were excruciatingly slow in delivering the negotiated amounts of agricultural products. By the following year, when the French finally agreed to enter the war as an American ally, Hortalez & Company was on the verge of bankruptcy and needed infusions of cash from the French government on three different occasions.

But supplies were reaching the American front and American troops. By December 1776, Beaumarchais had sent two hundred cannon and twenty brass mortars, plus a staggering three hundred thousand muskets, one hundred tons of gunpowder, thirty thousand uniforms, three thousand tents, and musket balls by the barrel. (The French were careful to file off any of their own markings on cannon, so they could not be traced back to them if captured by British troops.) The first delivery to reach American waters docked at Portsmouth in April 1777, the ships carrying sixty cannon, twelve thousand muskets, a large amount of gunpowder, and a stockpile of uniforms. This infusion of supplies particularly aided the Northern Army operating in the field opposite General Johnny Burgoyne and helped bring about his ultimate defeat at Saratoga that following fall. Through 1777 and 1778, Hortalez & Company supplied most of the war materiel used by the Continental Army. With the French and American treaties of friendship and alliance finally concluded by February 1778, much of the previously covert shipping of guns and cannon to the Americans could then be done in an overt fashion.

BELOW:
Baron Johann de Kalb (center) introducing the Marquis de Lafayette to Silas Deane.

Lafayette, You Are Here!

As Silas Deane negotiated with Beaumarchais to deliver skilled French officers to support Washington's forces in America, one of the most famous arrived in 1777. Marie-Joseph Paul Yves Roch Gilbert du Motier, best remembered as the Marquis de Lafayette, brought little military experience, but soon became one of General Washington's favorite officers. Lafayette was an enthusiastic supporter of the Americans and hated the British, whom he blamed for the death of his father.

Accompanying Lafayette to America was another officer, one older and perhaps a mentor to the younger French nobleman. Baron Johann de Kalb was Bavarian and had joined the French Army and worked his way up to general.

De Kalb was not actually new to America. Prior to the war, he had worked as an intelligence officer for the French and was dispatched to America in 1768 to observe the widening rift between the Americans and the British. For three years following his return in 1777, De Kalb shouldered responsibilities within the American military, serving in Delaware and Maryland and finally in the South under the command of General Horatio Gates. De Kalb was killed in the August 1780 Battle of Camden.

Although Baron De Kalb called himself such, in reality, he was no baron. He claimed the title to help elevate his status within the French military. Since he achieved the rank of general, it appears his claim to German aristocracy had worked in his favor.

RIGHT:

General Washington standing with Johann De Kalb, Baron von Steuben, Kazimierz Pulaski, Tadeusz Kościuszko, Lafayette, John Muhlenberg, and other officers.

During those important years when Deane was first on the scene in Paris, the French provided several other means of assistance to the Americans. They lent French military officers for covert operations. Deane negotiated with Beaumarchais to send seventeen French military engineers to North America to provide their skills to the Continental Army. They also provided ships to be used for military and covert, even paramilitary, actions, as well as access to French ports in the Caribbean. And finally, King Louis XVI paid for much of the undercover work done by the Americans during this period, to the tune of a two million livre loan delivered clandestinely.

⤙ ⚒ ⤚

THE HOUSE PAINTER PYROMANIAC

Silas Deane's days in Paris were typically filled with writing correspondences to connections in the city, London, or America. Clandestine meetings were commonplace, and his reports of such were written, of course, with invisible ink. But one would-be agent was a strange one indeed. Deane first met James Aitken when Aitken came to call at his house on the rue de L'Université in early November 1776. (He had come to Deane's home a couple of times before, but Deane's wary valet, put off by the stranger's appearance, had turned him away.) Taking in the stranger, Deane later described his appearance: "His dress no way recommended him at Paris."[139]

The modern-day phrase "shabby chic" might begin to describe the thin, twenty-five-year-old standing before Deane. His hair was a scatter of red straw, long and dirty, topped by a fantail cap, and his face was mottled with freckles. He wore a dirty, ox-blood-colored jacket that hardly fit him. He paced the floor of Deane's study rambling incoherently in a thick Scottish accent. Only later did Deane realize that Aitken was trying to speak in a form of code, concerned that someone in the household—perhaps that judgmental valet—might understand his purpose in coming. What Aitken was offering was his services as a saboteur.

Aitken was a slippery type, one who lied with such ease that even the most skeptical could easily be taken in. He explained that he had recently lived in America and had served in the king's forces in Virginia, but had since turned in support of the American cause. As it turns out, he had lived in America (he hailed from North Carolina), he and had joined up with a unit of Loyalist Scots. On no fewer than three occasions, however, he had enlisted in the British army, then immediately took off after collecting his enlistment bonus. Lately, he had come to Britain in search of an officer's commission and was turned down. So he had now decided to offer himself to the Americans. He was, by trade, an itinerant house painter—he was known locally as "John the Painter"—but also a criminal with a list of crimes as long as his painting arm. He was a burglar, shoplifter, stagecoach robber, and all-around no-good who had once shot a dog and raped a shepherdess. To round out his criminal record, he was a pyromaniac.

An Invisible Piece of Spy Craft

As an intelligence agent operating in France, Silas Deane was thrust into a world in which espionage had been practiced for centuries and the artistry involved was intricate, well-tested, and sophisticated. Among the most common practices was the use of invisible ink, including the type the British Secret Service supplied to Dr. Edward Bancroft. Fortunately, Deane had a significant and skilled (albeit indirect) provider of invisible ink, John Jay's brother.

Dr. James Jay was an expert in invisible ink. Born in New York City, he studied medicine in Great Britain and received his degree from the University of Edinburgh, a leading medical school during the late eighteenth century. He returned to New York in 1756 and commenced his medical practice. But he often had trouble keeping patients, as many thought him to be "haughty, proud, overbearing, supercilious, pedantic, vain and ambitious."[137] It seems his fees were too high as well. With few patients other than his own relatives, Jay decided to pack his practice up and move back to England.

Although living in London, Jay developed a sympathy for the Patriot cause and began working on a formula for an invisible ink that he could use to write messages to his brother John. He would report on English responses to the unfolding protests in Boston and other hot spots in the colonies. In some of his secret correspondence, James Jay communicated to the Continental Congress that the British had no intentions of backing down in the face of colonial protests. In his words, it was the "determination of the British Ministry to reduce the Colonies to unconditional submission."[138]

Prior to Silas Deane's mission to Paris, James Jay had sent a significant amount of invisible ink to his brother, John. As Deane prepared to set sail for Europe in April 1776, John Jay provided him with bottles of the stuff.

Deane was naturally skeptical about Aitken, given his appearance, his ramblings, and the mere fact that he did not know anything about him. But when Aitken hinted that he had some intelligence to pass on, something about British ports, Deane invited him back the next day. This time, they met outdoors, on the Pont Neuf, one of the most famous bridges crossing over to the Île de la Cité. Here, no one could overhear their conversation.

Aitken came to his point quickly. He intended to set fire to the British Navy dockyards in Portsmouth and Plymouth, both located on the

John the Painter's Incendiary Devices

How, exactly, were John the Painter's time bombs constructed? Once he received money and a green light from Deane to pursue his mission to burn British Naval dockyards, Aitken headed straight for England, where he hired a Canterbury tinkerer-mechanic to build his devices.

Aitken had drawn out simple sketches of his contraptions, which were to be fashioned out of tin, measuring under ten inches in length and three by four inches around, and having a similar look to a simple lantern. Inside these containers, the saboteur placed a highly flammable combination of turpentine and other paint materials that, when heated, would build in temperature for hours until finally flashing out into flames.

Once Aitken put them to their designated purpose, the small devices worked extremely well, helping John the Painter become the only saboteur during the American Revolutionary War who managed to inflict damage on the British fleet on British soil.

southwest coast, as well as Chatham, Deptford, and Woolwich, situated closer to London. He had things all worked out. Aitken had even created a delayed-action device that would cause a fire to ignite long after he had set the pyrotechnic piece in place. It was small and easily concealed, and several such devices could be placed secretly throughout a single dockyard, burst into flames in a synchronized order, and spread fire and chaos from wharf to wharf, ship to ship.

Deane was intrigued, even if still skeptical. But he had little reason not to sanction and support Aitken's plans. Although John the Painter might be little more than a common thief and highwayman, America was at war with Great Britain and a peculiar Scot was offering his services as an arsonist-saboteur. (He came armed with the devices to show he was serious.) As Deane wrote later, he agreed to support Aitken, with "motives no less than a desire to weaken a declared enemy, and to preserve my country, by every means in my power, from the horrors, and distress of fire and desolation."[140]

Soon, Aitken's short career as a saboteur in service to America commenced, with Deane providing him with the codename Zero and handing him seventy-two livres, equivalent to about $500 in today's money. He also gave Aitken Edward Bancroft's name and address in London—Number 4,

Downing Street. Once he returned to England, he had the devices built in Canterbury. By December 6, he put them to their purposes, using one to set fire to the dockyard in Portsmouth and another pair in a local residential neighborhood to provide a distraction to authorities. What Aitken had not told Deane was that he intended not only to destroy the dockyards, but the entire town as well. Poor matches kept him from setting the neighborhood ablaze, but he did manage to set fire to the dockyard, resulting in the destruction of a rope walk, a building in which rope was produced for ship rigging. Otherwise, the dockyard was undamaged.

The following day Aitken made a serious mistake. He appeared on Edward Bancroft's doorstep, where he bragged about the dockyard fire. He also said Deane had told him that Bancroft would provide him money and a safe house. Of course, Bancroft was uncertain how to respond. He was, after all, a double agent who did not want to reveal his cover. Just to have Aitken at his door was problematic enough because Bancroft knew that British agents sometimes kept watch on his house to make certain he did not turn traitor. Bancroft decided to refuse Aitken. News of the fire in Portsmouth had not otherwise reached him, so he had no way of confirming the story of the strange man making wild-eyed claims. Not wanting to lose an opportunity, just in case, Bancroft agreed to meet with Aitken the following day.

They met at an entirely unlikely location, the Salopian Coffee House on Charing Cross Road, one too public for secret agents uncertain of one another and their true loyalties. (Naval officers frequented the shop and the Admiralty offices were situated across the street.) Bancroft and Aitken were both uncomfortable when they sat down together. Each likely wondered if the other was actually setting him up for a fall. But Bancroft spoke in a soft voice, leaning in toward Aitken. He explained would not provide him money and would not hide him from British authorities. Aitken was never to return to Bancroft's residence, and Bancroft even suggested strongly that Aitken stop his sabotage.

An indignant Aitken rose from the table and shouted angrily at Bancroft, telling him that he would strike again soon, this time at Plymouth, then he stormed out of the coffeehouse. Bancroft reported his meetings with Aitken to his handlers. It appears that nothing was done by British authorities to try and apprehend him. To do so might have exposed Bancroft as a spy in the service of king and country.

Within a month, Aitken was caught. He had tried to plant his incendiary devices at the Plymouth dockyard, but had failed, as the facility was crawling with Redcoat guards. He had moved on to Bristol, where he attempted burning a Jamaican merchant ship, *Savannah*, on January 15, 1777. The next night he set fire to a local warehouse, one used by a bookseller, not the British navy. Soon, the British Secret Service was on his trail, offering a fifty-pound reward and circulating a broadside describing his actions, a physical description, and his name—John the Painter. By February 3, the dragnet closed, and Aitken was arrested, initially on suspicion of burglary. To tighten up their case, British officials planted a British agent in Clerkenwell Prison, disguised as an American visitor to the jail. After chatting up Aitken, the visitor returned daily, and the two became friends. In time, John the Painter confessed his actions, and the agent informed the authorities.

By March, Aitken was on trial, the informant testified, and the career criminal was convicted and sentenced to death. During the proceedings, the British prosecution tried to connect Aitken with Deane. At one point, the informant accused Deane of having paid Aitken £300 to support him in his sabotage, to which Aitken responded loudly: "Consider in the sight of God what you say concerning Silas Deane!" The prosecutor was direct in his response: "You need not be afraid, Silas Deane is not here, but he will be hanged in due time."[141] Before his execution, Aitken made a full confession to authorities and even mentioned Deane and Bancroft by name. He was hanged on March 10, 1777, at Portsmouth, suspended from a sixty-foot-tall ship mast, which "was erected at the Main Gate so that he could see the destruction as he passed from this world to the next."[142] Aitken may have been dead, but he was not soon forgotten: his body was placed in a cage suspended high aloft the dockyard, where it remained for months.

PORTS, SHIPS, PRIVATEERS

One of the more involved aspects of Silas Deane's work in Paris (with Benjamin Franklin providing his own sort of support), was the pursuit of strategies that might hamper the operation of Great Britain's most potent weapon—its navy. Comprised of hundreds of great sailing ships—from sloops and frigates to second raters and behemoth man-of-war vessels bristling with cannon—its presence on the high seas gave Britain an international dominance and control the Americans found difficult to counter. Unable to match the English ship for ship, Congress knew it had to work out ways to minimize the navy's impact. Deane was soon placed in the middle of this effort.

As large as the British navy was, it simply did not boast enough ships both to protect English merchant ships plying international waters and blockade the entire American seaboard. Deane and others arranged for ports beyond the reach of the British to be made secretly available for American ships. From these clandestine bases, American vessels could harass British merchant ships.

French involvement in such activities was a bit tricky. In 1713, the French had signed a treaty with the British in which they agreed not to accept privateered British ships and cargoes. However, the agreement did not preclude the French from opening up their ports to Americans engaging in the practice of search and seizure on the seas, so Deane worked behind the scenes to secure such ports, many of them situated in the Caribbean. Also, Congress officially sanctioned privateers to be used against the English; these were essentially privately owned ships that might prey on and seize British ships, then sell the spoils of war—the ship and its contents—while pocketing the booty. (General Washington himself even invested in a privateering ship.) Sometimes Franklin and Deane worked together on similar covert projects, all in support of the American revolutionary cause.

In time, such French ports as Brest, Saint-Malo, L'Orient, Nantes, and Le Havre were opened to the Americans and closed to the British. The British protested such moves in official diplomatic circles, even handing the French lists of specific ships, their owners, and captains. But the French, along with Deane, had set up a system with at least one degree of removal from the French government, allowing them an element of plausible deniability.

Access to French ports proved a boon to the Americans and their plucky privateers. Sometimes captured British vessels became American naval ships. Usually, though, merchant ship cargoes were sold and the profits divided between the privateers and the Continental Congress, which used the monies to help finance their war effort. The wait for the first successful American privateer was not a lengthy one, as a Captain Lambert Wickes (whose ship had delivered Dr. Franklin to Paris from

America) captured four smaller British ships in January 1777 and auctioned the cargoes to eager French merchants. Wickes also seized a Royal Mail packet plying waters between England and Portugal.

With such successes, Deane was soon encouraging more American captains to do the same, as well as the captains of foreign vessels, including the Spanish and French. Before the end of 1777 several privateers were trolling the waters surrounding Great Britain, concentrating on the English Channel, and new captures happened with regularity. One American privateering vessel alone managed to capture eighteen British ships.

While Franklin and Deane sometimes worked side by side, the great man from Philadelphia also pursued his own clandestine operations. As a favorite among the French court, French aristocrats, and other power players, Franklin gained support for many American revolutionary efforts. Franklin also had supporters inside Britain, especially among the Whigs in Parliament, many of whom had rubbed shoulders with him for decades. Such British contacts had to be made discreetly, often through go-betweens and mail drops, to allow a degree of separation between Franklin and the person of influence. Some of Franklin's more well-placed contacts were Lord

William Petty Fitzmaurice Shelburne, a former British secretary of state; Lord Charles Pratt Camden, former lord chancellor; and Thomas Walpole, a London banker of singular influence. By 1778, Franklin even sent an agent, Jonathan Austin, to work closely with Lord Shelburne, who twisted arms among his fellow members of Parliament in support of the Americans.

Such individuals also fed information to Franklin. One such piece of intelligence was crucial in Franklin finally convincing the French to sign a treaty of alliance with the Continental Congress. Franklin informed the French that, according to one of his men in Parliament, one British general, Lord Charles Cornwallis, had stated that the defeat of the rebels in America was a lost cause.

Franklin also operated a propaganda campaign of disinformation against the British, an effort that sometimes required his skills as a professional printer. Similar to many acts of espionage, Franklin disguised the true authorship of many of the documents he and his associates produced, creating a type of black propaganda (see "Black Propaganda," page 173). To facilitate publication of false documents, he set up a printing press operation in the cellar of the building housing the American Paris Commission. He went to great lengths to purchase paper from the Dutch, as well as print type (he also collected the same from sources in Great Britain). Multiple pamphlets and newspaper copies flew off of Franklin's Parisian press, all spinning propaganda designed to demoralize and even demonize the British. News of the American war effort was glowing, while the British were cast in a negative vein. Franklin even wrote articles for publications that were not from his press, including a regular column he penned for a French periodical published in Belgium, *Affaires de l'Angleterre et de l'Amerique*, which was little more than a propaganda front for the Americans, one funded by King Louis's government.

Franklin's false words fanned the flames of animosity between the Americans and the British. In one bit of propaganda, produced in 1777, Franklin produced a letter allegedly written by a German prince to Hessian troops stationed in America, in which he doubts the published British accounts of German casualties, and suggests they have been falsified at a low figure. He also claimed he had not been paid fully for German mercenaries he had provided to the British military. The letter was disseminated all over Europe and America, where it was published multiple times. As a result, the

British government was castigated for "lying" about its German troops, and the letter may even have caused some Hessians in America to desert.

In an attempt to cast a dim eye on British strategy in the war, Franklin produced another masterpiece of elaborate propaganda in 1782. He designed a completely false issue of a Boston newspaper, realistic in every detail, down to the advertisements. The issue included a fake article purporting scalp buying by the British governor of Canada. It said the governor was paying Indians for each lifted hair, including those of women and children. Franklin also convinced others to plant false tales of British injustices and deprivations in their publications. A Swiss journalist, Charles Dumas, published such stories in the Dutch press.

⁓ ※ ⁓

OTHER BRITISH AGENTS

As Franklin and Deane carried out their activities in support of the American cause, the British became well aware of many of their efforts. Some of this insight was delivered by Bancroft in his regular reports that he bottled and buried in the Tuileries, but the British Secret Service also utilized other agents to keep tabs on the Americans in Paris. The list includes a man of the cloth, an American named Reverend John Vardill, who was an Anglican minister. (He was also the former assistant rector of Trinity Church in New York City.) The reverend enlisted two additional agents—Jacobus Van Zandt, a merchant who moved under the code name "George Lupton," and Captain Joseph Hynson, a ship's captain from Maryland. Van Zandt claimed to have worked as a spy in New York City, using his cover as one of the Sons of Liberty to gain access and information.

Van Zandt was dispatched to Paris to become friends with Silas Deane, which he managed to accomplish. In time, Van Zandt found himself in Deane's apartment and was able to get Deane out of his presence long enough to riffle through his desk and whisk away some documents. But Van Zandt rarely ever provided his handlers with any other information beyond what they had already received from Bancroft. Deane eventually felt Van Zandt's questions to be too probing, and he cut off contact with the Loyalist spy in early 1778.

Black Propaganda

Benjamin Franklin's false publications, including pamphlets, fake newspapers, and leaked letters fall into a special category of government-sponsored misinformation called black propaganda. By definition, it refers to the disseminating of false information that appears to originate from sources on one side of a conflict when, in fact, it has been produced by the other side. By intent, it hopefully embarrasses or misrepresents the enemy.

Usually black propaganda is covert, because it shields the originator's identity. Those who produce such materials must be cautious, however, in what they print. The information must be believable; it has to fall within the realm of possibility.

Behind all black propaganda is a person or group intent on influencing another group,. and to an extent, its mission is psychological—to turn the minds of a public against one's enemy without their conscious awareness of it.

As for Captain Hynson, he proved to be the more successful of Vardill's agents. He, too, inveigled himself with Franklin and Deane, in his case, for about six months. Although he gained information from some sources other than Franklin and Deane, Hynson did pass on intelligence regarding American plans to purchase European ships. But his singular coup came in October 1777 when he stole the Paris Commission's official correspondence to the Continental Congress, papers covering the first six months of 1777. Captain Hynson managed to make friends with another American, Captain Folger, who was slated to deliver the papers to Congress. During a social occasion, Hynson accessed Folger's dispatch pouch, stole the documents, and replaced them with blank sheets of paper. Folger did not realize he had been duped until he arrived in America. The correspondence was eventually presented to King George III, and Hynson was rewarded with a payment of £200 pounds and a lifelong pension of £200 pounds annually.

One source for Captain Hynson was William Carmichael, who served both Franklin and Deane as a clerk at the Paris Commission from late 1776 to the end of 1777. He handled important papers constantly and managed to route materials to his handlers concerning American privateers and other sensitive data. It is unclear if Carmichael was in direct service to the British or simply worked for Rev. Vardill, but the results were the same. He spied covertly and passed information. It was the French intelligence service that finally picked up Carmichael's scent and informed Franklin that he should dismiss him. Franklin did so, and Carmichael was sent back to America. Ironically, Carmichael was soon elected as a Maryland representative to Congress and, by 1779, was working as a secretary for American diplomat John Jay in Madrid. Eventually, Jay felt he could not trust Carmichael and released him.

～ ※ ～

LEE AND HIS INTELLIGENCE EFFORTS

Even as Franklin and Deane collected intelligence in Paris—although they did not always work well together (see "A Lack of Teamwork," opposite)—Arthur Lee was at work in London. He was under siege by the British Secret Service who repeatedly tried to place its agents close to him. Indeed, they succeeded in planting a British army officer, Major John Thornton, as his private secretary.

In the summer of 1777, Lee was on a mission in Berlin to the court of King Frederick the Great, trying to drum up official Prussian support for the American cause. Lee took residence in a local hotel. When the British ambassador in Berlin, Hugh Elliot, was informed of Lee's arrival, he immediately went to work, lining up an embassy servant, a local German, to bribe hotel employees to keep watch on Lee and report on his comings and goings. Elliot then told the German servant to obtain the key to Lee's room and make a copy of it. On a day Lee was scheduled to be out of town, the servant went in and stole Lee's personal journal, delivered it to Elliot, and a team of secretaries was tasked with copying out the pages.

But the journal proved longer than Elliot anticipated. With Lee scheduled to return before the copying was complete, Elliot went to the hotel where he met Lee in the lobby and tried to detain him. Making some flimsy excuse that he was desperate to talk to someone in English, Elliot managed to hold up Lee for two hours!

When Lee finally reached his room, he soon discovered his journal was missing, and he informed the local police of the theft. With the copying finally completed, Elliot then returned to the hotel in disguise and gave the journal to a hotel employee who returned it to Lee, telling him the volume had been left outside his door. Lee was unconvinced. In time, a police investigation revealed that Ambassador Elliot had been spotted in the hotel, and Lee then understood what had taken place. He reported the incident to Frederick the Great, who publicly chastised the British ambassador for his illegal and clandestine activities. Back in England, George III also berated Elliot publicly, while privately paying him £1,000 for special services rendered.

In the end, the three American commissioners—Benjamin Franklin, Arthur Lee, and Silas Deane—were able to collect, over several years, a significant amount of actionable intelligence, while engaging in counterintelligence, including the dissemination of black propaganda. They worked alongside French intelligence and ultimately massaged such connections into a pair of alliances, both military and commercial. This success alone, the delivery of French support in the form of soldiers, supplies, ships, and money would prove indispensable to the American war effort and, likely, helped turn the tide of war in favor of Washington, his army, and the new nation of the United States.

A Lack of Teamwork

Through several crucial years of the American Revolutionary War, the men behind the Paris Commission managed to have a singular impact on the war effort through diplomacy as well as intelligence gathering. However, the three agents spearheading the commission—Franklin, Deane, and Lee—did not always work well as a team.

Franklin and Lee sometimes rubbed each other the wrong way. The aging Philadelphia printer considered Lee "jealous, suspicious, malignant, and quarrelsome."[143] Lee and Deane sometimes argued strongly with one another. In time, Lee accused Deane of malfeasance, which led to Deane's recall back to America, followed by a congressional hearing that left him very bitter.

Perhaps the most difficult of the three men was Lee. A man driven by an unhealthy ego, many people found him difficult to deal with, and neither Franklin nor Deane could be accused of liking him much. Perhaps, considering his role as an intelligence agent, one of his best personal traits was that he was a naturally suspicious man. He did not trust someone until he had established a friendship with him.

CHAPTER SEVEN

Forming the Culper Ring

A NEED FOR INTELLIGENCE

ven after the British ran him and his makeshift army out of New York City during the fall of 1776, General George Washington never fully gave up on the city. The lower tip of Manhattan may have become the de facto headquarters of the British army in North America, but what went on in its streets, within its barracks and coffee-houses, as well as aboard the dozens of naval vessels that lined its port facilities, was still of primary interest to Washington, along with a need to know what General Howe was planning next.

The city provided an extraordinarily secure base of operations for the British, allowing for superior communications capabilities and logistical support. The British could control the city's services as well as the comings and goings of everyone entering or leaving the island. There were also plenty of opportunities for Howe's troops to commandeer shelter, take respite in the city's many taverns and coffee shops, and satisfy their sexual whims, for the city was crowded with prostitutes ready to offer

their services to either side. The British, after all, could offer cold, hard currency. In short, much worth knowing was taking place between the East and Hudson Rivers, and Washington needed to find out as much as possible. He needed eyes and spies on the streets of New York.

❧ ✳ ❧

In and Out of New York

Despite the significant number of Tories in New York, Washington was comforted by the fact that the city had been a significant beehive of Patriot activity prior to the opening of the war. If Boston's Sons of Liberty chapter had been the most antagonistic toward British policy and the Redcoats, New York might have run a close second. Its chapter had been large and loud, at one point tearing down a leaden statue of King George III and melting it down for bullets. Some of these inhabitants lived in such neighborhoods as Flatbush, Perth Amboy, and Harlem Heights and were more than willing to provide any information that might help the Continental Army understand what was taking place in the city, including the number of Redcoats, their deployment, and other such tactical and logistic details that a commander such as Washington longed to know. As Howe and his officer staff made decisions and plotted strategies, the citizens of New York sought to uncover that information as quickly as possible, then transmit it to Washington's headquarters over in the rural outback of Pennsylvania.

Despite British efforts to control the movement of civilians in and out of New York City, it was impossible to simply cut off all outsiders. With thousands of British troops on hand, the city relied on constant and regular deliveries of food, fuel, and other necessities in order to continue living in the relative comfort Howe and his forces had come to expect. Security was complicated by farmers delivering produce and fishermen bringing in fresh catches from the sea. The city was a sieve that offered opportunities for spies to ply their trade on the streets, in the coffeehouses, and other dens frequented by the British.

❧ ✳ ❧

SPYMASTER SACKETT

To gain needed intelligence concerning Howe and his forces, Washington began taking steps in early 1777 to enlist potential agents. One of the first to make his espionage payroll was Nathaniel Sackett, who had already worked in 1776 for John Jay's secret organization, the New York Committee for Detecting and Defeating Conspiracies. With Jay's organization now defunct, Sackett met with Washington at his headquarters in Morristown, New Jersey, on February 3, 1777. Together, the two men made plans for a spy network to operate in and around New York City. When Sackett bade Washington farewell the following day, he was in the general's employ, having secured a monthly salary of $50 (equivalent to about $800 in today's money), as Washington explained, "for your care and trouble in this business,"[144] and an operating fund of $500 for any expenses he might incur. Sackett was in business once again and would report to General Washington, who anticipated "the earliest and best Intelligence of the designs of the Enemy."[145]

Sackett wasted little time getting agents into the city, usually under the cover of some merchant, farmer, or produce dealer. By March, he had several such individuals on his payroll, including a surveyor who entered the city on March 7, where he was to secure lodging, then "get a license to carry on a secret trade for poultry to enable him to convey our intelligence once or twice a week."[146] The British needed food, and a spy who entered the city under the cover of a chicken supplier (a significant black-market enterprise at the time) would face little scrutiny. But after a month in the city, the spy did not deliver a single report. Sackett's inveigled egg man, as far as the record shows, never reported back. What happened to him is unknown.

But Sackett had other spies in the offing. He soon dispatched a pair of agents ready for service. Both were natives of the New York area and one had a son who was a colonel serving the British. Washington's orders stated the mission clearly—the spy was to make contact with "Principal Torys near the enemies Lines—in order to get letters of Recommendation to some Principle Gentlemen in the enemies service."[147] Easy enough, given his son's role. Then, he was to deliver to the British eight or ten men operating undercover as deserters from the American side. Unfortunately, the record does not reveal what, if anything, Sackett's new spies accomplished.

But the operation seems to be well considered, including believable covers and multi-layered contacts, indicating "how much the American intelligence service had learned since Nathan Hale had been sent, unprepared, to a useless death."[148]

Others were also employed as spies under Sackett's guidance, including a Hessian who had lived in America for forty years. He was sent into the city to secure information, encourage fellow Hessians to desert from the British military, and otherwise "make use of the Deserters as pipes to convey Intelligence."[149] Another spy was a woman who was married to a New York Tory. Sackett sent her into the city to register complaints to British officials that some of her personal property had been confiscated (which was actually true). Finding herself inside the British encampments, the woman gathered what information she could. By late March, she left and reported directly to Sackett that the British were fabricating a significant number of flat-bottomed boats, and that these were to be used on an assault against Philadelphia. She had accomplished one of the few coups of Sackett's early efforts to establish a spy network in the city.

Sackett moved immediately on her intelligence report. By April 7, he sent a report to Washington. Within days, General Washington had sent General Thomas Mifflin to Philadelphia to establish yet another spy network. By the time General Howe and his men reached the Pennsylvania city, American spies were already in place and waiting. From the very day the British occupied Philadelphia—on September 26, 1777—spy reports were circulating throughout the city, sometimes with several reaching Washington on a single day. The mysterious woman in New York could be thanked for it all.

Meanwhile, Sackett's agents were active elsewhere, including in New Brunswick. While they worked the town, Washington sent his own agent to the city, disguised as a "Pennsylvania provision merchant." Unfortunately he was captured by the British in early June. During the previous weeks, however, the "merchant" spy had worked at convincing Hessians to desert. His cover was blown when he offered a Hessian grenadier fifty pounds to desert his ranks, then deliver intelligence to the Americans detailing the location of enemy forces, their number, the locations of their sentries and such. The Patriot agent was exposed and arrested. No record exists concerning whether he was executed or not.

Although Sackett spent months in service to Washington during 1777, before year's end, the network seems to have closed up shop. At least no record of it has survived today. Perhaps records were destroyed, maybe even purposefully to shield the identities of the agents after the war. Or perhaps Sackett's network was absorbed into other spy rings.

⁓ ※ ⁓

HUNTER AND THE "CHARACTERS"

Others also operated spy rings in New York City in 1777, including several Continental Army and militia officers in the New York and Connecticut area. Some contacts operated as double agents, functioning as trusted couriers for the British and delivering messages from one Redcoat outpost to another. Washington not only gained inside information from such dual agents, but he also utilized them to spread disinformation among the British ranks.

Captain Elijah Hunter of the 2nd New York Militia was one of the best of these double agents. Hunter had allegedly "retired" from military service in December 1776, but had instead likely become a field agent at that time. He may have spied for John Jay during 1778. By early 1779, he had gained the confidence of General Clinton as well as New York governor William Tryon, a staunch Tory. Tryon "convinced" Hunter to operate as a merchant who traded between Washington's Pennsylvania headquarters and Philadelphia; he was "to act apparently zealous for America—not to shake the Confidence of his Countrymen."[150] In the meantime, Hunter was really serving Washington. At first, the general did not trust Hunter, even though he had a letter from John Jay. The problem was that, by nature, double agents are difficult to trust. He wrote that it is "necessary to be very circumspect with double spies." Still, Washington believed Hunter to be "a sensible man capable of rendering important services, if he is sincerely disposed to do it."[151] A spymaster such as Washington certainly wanted to be on the side duping the enemy rather than on the receiving end of treachery.

Despite Washington's early doubts, he did not have to wait long before Hunter's spying yielded fruit. By September, he had managed to snatch up a letter written by one of Britain's best cavalry officers operating in America, Colonel Banastre Tarleton. He delivered the missive to Washington, the contents were copied, and the letter returned with the cavalry officer none the wiser. Such intelligence coups produced information needed by the Continental Army regarding troop movements and plans for future deployments. Hunter did not consistently act alone in the field, instead relying on a gang of additional agents, whom Washington referred to as "the Characters."[152]

As a courier for the British, he delivered communiqués between General Henry Clinton in New York and military officials in Canada. Sometimes disinformation was his best field tactic. During the summer of 1779, General Washington used Hunter to just such a purpose. The British had managed to capture several key Continental outposts along the Hudson River and were moving dangerously close to West Point, the key to an American presence on the river. Washington worked up a plan to throw off General Clinton's advancement. Hunter engaged in a bit of "feed material," a modern term for disinformation in which true and false information are blended into one report, in such a way that the true information does not provide real aid or new information. In his report Hunter informed the British of the locations of four American supply points in the Hudson Valley—which did exist—but also that Washington had the capacity to launch five thousand men in boats up the Hudson with only two hours' notice—which was false. The point was ultimately to discourage General Henry Clinton from ordering his men to move against those American points. In the end, the ploy worked.

While Hunter was a successful spy for Washington, he was never able to produce a significant amount of actionable intelligence. He remained in the field for more than two years and General Clinton seems never to have been the wiser. Hunter's business as a double agent was delicate. Any suspicion his actions might have raised could have exposed him immediately. On one occasion, though, Hunter took a rather brazen step, asking Clinton to provide him with a military escort for an excursion into Westchester County. While there, Hunter did little but report directly to Washington at his headquarters. When the war ended, Washington recognized Hunter's spying with a certificate honoring his service to his young country.

～ ※ ～

NEW YORK SPIES

If Hunter, Nathaniel Sackett's spies, and other early agents were only marginally effective, two individuals were able to operate in New York City with more success—Lieutenant Lewis J. Costigin, a lifelong resident and local merchant, and John Mersereau, who had already done some spying for Washington the previous year, prior to the British occupation of the city.

Costigin's actions proved to be rather unorthodox, even brazen. A lieutenant in the Continental Army, he had been recruited by Washington in January 1777 to operate as a spy in New Brunswick. The Battle of Trenton had taken place just weeks earlier and New Jersey was still occupied by a significant number of British and Hessian troops. New Brunswick was familiar to Costigin, where people had known him as a merchant prior to the war.

Costigin chose a unique method to get inside British-occupied New York City. He managed to get himself captured, while still in uniform, by the British, after which he was processed as a prisoner of war in the city. Once he was "paroled," with the expectation that he would not fight again for the Americans, he was free to roam the city, until a possible prisoner exchange could be made. By the fall of 1778, he was swapped for a British officer.

But Costigin did not leave New York, choosing instead to remain in the city, still in his uniform. This gave him continued access to information from citizens, British officers, and even government officials with whom he had made "friends" during the twenty months of his captivity. (In the preceding months, while paroled, Costigin had not been legally free to collect information and deliver it to the Americans.)

Why the British allowed Costigin to remain in New York is a mystery. Likely he just fell through the cracks of British bureaucracy. Costigin had become such a fixture that, following his official prisoner exchange, no one thought it odd or out of place for him still to be seen in the city's coffeehouses and taverns or on the streets themselves.

Through the remainder of 1778, Costigin ran with no restrictions as an agent for the Americans. He filed regular reports, usually signing them "Z." A few reports have survived in Washington's official papers and include those dated November 16 and December 7, 16, and 19, 1778. They contain the usual facts vital to American intelligence—the movements and deployments of British forces throughout the New York area, shipments of military supplies entering the city, and food rations and supply information, to name a few. How, exactly, Costigin was able to deliver his reports to Washington is unknown, but it is known that they were routed through two subordinate officers, Colonel Matthias Ogden and General Lord Stirling. Costigan would remain an agent, in his words, "as long as he thought it safe."[153] By January 1779, he left the spy service.

As for John Mersereau, spying seems to have run in the family. Back in 1776, Captain John Mersereau (his uncle) had spied for Washington in New York, with Lieutenant Colonel Thomas Knowlton as his handler. Now, John Mersereau (the younger) was in the spy business, referring to himself as John LaGrange Mersereau, ostensibly to avoid confusion with his uncle. The younger John was soon installed in New Brunswick as an agent, but Washington's expectations were for Mersereau to find his way across the river to Staten Island, where his father, Joshua Mersereau, had worked as a businessman. From Staten Island, John was to land in Manhattan. Over a period of eighteen months, Mersereau proved himself a successful agent. Eventually, the Mersereaus ran a family-based spy ring that included the father and son, as well as a brother to John the younger.

From Staten Island, John Mersereau gathered information routed through a courier named John Parker, one of John's former apprentices in shipbuilding. After a handful of deliveries behind American lines, Parker was captured in Amboy and clapped away in a British prison. Mersereau visited his friend during his confinement, bringing him clothing and food, but Parker subsequently died, as John noted: "It was of no use, for he should not live long."[154]

Having lost his courier, Mersereau began delivering his reports himself. According to his memoirs, he regularly rowed across the Hudson on a raft, his papers sealed away in a bottle, which he towed behind him on a string. This way, if stopped by a British patrol or other interested party, he could cut the cord and the incriminating bottle would simply sink to the river bottom. In the river, he sometimes landed on Shooter's Island, where he made dead drops, leaving reports beneath a large rock. In exchange, he could also pick up new orders from his handler. Once he dropped his reports on the island, he signaled an accomplice over in New Jersey by a lantern system.

On one occasion, Mersereau made a poor choice and was almost caught for his indiscretion. Receiving word from a friend that his father was visiting in the town of Elizabeth, New Jersey, John decided to pay him a call and stole a small boat he found in the weeds along the Staten Island river bank. After his visit, he hid out in a New Jersey barn, then headed back to Staten Island. In the meantime, the skiff he had used had been reported stolen, and the British had posted a sentry near the location of the missing boat. As Mersereau made landfall, the guard called out to him, but John did not stay around to explain himself. The sentry then fired a shot. John wrote later: "I fled on my hands & feet to a ditch, along which I could run without being much exposed to his fire."[155] Musket fire echoed across the water and a ball struck a fence post near Mersereau's head, causing him to panic. He leaped to his feet and sprinted for home, with several pursuers on his heels. At last, he found his lodgings in the dark, and ran to his room, hoping that those following him had not seen him at the house. But he soon heard angry voices, including that of a British officer who lodged in the same household as Mersereau. The Redcoat major was roaring drunk, and he had not heard Mersereau enter. Ironically, he became the American spy's salvation. In a tirade, the officer swore profusely, assuring the strangers at the door "there were no rebels in the house where he lodged."[156] Mersereau had escaped, thanks to a combination of alcohol, British assuredness, duplicity, and sheer luck.

Following several more close calls and misadventures, John Mersereau began to fear detection, even as British authorities were starting to smell a traitor in their midst. He made his escape behind American lines and was even available to help in monitoring captured British troops from the Battle of Saratoga. Although he was unable to don once again the uniform of the Continental Army, due to a condition in his right arm that kept him from being able to shoulder a musket, Mersereau had done his duty as a successful intelligence agent.

Even as John Mersereau the younger bowed out of the spy game, other members of his family stepped up, including a sixteen-year-old brother who continued his older sibling's exploits, including rowing at night across the Hudson River, eluding British patrols, and delivering materials to General Washington. He had help from his father's uncle, Paul Mersereau, who lived on Staten Island and managed to operate under the noses of the British without drawing any undue attention to himself.

College Classmates, Future Spies

Both Nathan Hale and Benjamin Tallmadge had more in common than their service to General Washington as spies during the Revolutionary War. Each had known the other before the war and had, in fact, been classmates at Yale. Tallmadge was a minister's son who came to college with much learning already under his belt, which ironically, caused him to get into trouble with school officials. The explanation is found in his own words: "being so well versed in the Latin and Greek languages, I had not much occasion to study during the first two years of my collegiate life."[157] Perhaps another contributing factor in his behavior was his age. When Tallmadge entered Yale, he was only fifteen years old.

Tallmadge's troublemaking sometimes happened alongside Nathan Hale and Hale's older brother, Enoch, who also attended Yale. On one occasion, the three college comrades were disciplined for breaking windows in a tavern after they had consumed too much alcohol. They paid fines of a shilling and five pence, an amount that was a bit steep for such college students. Tallmadge even had to pay an additional seven pence for also having destroyed additional property on the Yale campus that same evening.

By the time Tallmadge graduated, all appears to have been forgiven regarding his behavior at Yale. The college's president even invited him to speak at the graduation ceremony.

Enter Benjamin Tallmadge

In the end, General Washington maintained several spies in New York, many operating out of Staten Island. In a communication to Congress on July 5, 1777, he explained: "I keep people constantly on Staten Island, who give me daily information of the operations of the enemy."[158] By late July, Washington issued orders to Colonel Elias Dayton, his chief espionage officer in New Jersey, to dispatch twenty spies to Staten Island for the purpose of collecting information such as troop strength and their locations.

These various agents and subagents who spied on behalf of General Washington in and around New York City still were producing only limited intelligence. It was a crazy quilt of a system that was, indeed, no real system at all. What Washington really needed was a single organization

of spies, one that could produce coordinated efforts and consistent action-able intelligence. To that end, he began putting together the pieces and personalities of just such a system by the summer of 1778. It would be known as the Culper Ring, and its members, a small cadre of half a dozen individuals with overlapping relationships, would come to symbolize the best of American spying during the Revolutionary War.

Fortunately, when Washington set out to organize an elaborate, efficient spy ring, he already had men around him who could pull the various parts of such a system together. First, he gave the assignment to Brigadier General Charles Scott. A veteran of the French and Indian War, Scott was a man of much military experience, a capable commander whom Washington knew well. But Scott had some drawbacks. He lacked imagination and was a man many found difficult, even abrasive. And, if Washington's spy ring was going to center its activities in and around New York City, Scott was at a disadvantage. He had troublingly little firsthand knowledge of the back roads and waterways of Manhattan, Connecticut, or Long Island—the very places he would have to know as well as the back of his hand. As Scott would suddenly leave active duty in November, his appointment proved a moot point in the end.

A replacement was soon appointed. Captain Benjamin Tallmadge was an officer in the Second Light Dragoons, a unit assigned along the coast of Connecticut on Long Island Sound. His role as cavalry officer would provide him with an adequate cover. Tallmadge had been present at Scott and Washington's first meeting on August 25, in which they discussed the new spy ring, so he had been in on the planning from day one. The young captain (who would one day achieve the rank of major) seemed up to the task. He was intelligent, a dashing individual and a stalwart supporter of the Patriot cause, having enlisted in the summer of 1776, in time to see action in the Battle of Brooklyn Heights just weeks later. He emerged from the fight shaken and reflective, writing: "This was the first time in my life that I had witnessed the awful scene of a battle, when man was engaged to destroy his fellow-man. I well remember my sensations on the occasion, for they were solemn beyond description, and very hardly could I bring my mind to be willing to attempt the life of a fellow-creature."[159] The fighting in the streets of New York City that fall left him damaged in another way as well. Tallmadge's brother, William, was a sergeant in Washington's army, and he was captured by the British during the fighting in the city, and subsequently died, at the age of twenty-four, onboard a filthy prison ship. The family loss filled Tallmadge with a strong desire for revenge.

A fellow Continental described him with glowing sentiment: "[Tallmadge] was a large, strong, and powerful man and rode a large bay horse which he took from the British. He was a brave officer, and there was no flinch in him. He was a man of few words, but decided and energetic, and what he said was to the purpose."[160] Such a description fits a potential spymaster—someone who is bold, who keeps his own counsel, is determined, dogged, and who stays focused and on point. In a sense, Tallmadge had an emotional stake in the new spy organization. Nathan

Hale, whom the British had hanged, had been a close friend of his. (They had both taught school in Connecticut before the war.) Yet, despite possessing attributes that might have qualified him as a handler of spies, as a spymaster, he would have to learn on the fly.

A Dashing Dragoon

Before his recruitment into spy service for Washington, and even afterward, Benjamin Tallmadge served as a cavalry officer, a captain of the Second Dragoons. Congress had authorized four such units and those who served in their ranks were typically recognized for their dash and the cut of their uniforms. Tallmadge and his men wore "dark blue coats, lighter breeches, and knee-high black boots with silver spurs," their heads covered with metal helmets "stylishly decorated with a white horsehair plume sprouting from their crested peaks."[161] As an officer, Tallmadge also wore a deep red sash around his waist.

These were men armed to the teeth, as each carried a gleaming cavalry saber, perhaps a couple of flintlock pistols, and a short musket. Such well-accoutered men on horseback could not help but draw attention to themselves. To make certain of it, Tallmadge himself insisted that his unit ride astride matching mounts, "composed entirely of dapple gray horses . . . with black straps and black bear-skin holster-covers."[162] Reflecting years later in his memoir, Tallmadge reminisced: "I have no hesitation in acknowledging that I was very proud of this command."[163]

RECRUITING THE SECRET SIX

Tallmadge was technically reentering the espionage arena that summer of 1778. During the spring of 1777, he had worked for Nathaniel Sackett on Long Island. With his cover as a cavalry officer (he was then a captain), Tallmadge made regular visits across Long Island Sound to see various men about buying horses. Meanwhile, he engaged in various espionage missions. One of his early assignments was to provide security for Major John Clark, whom Washington dispatched to Long Island (then occupied by the British) to collect intelligence on the Redcoats stationed there. On

February 25, Clark hired a local whaleboatman named Caleb Brewster to row across the sound and deliver a secret message to Tallmadge. The following year, as Tallmadge formed his spy ring for Washington, he recruited Brewster as one of the Culper Ring.

The organizational structure of the Culper Ring—the core members of the network would be known as the "Secret Six"—was kept simple, which was one of Washington's cardinal rules regarding such operations. (As for the name, it was Washington's pick, referring to Culpeper, Virginia, the county bordering Stafford County on the west, where Washington had grown up and had done some survey work.) Any such organization that involved too many layers and too many individuals ran a greater risk of exposure. Tallmadge became the ring's managing case officer, the individual who would make direct contact with the agents themselves. Rarely did Washington meet with the ring members directly, allowing a degree of separation and a plausible deniability for any man accused of spying for Washington. Tallmadge would report directly to Washington, who served as the ring's senior intelligence officer, a spymaster. And master he was, for Washington remained directly involved in the operation. Reports were directed through Tallmadge as a third party, but were for the general's eyes only.

Compartmentation was Washington's watchword for his new spy organization. To ensure success, the general believed that, as much as possible, the various agents in Tallmadge's spy ring should not know one another's real names. That way, if an agent were captured and interrogated, he or she could not possibly name names. In an early communication to Tallmadge, he made a specific point about this single most important factor. That message, dated November 20, 1778, read: "You will be pleased to observe the strictest silence with respect to C——, as you are to be the only person intrusted with the knowledge or conveyance of his letter."[164] The mysterious "C——" was an allusion to the first of a handful of spies Tallmadge recruited into his ring, a trusted friend named Abraham Woodhull. The "C" was in reference to his cover name, Samuel Culper.

Tallmadge tagged Woodhull because he was from Tallmadge's hometown, Setauket, on Long Island. When they were younger, they had been neighbors. Other than this shared history, Tallmadge and Woodhull were

Right:
Letter from Benjamin Tallmadge to George Washington on June 27, 1779: "The inclosed contains matter for our knowledge only."

62:13

New Windsor June 27th 1779.

Sir,

I observe what you say respecting your position at Bedford — and the fatigue of the horse — with regard to the first, when Bedford was pointed out, it was descriptive only of a central place between the two Rivers, and as near the enemy as you could with military prudence take post for the purpose of covering the inhabitants, & preventing the ravages of small parties. — The judgment of the Officer commanding, is, under the idea just expressed, to direct the particular spot & choice of ground which ought to be varied continually, while you are near enough the enemy to give assistance to the people — With respect to the second matter I have only to add that I do not wish to have the horse unnecessarily exposed, or fatigued, but if in the discharge of accustomed duties they should get worn down, there is no help for it. — Col. Moylans Regiment is on its march to join you, which will render the duty easier and Yr Troops there more respectable. —

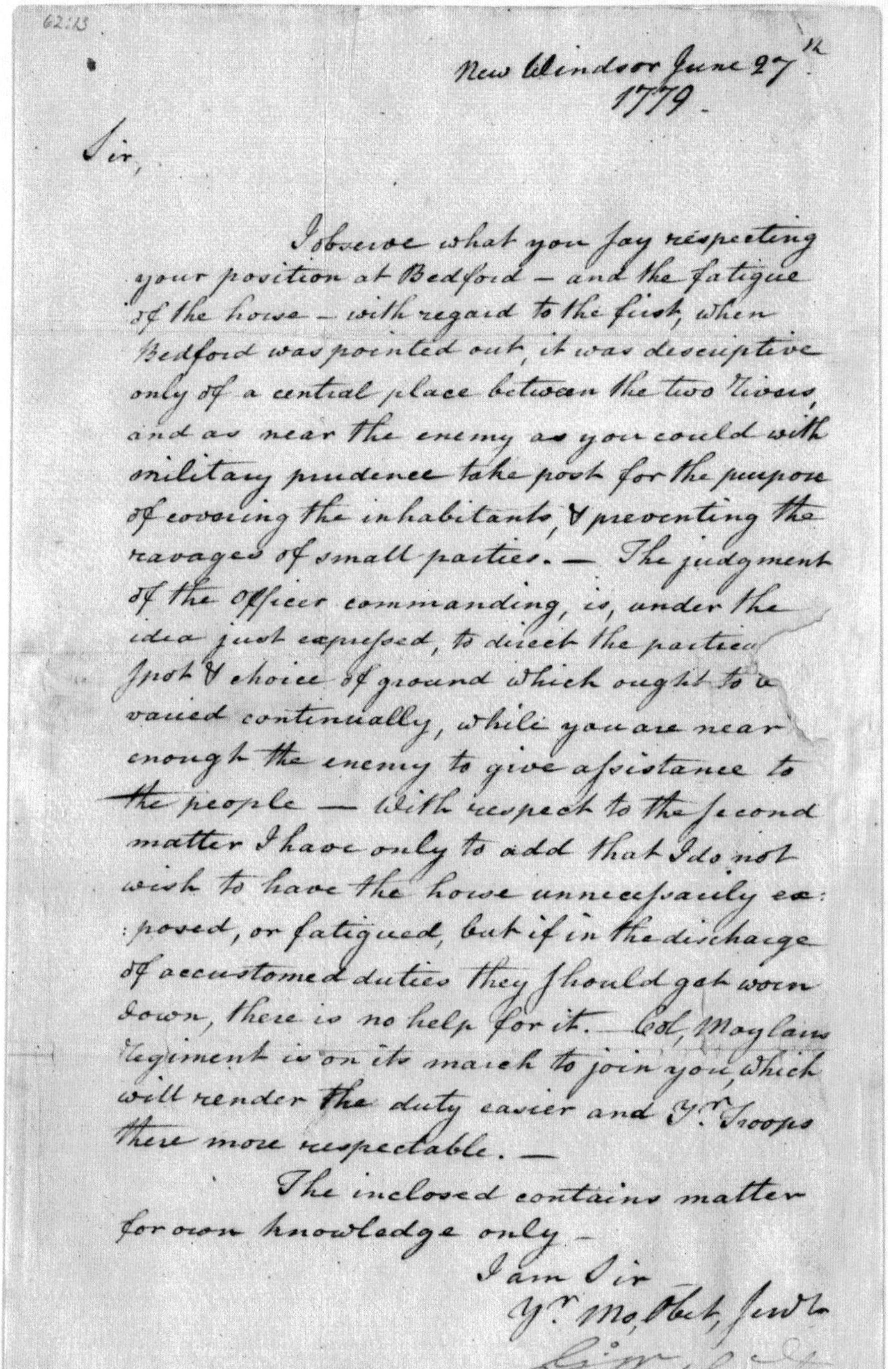

The inclosed contains matter for own knowledge only —

I am Sir

Yr Mo. Obet, Servt

G Washington

two inherently different men. Abraham, by accounts, was taciturn where Tallmadge was optimistic, even jolly. He was thirty years old, a bachelor who enjoyed his personal freedom. He had remained out of military service, because he hated the idea of taking orders from anyone. Once the war opened, Woodhull continued his work as a farmer-merchant, selling his vegetables and hogs to the British Army on the island. When Tallmadge made the decision to contact his old acquaintance, he found him under lock and key, as he had been thrown in a local jail for doing business with the Redcoats. He had had to negotiate with Connecticut officials for Woodhull's release.

～ ※ ～

A Man at the Oars

Some of the Secret Six's most dangerous activities took place on the water. Messages and other intelligence had to pass from Long Island to Connecticut or New York without the detection of any agent's boat. This required the recruiting of another of the Culper Ring, a brash individual who had prior espionage experience. Caleb Brewster was a man of the sea. Today, he likely would have made a good longshoreman. Or perhaps a Navy SEAL. He ran a smuggling ring between Long Island and Connecticut and had repeatedly evaded capture by the British before Abraham Woodhull approached him about spying for Washington. Brewster was a loud, excitable man, who was known by locals to love the thrill of a boat chase from time to time, with British officials rowing after, but never overtaking him.

Brewster and Woodhull had crossed paths a few years prior to 1779. In June 1775, before the Battle of Bunker Hill, both men had signed the same document, a circular letter signaling their intent to fight for the American cause against King George III. Remembering Brewster as a man of high spirits, anti-British resolve, and special skills, Woodhull approached him in November 1778. By that point Brewster was already providing intelligence to Washington concerning British ship movements within the waters of Long Island Sound. His new assignment made him one of the Secret Six.

Brewster became the master of his own small group of watermen in service to the ring. While the British already knew about Brewster and his overt smuggling activities, they never realized he was transporting intelligence for Washington. No one knew the sound like Brewster. He knew how to sail its waters in all weather conditions and was familiar with its currents. He had a knack for evading British and Tory naval vessels and boat crews, as well as self-appointed privateers and profiteers, such as himself, between its shores. In effect, Brewster served as Charon, a ferryman for American intelligence.

Woodhull managed to snag another recruit into the ring by convincing his friend, Austin Roe, to work as a spy. (Roe and Brewster were neighbors in Setauket.) Like Brewster, he was a high-spirited Patriot, even as everyone knew him as a solid businessman—a married, comfortably middle-class tavern keeper. As such, he could keep visitors overnight without raising suspicion, and some of those taking rooms could easily be undercover contacts.

Roe was hesitant to join the ring at first. He was dependent on his tavern-inn for his living, and he could not afford to jeopardize his business by being caught as a spy. But he soon signed on. Now three fellow acquaintances from Long Island—Woodhull, Brewster, and Roe—would soon join ranks with a fourth agent, Tallmadge's man in Manhattan, Robert Townsend.

That several of the Culper Ring's members were businessmen was extremely consequential to the spy organization's success. Being engaged in trade and interacting with customers, some of whom were British officers, provided them both opportunity and cover. Roe ran a tavern and sometimes needed to cross over into New York City to purchase supplies and other items. Any British sentry or patrol stopping him on the roads and asking for identification and the nature of his business would get easy answers. Roe's business *was* business. And one of his suppliers was Townsend. Woodhull sold his agricultural produce in the city. Brewster plied the waters of the sound for profit, carrying cargo and passengers. As these men moved from place to place, they had legitimate reasons. Spying just had to be the reason they kept secret to themselves.

Between November 1778 and January 1779, the first three members of the Culper Ring—ultimately the spy network known as the Secret

Six—was in place and active in the field. Following their recruitment, with Tallmadge as the spy master, months passed before Tallmadge appointed another member of the Ring. Washington was patient with him on this score, for he knew that the process needed to be careful, systematic, and well considered. One wrong decision could jeopardize the entire operation. This fourth agent was finally chosen in June 1779. In fact, Woodhull himself helped select the man who would help shoulder the burden of spying on the British and collecting intelligence.

This additional agent, Robert Townsend, was well chosen. He hailed from Long Island's Oyster Bay and had become a member of the local Sons of Liberty chapter by the early 1770s. At the time of his recruitment, he was a partner in a merchant house in New York City that sold dry goods and food. Oakman & Townsend sold to the locals as well as the British. His business was located near the East River, close to Peck Slip, one of several docks in that area of Manhattan. Townsend was also a partner in a second New York City business, a coffee shop he owned with James Rivington, a New York Tory who published a Loyalist newspaper, the *Royal Gazette*. In short, he was a man with solid business roots in the city, which lessened the necessity of him having to explain any comings and goings across the city or over to Long Island, where he had family. As for the coffeehouse, it represented a funnel for information about the British. Among some of Rivington's best customers were British officers, many of whom were perfectly comfortable to talk openly about the very things Townsend might be interested in finding out. One of those British officers was a young major named John André, who served as the chief British intelligence officer in New York. One day, he would assist in the defection of one of America's most famous traitors, Benedict Arnold.

Thus, while Woodhull was based out of Setauket on Long Island, Townsend was a merchant active on the British-occupied streets of New York City. Technically, part of his cover was his religion. He was a Quaker, a member of the Society of Friends, a Christian sect that eschewed war. As such, the British believed those of such a religious bent would not participate in the revolution and certainly not a war against King George. Some Quakers made exceptions of themselves, and Townsend was one of them. To further redirect any possible British suspicion of his intelligence gathering in New York, Townsend joined a Tory militia unit in 1780 and even penned Loyalist essays for Rivington's *Royal Gazette*. When Townsend was recruited, he was given the code name "Culper Jr." and Woodhull became "Culper Sr." As for Tallmadge, he, too, had a code name—"John Bolton."

⤳ ※ ⤆

THE MYSTERIOUS AGENT 355

With Tallmadge as handler, the Culper Ring had grown to four agents, including three who were already friends before their recruitment. Townsend was well known to Tallmadge, so he was someone the major could trust. Now they recruited a fifth member, and she was the most mysterious of them all.

The female agent came onboard not long after Townsend's recruitment. In fact, Townsend may have been the first to mention her to Woodhull. It's possible she was a young Long Island socialite, whom Woodhull describes for the first time in a letter dated August 15, 1779. Woodhull refers to her vaguely: "I do not think [the vigilance] will continue long so I intend to visit New York . . . and think by the assistance of a 355 of my acquaintance, shall be able to outwit them all."[165] She is barely mentioned in Townsend and Woodhull's documents, but she would prove a valuable addition to the ring. Her name is not provided, as secrecy and code names were standard operating procedure for the Culper Ring. She was dubbed "Agent 355"; the number "355" being code for "lady."

Yet for all this secrecy, some historians are fairly certain of Agent 355's identity. She is thought to have been Anna Strong, of Setauket, New York. She and Abraham Woodhull were neighbors, and her husband was Selah Strong, a solid Patriot who had served in the provincial Congress prior to the war. He had been subsequently arrested and at the time of Anna's recruitment was being held on a British prison ship. In a sense, Anna and Abraham were related. Her husband's mother was Hannah Woodhull, the oldest sister to Abraham Woodhull's cousin, General Nathaniel Woodhull. (After the war, Selah Strong's sister, Susannah, would marry Benjamin Tallmadge's father.)

Not all historians are in agreement about the identity of Agent 355. Accounts indicate she may have spent time in Manhattan where she could have interacted socially with British officers and New York Loyalists. If that were the case, it is thought doubtful that Strong was Agent 355. As one historian writes: "It seems quite unlikely that the fortyish housewife, mother, and spouse of a well-known Patriot rabble-rouser would have ventured from Long Island to Manhattan to attend parties where she would have rubbed elbows with Loyalist elite and gained the trust of high-ranking British officers."[166] A suggestion has been made that Agent 355 may have actually resided in Manhattan, was perhaps the daughter or spouse of a Loyalist, and may even have been an acquaintance of Major John André, the British intelligence chief. But, whoever she was, Agent 355, then, as now, remains a mystery.

༄ ❈ ༄

The Last Recruit to the Secret Six

Since Townsend operated a coffeehouse in which British officers commonly gathered, he would have to appear above question or suspect. He also needed to be able to move about the streets of New York, observe the specific deployments and numbers of the British Redcoats, and even write down such details without drawing attention to himself. He soon hit on a means to accomplish both: James Rivington.

Rivington was a silent partner in Townsend's coffee business and operated a print shop just down the street. He had arrived in America during the latter days of the French and Indian War to seek a new livelihood after a failed investment in a horse racing business. First he tried operating a print shop in Philadelphia, but soon packed up and moved to New York. By 1773, he was the editor of the *Royal Gazette*, which published under the banner line "Open and Uninfluenced." At first his paper was meant to be, as they say, fair and balanced. But as war between America and Great Britain inched ever closer, his true colors came out. He was the king's man. Editorials took on a decidedly Tory bent, which led to his being targeted by the Sons of Liberty. Not only did they mock him in their publications, but they even attacked his place of business. In May, a mob raided his print shop. On November 23, 1775, they again hit his print shop, making a wreck of the place, destroying his printing presses, and even burning his house to the ground. The mob of two hundred angry Sons of Liberty took all Rivington's lead type and later melted the letters into bullets. A frightened Rivington soon left New York for England and did not return until he perceived the coast was clear in 1777. Once again, he opened a print shop, as well as an adjacent sister enterprise—a coffeehouse.

Once recruited into the Culper Ring, Townsend walked down to the print shop and offered his services to Rivington. Townsend was a natural-born writer, so he was soon penning local human-interest articles. It was a brilliant cover. As a "journalist," everyone who knew Townsend suddenly expected to see him out and about on the streets, pencil in hand, taking notes, talking to anyone of interest, but all the while he was committing facts and figures to paper concerning the British military presence on the southern tip of Manhattan. In time, Townsend would even recruit Rivington into the ranks of the Secret Six.

Given the clandestine nature of one spy recruiting another spy, the details of Townsend's enlistment of his business partner, Rivington, are largely unknown. Rivington's name appears as the last one added to the Culper Ring's code system. In order, the code numbers of the Ring's members were Tallmadge (721), Woodhull (722), Townsend (723), Roe (724), Brewster (725), and Rivington (726). The oddity in the system will be the female recruit, who is never named, but referred to by the code number for "lady," (355).

Given Rivington's seeming dyed-in-the-wool Toryism, Townsend's turning Rivington into a Patriot spy is testament to his abilities. If Townsend had midjudged his Partner, he would have exposed himself as a Patriot spy. Certainly, once Rivington did agree to serve in the Culper Ring, he had an ironclad cover as a known and vociferous Loyalist.

⌒ ※ ⌒

A Spy, a Woman, and a Chase Scene

Even before General Washington recruited Major Benjamin Tallmadge as the Culper Ring's handler, Tallmadge had already been involved in a bit of spy action of his own. In the spring of 1777, following an April attack on his cavalry unit, he was handed a unique assignment. Writing in his memoirs, he described how "a country girl had gone into Philadelphia; with eggs, instructed to obtain some information respecting the enemy."[167] Tallmadge was assigned to reconnoiter with the woman at a local inn, the Rising Sun Tavern, where she would pass her information to him.

Unfortunately, this meeting placed Captain Tallmadge at the wrong place at the wrong time. The British lines were within sight of the tavern and several Redcoats spotted Tallmadge entering. The alarm was raised and, as British soldiers ran toward the tavern to capture Tallmadge and the young woman, the American officer swung into action—literally.

Hurriedly, Tallmadge emerged from the tavern, pursuers on his heels. He leapt on his horse, then, in a single motion, and swung the young lady up behind him on his saddle. Spurring his mount, Tallmadge and his fellow spy took off with the British following in hot pursuit. The chase went on for three miles. Entering Germantown, the woman jumped off the horse and was soon gone. Tallmadge managed to elude his pursuers.

The adrenaline-charged escape on horseback, fed by whip and spur, left its mark on Tallmadge. The experience thrilled him, as he later wrote: "During the whole ride although there was considerable firing of pistols, and not a little wheeling and charging, she remained unmoved, and never once complained for fear after she mounted my horse. I was delighted with this transaction, and received many compliments from those who became acquainted with it."[168]

Tallmadge had gotten his first taste of the excitement that sometimes came with Revolutionary-era espionage.

AGENTS IN THE FIELD

The summer of 1779 saw Woodhull and Townsend in action. Usually Woodhull was his contact in the field; the Setauket farmer would come to his coffeehouse to receive reports. Townsend's shop ledger mentions Woodhull visiting on July 18, and August 15 and 31. (Undoubtedly, they met more often. Such a ledger would need to indicate some such visits, but not too many to make Woodhull's stops suspicious.) In a July 15th report to Washington, Townsend states: "I saw S. C. Senr. [Samuel Culper, aka Woodhull] a few days ago, and informed him of the arrival of 10 sail of vessels from the West Indies, with Rum, &c. and a small fleet from Halifax, but no Troops."[169] Mindful of gathering intelligence without raising British suspicions, Townsend was a man of detail and delicate interaction, as mirrored in one of his reports dated August 6, 1779, regarding troop numbers: "You may think that I have not taken sufficient pains to obtain it. I assure you that I have, and find it more difficult than I expected. It is some measure owing to my not having got into a regular line of getting intelligence. To depend upon common reports would not do. I saw and conversed with two officers of different corps from Kingsbridge from neither of whom I could obtain an account of the situation of the army there. I was afraid of being too particular."[170]

During the months preceding the selection of Townsend as an agent, Woodhull had been busily engaging in his early spying. Traveling on agricultural business from Long Island to New York City, Woodhull had sent reports with significant details regarding the British. On November 23, 1778, he sent one such report through Tallmadge to Washington concerning British defensive positions on Long Island. But the real coup was his discovery that the British had managed to decode the French cipher system. By 1778, the French government had joined in support of the American revolution. They began sending men, materiel, money, and something extremely valuable to the American cause—naval vessels. Already, the French admiral Charles Hector, comte d'Estaing, had been sent to America with ships. Woodhull discovered that the British had intercepted and deciphered some messages he sent back to Paris. By late February 1779, Woodhull sent another long report to Washington with more intelligence regarding British

An Incentive to Spy

While Abraham Woodhull had several motivations for becoming a spy and member of the Culper Ring, one was personal, about his family, or rather, one member of his family—General Nathaniel Woodhull. Abraham sought to avenge his cousin's tragic death.

The general was a veteran of the French and Indian War who had joined the Patriot cause as the animosity between the Americans and the British flared up during the 1760s and 1770s. He became the president of the Patriot Provincial Convention, but was at heart a bit of a moderate. When Congress disseminated copies of the Declaration of Independence for state conventions to sign during the summer of 1776, Woodhull had thought the move to cut the political ties with Great Britain to be too radical. But he was still a spirited supporter of the American cause.

Just two months following the signing of the Declaration of Independence, General Woodhull was stationed on Long Island. The British were coming. In an attempt to keep valuable stores of grain from falling into the hands of the Redcoat army, Woodhull, serving with the Suffolk militia, was assigned to destroy these supplies. For days, he and his men zipped back and forth along the western reaches of Long Island. On August 28, he had reached Jamaica, Long Island (now part of Queens), and chose to stay overnight at a local tavern-inn. While at the inn, the British 17th Light Dragoons and the 71st Foot surrounded the establishment. Woodhull tried to break out and was shot in the head and arm, then taken prisoner. Other accounts written later describe him being attacked after he refused to surrender his weapons, "wounded on the head with a cutlass, and had a bayonet thrust through his arm." The vicious attack may have been preceded by a British major ordering Woodhull to state: "God save the King," with the general responding: "God save us all."[171] The severely wounded Woodhull was carried to the Church of New Utrecht, where he failed to receive medical attention or even food. A doctor and fellow prisoner, Silas Holmes, observed him and "the wounded prisoners . . . [who] were wallowing in their own filth, and breathed an infected and putrid air."[172] He died a few weeks later on September 20.

Abraham became aware of the maltreatment his cousin had suffered through various Patriot publications. So, when the offer to join the Culper Ring came, "Woodhull single-mindedly devoted himself to destroying the British, their allies, and all that they stood for by spying the daylights out of them."[173]

troop positions in New York City, as well as on Long Island, plus information on British naval operations.

During his days as a spy for Washington, Woodhull was often concerned about his safety and anonymity. He appears to have been a bit on the nervous side by nature, and being a spy did not help alleviate his fears—and even paranoia. In early June 1779, he had nearly been captured by the Queen's Rangers. A Loyalist prisoner of war who had been released recently from a Connecticut prison had pointed out Woodhull. Rangers barged into his home, only to find Woodhull's aged father, whom they roughed up.

Both Woodhull and Townsend chose to perform duties as espionage agents for several reasons. It must be understood by the modern reader that many people in their day thought spying to be a sordid business. After all, those who worked as spies performed duties that included subterfuge, lying, and a variety of other forms of trickery. These individuals were thought to be untrustworthy, for the easier such activities came to an agent, the more second nature they were to him. But both men believed in the causes symbolized by the American Revolution. They took money for their services—sort of. Townsend, ever the businessman, wanted to be reimbursed for his expenses. So did Woodhull, although he was much more patient when monies were not immediately forthcoming from Washington or Congress.

With the approach of the autumn of 1779, with Tallmadge as their handler, all the members of the Culper Ring, those comprising the Secret Six—Abraham Woodhull, Caleb Brewster, Austin Roe, Robert Townsend, Agent 355 and James Rivington—were recruited and in place. Woodhull had already been collecting intelligence for several months prior to Agent 355's recruitment. Now, these intrepid Patriots, both military and civilian, were ready to work together as agents of General Washington. Over the next several years, and even until the end of the Revolutionary War, the Culper Ring would see success and failure, close calls and clandestine contacts. Working in the shadows, writing in code, and remaining off the British radar, these six agents spying across the sound would accomplish more than anyone could possibly have imagined.

∽ ※ ∾

A Man Named Hercules

Though the interlocking connections among the agents comprising the Secret Six stretched from Manhattan to Connecticut to Long Island, they did not operate alone in the greater New York City region. Other agents—perhaps "subagents" is a suitable term—worked on the fringes of the organization, sometimes plying their spy trade with only one agent, known only to that single operative. One such individual was Hercules Mulligan.

Mulligan came onboard during the summer of 1779, just six weeks following Robert Townsend's recruitment. Woodhull mentions him for the first time that summer in a letter to Tallmadge dated August 12, naming him as "an acquaintance of [Alexander] Hamilton's," who had already handed off intelligence stating that "4 or 5 regiments were embarking, generally said for Quebec [and] had taken altogether thick clothing, yet nevertheless he thought most likely for Georgia, and believed they all had but a short time to stay here."[174] Mulligan soon became a valuable agent to the Secret Six. He did not typically write out reports that might be captured by the enemy and expose either himself or someone else in the Ring, but delivered information directly to Townsend or through another agent. (The identity of this other agent remains a mystery even today, but this person—according to Mulligan's own son, John, who wrote years later about his father's intelligence-gathering activities—may have reported Mulligan's findings directly to General Washington.)

The story of how Mulligan came to America and eventually fell into the spying game is one worth the telling. Born in Ireland in 1740, Hercules migrated with his family to New York when he was only six. He and his two brothers all grew up to be merchants. By the 1760s, he was working for the import business Kortwright & Company, a firm that ran seven company ships between New York and the West Indies.

During the 1760s, Mulligan not only began to make his fortune in the West Indian trade, he was also a young man ready to join the ever-expanding rebellion. During the Stamp Act Crisis, he published an inflammatory anti–Stamp Act newspaper. By 1770, he had joined the Sons of Liberty, which eschewed such tactics as boycotts against British goods in favor of more aggressive, even violent means.

In 1773, Hercules bought out his partners and took over full ownership of the company. That same year, he met Alexander Hamilton, then a young man of eighteen, recently arrived from the Virgin Islands where he had grown up. The bright and energetic Hamilton had worked for the company on St. Croix and had been brought to New York to attend King's College (today's Columbia University). Soon, he was boarding in Mulligan's household while attending school, and the two men—despite an age gap of fifteen years—became good friends.

The following year, Mulligan opened the doors to a new men's clothing store in New York, one that tailored to the city's best-dressed men. His emporium carried everything for the dapper man about town, including "superfine cloths of the most fashionable colours" and a varied array of accessories, such as "a large assortment of gold and silver fringe ornaments with bullion knots" and "epaulets for gentlemen of the army and militia."[175] Mulligan soon married Elizabeth Sanders, whose father was Admiral Sanders of the Royal Navy. New York's tailor to the elite now had connections with British officers both by trade and marriage.

In 1775, with the outbreak of the war, both Mulligan and Hamilton expressed support for the Patriot cause, and even stole a cannon together from New York's Battery. By the following year, Mulligan helped Hamilton gain his officer's commission in the Continental ranks. (Together, the two recruited twenty-five new men for Washington's Army.) A known Patriot, Mulligan was captured by Tories as he and his family tried to leave New York City following Washington's evacuation of Manhattan in the fall of 1776, but he was soon released. Given the circumstances, Hercules pretended to a change of heart. He would stay on in New York and continue to serve his Loyalist and British officer clientele. By 1779, he found his way into the shadowy world of intelligence gathering as a peripheral connection of the Culpers.

MEANS AND METHODS

As new subagents were added, the members of the Culper Ring worked out the distribution of tasks necessary for their success. Much is known today about how the group operated. Even if the records do not tell the whole story of the inner workings of the Secret Six, one fact is clear—the cover stories of the ring members tended to work for them, typically raising only rare suspicions on the part of the British. Often, agents such as Woodhull passed easily through British security checkpoints and were rarely searched. On the other hand, small units operating independently of British authority, such as Tory or Patriot groups or even simple thieves and highwaymen, posed a greater risk to the Culper Ring. Such individuals were usually looking for valuables hidden on those they stopped, so their searches might inadvertently turn up documents and other damning evidence of espionage. On one occasion, Woodhull was stopped just beyond British lines by a group of no-goods who forced him to surrender to a complete search of his person. As they rifled through every nook and cranny of his clothing and boots, he could only hope they did not discover the location of the reports and spy papers he had hidden away. They did not, and he was allowed to pass. The documents had been squirreled away under his horse's saddle.

To aid the group in passing information to Washington, Tallmadge went to great lengths putting together a communication system, one that included such spy craft as invisible ink, the sympathetic stain on which agents on both sides relied. He handed out bottles—rationed might be a better word, as the availability of such "inks" seems to have often been in short supply—of chemical agents that worked together to first mask, then reveal secret messages. Several types of liquids were utilized, similar to the type created by John Jay's brother, Sir James (see "An Invisible Piece of Spy Craft," page 165). These specialized inks did not always mean communications were easily disguised. Sometimes the inks smeared and sometimes agents simply applied the liquids to paper incorrectly.

The Culper Ring utilized another important bit of spy craft, an elaborate system of coded words invented by Major Tallmadge. Many codes used during the American Revolutionary War were simple substitute systems, where one letter represented another letter. But such systems were, in the right hands, easy to break. (Such had been the downfall of Dr. Church.) Instead, Tallmadge worked up a system that utilized three-digit replacements for 763 words, either ones commonly used in the English language—the word "the," for example, was "625"—or words specific to their operations, such as locations or spy activities or the names of the agents themselves. He also included a substitute system for letters of the alphabet. Tallmadge wrote out the words included in more-or-less alphabetical order (for example, "light" [352] comes before "last" [353]). This is part of the code that he probably should have arranged differently, as it gave British decoders a clue as to the words being coded. Taking an example from the system, Tallmadge included the following words beginning with the letter D:

date	120	dispatch	130	dismount	140	disagree	150
day	121	distant	131	disarm	141	disorder	151
dead	122	danger	132	detect	142	dishonest	152
do	123	dislodge	133	defence	143	discover	153
die	124	dismiss	134	deceive	144	december	154
damage	125	dragoon	135	delay	145	demolish	155
doctor	126	detain	136	difficult	146	deliver	156
dirty	127	divert	137	disaprove	147	desolate	157
drummer	128	discourse	138	disregard	148	during	158
daily	129	disband	139	disappoint	149		

Obviously, Tallmadge chose his words carefully. Such words as "dead," "dispatch," "danger," "dragoon," "detain," "defence," "demolish," might come in handy in a spy report.

Local places, such as New York (727), Long Island (728), Setauket (729), Staten Island (732), Connecticut (735) and New Jersey (736) had to be included, as well as such relevant, if more distant, locales, including England (745), London (746), the West Indies (752), France (755), and Spain (756).

The three-number replacement code was also used to identify the members of the group, even though they already had code names. Abraham Woodhull, aka Samuel Culper Sr., was, in Tallmadge's code system, 722. Townsend, known as Culper Jr., was 723. Strangely, all five men who comprised the Secret Six had code names and code numbers. Only the female member of the group was known by her code number, the three-digit code for "lady." Anna Strong—if that was her identity—was simply known as "Agent 355."

Other than relying on a basically alphabetical system, the main problem with the code was that uncoded words could sometimes provide a clue as to a secret message's meaning. But, overall, the system worked. One typical coded message sent by Abraham Woodhull to General Washington read as follows:

729.29.15th 1779

Sir. Dqpeu Beyocpu agreeable to 28. Met

723. not far from 727. & received a 356. . . .

Every 356. Is opened at the entrance of 727.

And every 371. Is searched, that for the future.

Every 356. Must be 691. With the 286. Received.

The communication opens with the place and date. The three-digit code words "729" and "29" stand for "Setauket" and the month of August, respectively. Then, a person's name follows, that of Jonas Hawkins, a courier sometimes used by Austin Roe and other members of the Ring. So,

"Dqpeu Beyocpu" becomes "Jonas Hawkins." The body of the communiqué is sprinkled with three-digit code words, and the translation comes out on the other end as the following:

Setauket August 15th 1779

Sir. Jonas Hawkins agreeable to appointment

Met Culper Jr. not far from New York &

Received a letter . . . Every letter is opened

at the entrance of New York and every man

is searched, that for the future every letter

must be written with the ink received.[176]

Tallmadge's code served as a centerpiece of the spy craft with which his Ring operated. If the British captured a copy of the key, possibly every member of the Secret Six would have been exposed and possibly captured. To make certain it remained secret, Tallmadge only wrote out four copies. While the British never managed to get their hands on a copy of his code, through one mishap, he did lose several papers to the Redcoats, as well as a field agent. On July 2, 1779, Tallmadge and some of his dragoons engaged British forces in a skirmish, following a dawn raid by British units, along the border between New York and Connecticut. During the military melee, ten of Tallmadge's men were killed and eight taken prisoner. While the Connecticut Yankee escaped with his life, an entire saddlebag full of intelligence papers was seized, along with some money earmarked for Abraham Woodhull. Although Tallmadge's code was not discovered, the name and address of an agent named George Higday was. Eleven days later, the British caught up with Higday and arrested him. But he was a step ahead of the Redcoats, having destroyed all incriminating documents in his possession. He talked his way out of his situation, telling British authorities that he had, indeed, tried to volunteer for spy duty with Washington, but that no agreement had ever

Crying Over Spilled Ink

Invisible ink, which the members of the Secret Six relied on, always seemed in short supply. Unfortunately, a startled Woodhull once spilled a batch of the stuff when someone broke into his room.

On that evening, Woodhull was at his desk writing a letter to General Washington with the sympathetic stain. At the time, British soldiers were quartering in rooms in his home, so his clandestine work was taking place right under the enemy's noses. He had just finished his report, when the door to his room burst open, and a pair of individuals entered unannounced. Surprised and caught red-handed, Woodhull jumped to his feet and tried to cover up his papers. In his panic, he knocked over his writing table and the vial of invisible ink broke on the wooden floor.

Fortunately, the intruders were not snoopy British Redcoats, but two teenage girls, cousins of his who had observed that Woodhull, of late, had seemed nervous, even depressed. They had decided to surprise him by jumping into his room, hoping to make him laugh. The girls had not succeeded.

Later, after telling Tallmadge of the incident, his handler related the story to Washington: "Such an excessive fright and so great a turbulence of passions so wrought on poor Culper that he has hardly been in tolerable health since."[177] Not only were Woodhull's nerves further frayed by his two cousins, he had also lost a supply of the precious invisible ink he needed for his intelligence communications.

been reached. With no real proof, the British released Higday, who lived to spy another day.

Tallmadge's reliance on spy craft did not end with invisible ink and a code system that replaced words with three-digit stand-ins. He also suggested to his agents other ways of disguising secret materials, especially during transportation. (Some of his tips had come from Washington originally.) The trick involved taking single pages of secret documents and "hiding" them in unnoticeable places. One suggestion was for messages to be written with invisible ink on the blank pages of books, pamphlets, and other printed materials. Another was to transport a large amount of blank paper and place the potentially incriminating documents—again, those done in invisible ink—between the pages of these blank sheets. If these papers were discovered, they could easily be explained to any British authority who asked.

CHAPTER EIGHT

The Culper Ring
in Action

THE RING SWINGS INTO ACTION

PREVIOUS:
This c. 1781 engraving shows George Washington and officers looking toward the "half-ruined city of New York in the distance."

By late 1778, the entire complement of agents comprising the Culper Ring had been recruited and their joint intelligence efforts were soon in full swing. Others would be recruited in secondary roles as well. At the end of 1778, Major Tallmadge recruited another local Setauket citizen, Jonas Hawkins, to function as a courier between Woodhull and Brewster. Again, he represented a known entity, as Tallmadge, Woodhull, and Brewster had associated with him previously. He ran as a courier for the ring until September 1779, when he "retired" from his spy role. That same month, however, Woodhull's uncle, Captain Nathan Woodhull, who, in his mid-fifties, represented an older element within the organization, also began delivering reports. (His captaincy was, ironically, within the ranks of a Loyalist militia unit.)

While the spy missions of the Culper Ring did not always conform to the same pattern, a routine sometimes existed that required each agent to fill a prescribed role or two. An agent might pay a call to New York, to say, tavern keeper Austin Roe. He might meet with Townsend, either in his coffeehouse or elsewhere and return with a report to Long Island. Keeping a plausible cover for the agents in the loop, Roe might then drop off the report, not directly into Woodhull's hands, but at a designated "dead drop" located on his property, a meadow where Abraham's cattle grazed. Roe would bury the papers in a box under a tree. Woodhull would later arrive, checking on his cattle, and dig up the buried trove of documents.

The ring may have relied on another typical delivery system as well, depending on the identity of Agent 355. In this scenario, Brewster was informed that a report was ready to pick over on Long Island. Operating out of his base over in Fairfield, Connecticut, Brewster would launch a whaleboat into Long Island Sound and row toward Long Island. Reaching the Devil's Belt portion of Long Island, Brewster used a telescope to focus in on Anna Strong's clothesline. (The two were neighbors.) On the line, she would hang a black petticoat, indicating to Brewster that it was time to pick up a report. Then she hung out a series of white handkerchiefs along the line, each corresponding with a series of coves along the shoreline of Long Island—a secret signal that told him exactly where to row to find the documents in question—six coves, six handkerchiefs.

After dark, Brewster would go to the designated cove, pick up the stashed report, then row back across the sound to his rendezvous site near Fairfield, sometimes dodging British patrol boats. Once back in Fairfield, Brewster handed the messages to a designated courier, often one of his own boatmen, who would deliver the intelligence by horseback to Tallmadge. Then, Tallmadge, through a series of riders, each typically spaced fifteen miles apart, saw to the delivery of the documents to Washington, wherever his headquarters was at the time.

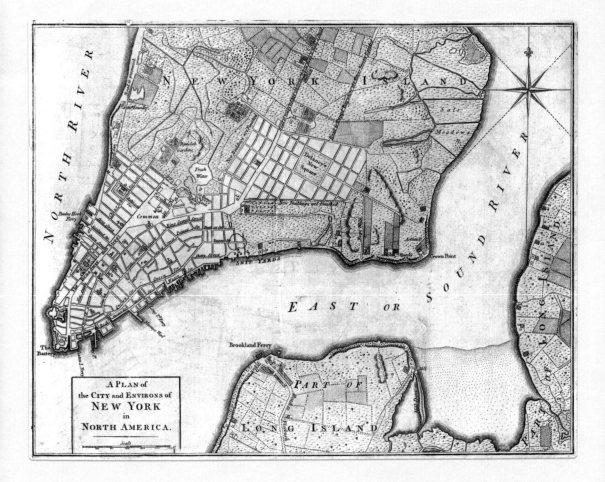

Whaleboat Wars

The members of the Culper Ring consistently faced risks in the field. By running agents between Long Island and the mainland, especially across the "Devil's Belt"—the notorious stretch of water between Setauket and the rocky coastline separating Fairfield and Stratford, Connecticut—members of the ring, especially Brewster, faced a unique challenge: privateers.

Following Washington's evacuation of New York City in the fall of 1776, Long Island Sound became the backdrop for a guerrilla-style conflict that came to be known as the "Whaleboat War." It all began as a natural extension of the Loyalist-Patriot conflict that unfolded in the choppy waters of the sound. By October 1776, the governors of New York and Connecticut issued privateer commissions to individuals willing to harass British and Tory ships and to engage in raids against land bases, destroying anything of value to the enemy, even as they commandeered supplies for the Continental Army and various militia units. Their craft of choice were whaleboats, the type common to New England, typically running thirty feet in length and manned by between a dozen and two dozen men each, plying eighteen-foot oars. Such boats were light, maneuverable, and sleek in the water. Brewster had been an early recruit, gaining a commission to privateer in November.

Some privateers were quite successful against the British, such as Connecticut colonel Jonathan Meigs who, in May 1777, raided one British post with 234 men rowing thirteen whaleboats, plus a pair of sloops, a foray resulting in the deaths of six of the enemy, the capture of ninety Loyalist militiamen, and the destruction of "120 tons of hay, corn, and oats, as well as a huge quantity of rum."[178] General Henry Clinton retaliated by issuing privateer commissions as well, offering rewards for those whaleboatmen who plundered the Patriots, so long as they did so short of "excesses, barbarities or irregularities."[179]

In time, such "barbarities" were taking place, none causing a greater howl than kidnappings and hostage takings. Tory privateers were the first to take up the practice, starting in May 1779, when two Loyalist captains, Bonnell and Glover, kidnapped General Gold Selleck Silliman, a Patriot commander stationed outside Fairfield, Connecticut. Soon, both sides were demanding ransom for hostages.

Caleb Brewster despised the practice and even wrote a letter to Governor Clinton about the harsh treatment inflicted on Patriot and Continental hostages. Tallmadge felt similarly. The sound became a battleground of raids and recriminations, harassment and hostage taking, and all this made it more difficult and dangerous for the Culper Ring to operate.

In 1779, Tallmadge reported to Washington how the "Whaleboat War" had recently interfered with the ring, as "the boat [used] for dispatches from C—— [Abraham Woodhull] has been chased quite across the Sound by these plunderers . . . while our crew has supposed them the enemy." All this made Woodhull jittery, as Tallmadge added: "C—— will not risk, nor 725 [the otherwise indefatigable Brewster] go over for dispatches."[180] In 1780, Brewster, preparing to pick up a communication from Woodhull, was attacked at 2:00 a.m. on August 17 by a pair of Tory privateers, including Captain Glover, who had kidnapped General Silliman.

Although Washington agreed the privateers were a problem, he did little to stop them, which led Brewster and Tallmadge to take action on their own. Lloyd's Neck, Long Island, was a known "headquarters" for Tory privateers, and the two members of the Culper Ring led a raid against the outpost in September 1779. Tallmadge delivered 130 of his dragoons on several vessels across the sound, including whaleboats under Brewster's command. The element of surprise worked in their favor, and the Culper Raid ended with the Tory whaleboats destroyed, their huts burned, and a small party of prisoners taken, all without the loss of a single Patriot life. While all this did not end the "Whaleboat War," Tallmadge and Brewster had inflicted a heavy blow to the Tory privateers.

ABOVE:
This sketch by a British officer shows Admiral Howe's fleet at anchor in New York Harbor just following the Battle of Long Island.

A British Nemesis

As Major Benjamin Tallmadge recruited agents into the Culper Ring, he was aware that he and his operatives had counterparts on the British side, agents who were often well-trained, intelligent, and adept in the ways of espionage and counterespionage. One such agent was, in fact, a regular customer at Townsend's coffeehouse. In the spring of 1779, while the Culper Ring was growing, British general Henry Clinton was appointing John André as his chief intelligence officer, making him as close to Tallmadge's British counterpart as anyone else among the Redcoats' ranks. André would prove himself as skilled in the spy game as the Americans.

Yet André was a different sort of spy. He was an artist—the son of a Swiss father and a beautiful Parisian mother—who enjoyed writing doggerel poetry and attending theatrical shows. He was accomplished, polished, popular as he moved about during social soirees. He charmed others easily. Born in 1750, he was raised to project an aura of culture and refinement. He was versed in multiple languages, studied hard, and his skill set ran the gamut from fencing to dancing, music to mathematics.

By the age of nineteen, André was living in London. Soon, his father died and left him with a tidy fortune. Set for life, but easily bored, André joined the British military, having purchased the rank of second lieutenant in the Royal Welch Fusiliers. He later transferred to the 7th Foot as a full lieutenant. His unit was dispatched to Canada in 1775, the war already underway in America.

In November 1775, Continental troops captured André and subsequently, as was common practice with officers on both sides of the war, placed him on parole, which gave him the opportunity to pay a visit to Philadelphia. While in the city, he met a vivacious young woman, the charming and refined daughter of local wealthy Tory Judge Edward Shippen, who had served in a variety of British colonial bureaucratic offices. At the time, Margaret "Peggy" Shippen was an eligible, unattached female whom André befriended, probably not with any romantic intentions. A few years later, she was married to a gallant American officer, but one who determined to follow a path leading to his turning traitor to the revolution—Benedict Arnold. And when the time came for Arnold to defect to the British, it was Major André who became his handler.

By late 1776, André was exchanged and was soon tapped as a staff officer at General Howe's New York headquarters. Fluent in German, he helped translate documents for the Hessians. When Howe finally packed his bags and returned to England, having had his fill of the Americans, André went to work for Henry Clinton from 1777 to 1778. (André was one of the British officers who gathered in Lydia Darragh's front parlor in December 1777, including the night she sneaked into a closet to eavesdrop on one of their late-night war councils.) He and Clinton got along nicely, the elder general taking André under his wing. Soon, André was Clinton's chief of staff. (The role was officially known as adjutant general.) With 1779 came his appointment as Clinton's intelligence chief. The paths of John André and the Culper Ring were destined to cross.

~ ※ ~

TOWNSEND EXPOSES A DOUBLE AGENT

From 1779 until the end of the Revolutionary War, the Culper Ring continuously delivered spy reports to General Washington, yet their total contribution to the success of the American cause is a difficult one to quantify. It is doubtless that the Secret Six and their clandestine operations did have an impact, and some of their missions had more dramatic effects than others. Three specific missions stand out among their successful ventures.

In mid-July 1779, Robert Townsend wrote a report to Washington (some of the information had been provided by Abraham Woodhull) that revealed how adept he was at subterfuge. In the report—the letter was actually sent by Woodhull directly to Tallmadge—Townsend informed the general of the presence of a British double agent named Christopher Duychenik. The agent in question had worked for the former royal governor of New York, William Tryon, who also served as a major general in a Loyalist militia unit. This Tory group had a reputation for its harsh raids along the Connecticut coast. Townsend exposed Duychenik as an operative spying for William Franklin, who ran an intelligence ring out of New Jersey. (William was the illegitimate son of Benjamin Franklin and former royal governor of New Jersey. At this time, the elder Franklin and his son were completely estranged.) Tryon also worked as part of William Franklin's spy network, as well as directly with General Henry Clinton's intelligence service and Major André.

In his report, which was delivered through Woodhull, Townsend reveals that "Christopher Duychenik, sailmaker at 10 [New York], formerly chairman of the Committee of Mechanics, is amongst you and is positively an agent for David Mathews, mayor of 10, under the direction of Tryon." Woodhull added: "Be very cautious how you handle [this information] for if it should get to the above mentioned persons ears C. Jr. [Townsend was Culper Jr.] tells me they would immediately suspect him."[181]

Townsend's information represented a spy coup worth crowing over. An American agent had somehow managed to penetrate the walls of secrecy surrounding rival British and Tory rings. Exactly how he had managed to do so is not entirely clear, and reasonably so. Townsend was emphatic about secrecy, understanding that loose lips cause slips. The extant record points away from any of the other full-time agents in the ring—Woodhull was involved, but perhaps only as a courier—leaving some other mystery person as the key.

Perhaps Rivington is a likely candidate. Few members of the Culper Ring had more continuous interaction with important British and Tory officers than Rivington. Another possibility is the man working inside one of the ring's two safe houses, Jacob Seaman. His wife's father was a member of a Loyalist intelligence organization, someone who would certainly have access to such valuable inside information as Duychenik's identity. Or perhaps the information came from William T. Robinson, a prominent New York City merchant, who ran in the highest of society circles, especially among the Tories. He was known to have passed information to the Culper Ring through a cutout named Joseph Lawrence, who lived in Bayside, Long Island. (Robinson was related to the Townsend family by marriage.) And maybe the informant was none other than Abraham Wooodhull's uncle, Nathan, who functioned as a double agent of sorts himself, since he served as an officer in a Tory militia unit and is known to have passed information to both Townsend and to his nephew. Regardless of where Townsend received his intelligence, it was an important discovery. Every double agent working against the American cause was problematic to the ultimate success of General Washington and of the revolution.

Culper Ring Safe Houses

With various agents among the Secret Six traveling regularly on missions into New York City, the ring needed access to other individuals they could trust in an emergency. To that end, two safe houses were worked out, both operating as boarding houses. Unfortunately, both houses also provided lodgings for British soldiers, so agents had to be cautious to whom they spoke and when.

One of the houses was operated by Amos and Mary Underhill. (The designation of their house was natural, as Mary was Abraham Woodhull's sister.) Townsend also did business with the Underhills, so either agent could meet with one or both of the couple without raising undue suspicion.

The other safe house was run by Jacob Seaman, who was married to the daughter of a Loyalist officer who worked counterintelligence in New York City. Townsend stayed in the Seaman house from time to time.

COUNTERING BRITISH COUNTERFEITERS

Certainly the Continental Army's performance on the various battlefields of the war helped determine which side—American or British—won the ultimate conflict. But spying played its part as well. Sabotage was a common espionage tool, and it could be played out in several different ways. One means of "sabotage" the British employed was economic—the devaluing of the Continental money supply. The chief method utilized was counterfeiting.

The British were masters of the art. They ran counterfeiting operations onboard ships and wherever else they could. The British published newspaper advertisements encouraging Loyalists traveling from one colony to another to carry counterfeit bills to spread their impact. (Abraham Woodhull even requested being reimbursed for his spying expenses in British currency, not Continental money.)

Not that Continental currency was difficult to replicate. Many times it was poorly printed and badly inked, produced by private printing offices

No.

TWO THIRDS

OF A DOLLAR,

According to
a Resolution of
CONGRESS,
passed at PHI-
LADELPHIA
February 17,
1776.

MIND YOUR BUSINESS

C

Two Thirds of a Dollar.

Two Thirds of a Dollar.

Philad. Printed by HALL
and SELLERS. 1776.

N.Carolina Currency.

Nº 2562 FOUR DOLLARS

By Authority of Congress
at Halifax April 2. 1776

TWELVE SHILLINGS   & SIX PENCE

Nº 12242

TWELVE SHILLINGS
AND SIX PENCE
Current Money of VIRGINIA,
PURSUANT to Ordinance of
CONVENTION
PASSED JULY 17 TH 1775.

John Dixon

SIX SHILLINGS.

To Counterfeit is Death.

Printed by JAMES ADAMS, 1776.

that received contracts from Congress. But one aspect of duplicating Continental money was a bit trickier. American money was printed almost exclusively in Philadelphia on a high-quality paper stock that the British found difficult to replicate. Throughout the war, the British continually made attempts to counterfeit the Patriot script, but the cheap paper they employed often gave away their efforts. Still, it was a matter of concern for the Americans. If the British could devalue American money through counterfeiting, then it would become more difficult for various officials to purchase food and other supplies for the army. Bad money might sink the entire revolution.

On November 29, 1779, Townsend delivered another important report to Tallmadge warning that the British had put their hands on a large quantity of a special paper stock, one that matched perfectly the type used by Congress, being the exact quality, weight, and thickness. As Townsend reported, "several reams of the paper made for the last emissions struck by Congress have been procured from Philadelphia."[182] In addition, the British might even have come into possession of a set of printing plates purloined from Philadelphia.

When word reached Washington, he moved immediately, delivering a report to Congress by December 7. Within months, Congress, concerned that the British had the capacity to produce quality Continental money that would be virtually undetectable, recalled all currency in circulation. This, of course, created another problem. The American economy was struggling during wartime, and a lack of money in circulation, even temporarily, would not help matters; however, the threat of counterfeit currency contaminating the money supply and causing undue inflation was even greater. Townsend, again, with the help of someone providing him with information, had once again managed a Culper coup. The ring had handed Washington, and Congress, vital economic intelligence while thwarting a major British plot. Once again, how had Townsend done it? From whom was he gaining his intelligence? The answer might lay in the hands of his own business partner, James Rivington.

A New York City entrepreneur who dispensed both coffee and news on the streets of New York, Rivington appeared to be a known quantity for the British. His coffeehouse was a haven of caffeine and conviviality for

OPPOSITE:
Examples of colonial currency.

British officers. His *Royal Gazette*, published under the moniker "Printer to the King's Most Excellent Majesty," railed against the Patriots while singing the praises of King George and His Majesty's men in uniform. But somewhere along the way, Rivington had turned.

Following his self-preserving exile to England in 1777, Rivington returned with a change of heart. What, exactly, had caused the New York newsman to shift his true loyalties is not clear. As one of the only associates of the Culper Ring to take payments for his information, perhaps money played a role. Whatever was behind this change in allegiances, it remained a secret to the British, as Rivington continued to publish his newspaper with editorials leaning in support of the British cause. (Rivington did manage to get into some trouble with British authorities in 1778 when he criticized General Howe's leadership.)

Rivington played a singular role in support of the Culper Ring. Townsend had recruited him not long after he had joined the ranks of the ring himself, sometime in the late summer of 1779. Once again, the talents of Robert Townsend may have come into play. How Townsend came to know (and trust) that Rivington had turned Patriot and then managed to talk him into taking the great risks inherent in spying for General Washington indicates that Townsend's powers of persuasion and, perhaps, elicitation were highly sharpened.

Townsend's partner in business and espionage soon proved invaluable. He provided books to members of the Ring that were used to hide messages in invisible ink on otherwise blank pages and endsheets. And he obviously managed to collect valuable intelligence from various contacts, whether they knew they were providing information to a Washington spy or not.

Long after the Revolutionary War, William Hooper, a congressman and signer of the Declaration of Independence, penned a letter to his friend, James Iredell, who would one day be named to the U.S. Supreme Court, in which he extolled the contributions Rivington made to the Culper Ring: "It has come out as there is now no longer any reason to conceal it that Rivington has been very useful to Gen. Washington by furnishing him with intelligence. The unusual confidence which the British placed in him owing in a great measure to his liberal abuse of the Americans gave him ample opportunities to obtain information which he has bountifully communicated to our friends."[183]

Rivington may have been the one to stumble onto the British currency plot because he was a printer. In 1775, concerned for the safety of his family because of the actions of the Sons of Liberty, Rivington had packed up his clan and sailed for England, where he stayed for two years. During the time he was away, the British had been utilizing his printing presses. According to a counterfeiter named Israel Young, the British established a money-copying workshop onboard a ship docked at New York, *Duchess of Gordon*. William Tryon directed the operation. Young later testified that he was told by an associate that he "had also seen Governour Tryon often, and that the Governour would talk very free with them; that they had on board a number of Rivington's types and one of his printers."[184] This alleged eyewitness also stated that "he himself had seen them printing . . . off [counterfeit money]; that they had a chest of it."[185]

How much did Rivington know about such counterfeiting operations? It is difficult to ascertain with certainty. Even if he was not involved on the inside with the operation, he was likely in the know. Were the British still utilizing his presses as late as 1778 or 1779? Unlikely. But, considering his contacts in the printing world, the British officers he knew as valued and sometimes talkative customers, it is unlikely he would not have found out about the latest counterfeiting operation and the British accessing the special quality paper. Knowing the British operated such counterfeiting rings, he probably kept his ear to the ground and even asked delicate questions in hopes of uncovering some new printing operation floating somewhere on the East River.

Of all the members of the Culper Ring, the New York printer had a unique worth. Rivington was known as a man with an ironic sense of humor, and it likely amused him to know that while Patriots raided his print shop and burned him in effigy, he was playing the British, writing pro-British editorials and articles, and even flattering one of his customers, spy John André, by publishing his love poems.

⁂

THE RING SAVES
THE FRENCH FLEET

Another of the Culper Ring's intelligence coups involved the arrival of a French fleet of naval vessels in the summer of 1780. With the success of the Franklin mission in Paris by early 1778—near to the time the Culper Ring was beginning to be organized—the French were soon supporting the American cause in as many ways as one could imagine, including money, guns, cannon, troops, and much-needed naval ships.

On April 6, 1780, the French had set sail from Brest, with Washington expecting them to arrive by early summer. Woodhull sent a report dated June 10 to Tallmadge of rumors concerning the anticipated arrival of the French: "You speak with some assurance that the French is hourly expected to our assistance—hope they may not fail us. . . . Thers [*sic*] a ground movement on foot in N. York. The troops are called from Lloyd's Neck and is said from every other distant post, and an embargo laid on all ships and small Sloops. It is suspected they are a going to quit N. York, or are going to make some diversion up the river, or are afraid of the French."[186]

Ironically, during these weeks of anticipation before the arrival of French ships and troops, the Culper Ring was at a low point of operation. In fact, Washington had officially ended their services. In the fall of 1779, Robert Townsend had entrusted a relative named James to deliver Secret Six reports, but young James had been exposed and the ring compromised. Townsend and Woodhull had a falling out, and Robert quit the organization in early May 1780. In a letter to Tallmadge, Woodhull informed his handler of the unfortunate turn of events: "I have had an interview with C. Junr. And am sorry to find he declines serving any longer."[187] One of the motivations behind Townsend's reluctance to continue working as a spy was the arrest of Hercules Mulligan. The man behind the grab was none other than Benedict Arnold, who had defected to the British. (More about his duplicity later.)

At the same time as Townsend's withdrawal from the Secret Six, Washington was frustrated with his agents. Prior to Culper Jr.'s resignation, Washington had expressed concerns to Tallmadge: "I should be exceedingly glad to hear from C. Junior, because all my accounts from other quarters are very defective as to the number of troops to be embarked, or, indeed, whether an embarkation is seriously in contemplation."[188] With Townsend out of the circle, the general was uncertain how the ring could function efficiently. On May 19, he sent a letter to Tallmadge, penned at his headquarters in Morristown, New Jersey: "As C. Junior has totally declined and C. Senior seems to wish to do it, I think the intercourse may be dropped. . . . I am endeavoring to open a communication with New York across Staten Island, but who are the agents in the City, I do not know."[189] Washington expressed his frustration by cutting off the only well-established group of agents he had in operation in New York City. They, especially Townsend and his connection, Woodhull, had been his eyes and ears in the city, then home to General Clinton's military headquarters. Now Washington was operating blind.

As for Woodhull, he seems to have been pleased with the turn of events. He had experienced more than one close call during his months as a spy—near detections, detainment on roads leading into the city, and even an incident where robbers took his money. These events made him periodically extremely nervous, even jittery. In his June 10 letter to Tallmadge, he sounded relieved that Washington might be closing down the Culper Ring: "I am happy to find that 711 [Washington's code name] is about to establish a more advantageous channel of intelligence than heretofore. I perceive that the former he intimates hath been of little service. Sorry we have been at so much cost and trouble for little or no purpose."[190] Woodhull's words sound as though he were slightly hurt at Washington's response to the efforts of the Secret Six, and he even mentions later in the letter some money he was still owed to cover his previous expenses. All signs pointed to the end of the Culpers.

～ ※ ～

Another Townsend Agent

One of the essential keys to the selection of agents within the Culper Ring was having a previous relationship with those chosen; it raised them, assumedly, above suspicion as a potential double agent. On one occasion, Robert Townsend needed a courier and he tagged a relative he could trust, a younger cousin named James Townsend. But the mission James became involved in did not go well.

One issue that plagued the organization was the length of time required to deliver messages to Washington. When the general became concerned, claiming information reached him so late that it was sometimes out of date, Townsend tried to shorten the process by utilizing James, who does not seem to have been up to the challenge.

In March 1780, James passed through British lines while acting as courier for his older cousin. Soon, reminiscent of the short-lived mission of Nathan Hale, he became involved in a conversation with strangers he believed were Loyalists, and he expressed his own loyalty to the British cause. Unfortunately, his audience was actually a group of Patriots, who took him captive, believing they had discovered a British spy in their midst. The Patriots searched him, then packed him off to Washington's headquarters.

Washington immediately recognized that among the papers young Townsend was carrying were sheets coded with invisible ink. In time, he was able to sort out the problem, taking pains to keep the true identity of one of his own agent's couriers a secret, but James was never utilized again on a mission.

BACK IN ACTION

The French fleet—its official name was the *Expedition Particulière*—arrived in America and docked at Newport, Rhode Island, on July 10, 1780 (just as Woodhull's report reached Washington), delivering a complement of 5,500 white-uniformed French troops under the command of Jean-Baptiste Donatien de Vimeur, comte de Rochambeau. The British were aware of the French navy, of course—they referred to the Gallic fleet as the "Special Expedition"—and General Henry Clinton, from his headquarters in New York, was soon making plans to respond.

That Clinton became aware of the approach of French ships and soldiers as quickly as he did was due to two men working in tandem—his chief intelligence officer, John André, and a traitorous American general who had decided to sell out the revolution and his fellow Continental soldiers, Benedict Arnold. Arnold, one of the heroes of the Battle of Saratoga, had learned of the French coming to New England directly from General Washington. He had subsequently penned a letter to André, telling the spymaster everything.

LEFT:
A c. 1834 portrait of Jean-Baptiste Donatien de Vimeur, comte de Rochambeau, who led French expeditionary forces in the latter part of the Revolution.

In the meantime, Washington had decided to reconsider his decision to close down the Culper Ring. Events were afoot and he needed, perhaps more than ever, to know what was going on in New York City. By July 11, he sent a letter to Tallmadge asking him to resuscitate the organization: "As we may every moment expect the arrival of the French Fleet a revival of correspondence with the Culpers will be of very great importance."[191] Uncertain whether all members of the ring would be willing to return to active duty, Washington speculated: "If the younger [Townsend, as Culper Jr.] cannot be engaged again, you will endeavor to prevail upon the older [Woodhull, as Culper Sr.] to give you information of the movements and position of the enemy upon Long Island—as whether they are all confined to the port at Brooklyn or whether they have any detached posts and where, and what is their strength at those posts—in short desire him to inform you of whatever comes under his notice and what seems worthy of communication."[192]

Fortunately, the Culpers responded positively, leaping into action almost immediately. Tallmadge had sent word through Brewster, who rowed across the sound to inform Woodhull. He was ill with a fever, so Austin Roe filled the breach, riding hard on horseback for more than fifty miles to inform Townsend that Washington wanted them back in service. As Agent 355 was operating out of New York City at the time, she, too, was informed. The agents scoured the city for intelligence. Within days, Townsend had news, which he passed to a recovered Woodhull, who sent it onto Brewster, who rowed, once again, across Long Island Sound, inspired to speed by Woodhull's personal addendum to his report: "The enclosed requires your immediate departure this day by all means let not an hour pass: for this day must not be lost. You have news of the greatest consequence perhaps that ever happened to your country."[193]

Indeed, Woodhull's report had important, even vital intelligence concerning the British and their response to the arrival of the French fleet. It is clear from the document's content that Townsend, Woodhull, Roe, Brewster, and Agent 355 had done their work well, despite Washington's earlier concerns. The British were making big plans:

[A]lso assures of the arrival of Admiral Graves with six ships of the line and is joined by three more out of New York, also one of 50 and two of 40 guns and has sailed for Rhode Island and is supposed they will be there before this can possibly reach you. Also 8000 Troops are this day embarking at Whitestone for the before mentioned port. I am told for certain that the French have only seven sail of the line. I greatly fear their destination.[194]

Woodhull knew his intelligence report was so crucial that he did not include Benjamin Tallmadge in the delivery circuit, but had Brewster deliver it directly to Washington's headquarters, handing the missive to one of his aides-de-camp, a young Alexander Hamilton.

Washington pondered his choices. Without hesitation, he sent word to Rochambeau, the French commander, of the British plan to attack. But how would he counter Clinton's movement of thousands of troops out of New York? He considered attacking the city, as it would be under-manned. But the American general was uncertain that he had enough troops, and his supply of ammunition, especially for his artillery, was low. His Excellency then chose another strategy, one worthy of a spy-master. He would engage in a bit of disinformation. What he needed was to make Clinton *believe* the Americans were going to counter his move into New England by attacking New York City with an army twelve thousand strong.

Washington set in motion a series of false moves. He put together a collection of misleading letters and other communiqués indicating he planned a full-scale attack on New York City while Clinton and thousands of his troops were away in New England. The general then selected a special courier and gave him instructions.

Within hours, a stranger entered a British outpost near the city and handed a package to the Redcoats. The individual stated he found the bundle on the road and thought, from the contents, that the British might be interested in the enclosed letters. It was all part of the plan. Perusing the documents, the ruse worked perfectly. Redcoats from the post delivered the package to their officers, and the documents soon reached officials in New York. Believing the city to be vulnerable, Clinton and the thousands he intended to attack the French in Newport were recalled back to the city. Even as the soldiers, British officials, and citizens of New York City waited, no attack was forthcoming. However, the French fleet was put on alert and sailed from Newport, out of harm's way.

It was the kind of thing George Washington had done before—the planting of false information to distract, confuse, and delay the enemy. And just as the clandestine tactic had worked previously, including Honeyman's duplicity with the Hessians at Trenton in December 1776, so it worked again. Washington had seen the light. He needed the Culper Ring and, despite previous setbacks and slow progress on the intelligence-gathering front, the Secret Six had moved deftly back into service and had helped save the French fleet in America. Few American espionage coups would ever match this one pulled off by Townsend, Woodhull, and the rest of the Culper Gang.

~ ❊ ~

BENEDICT ARNOLD, AMERICAN TRAITOR

Even as the Culper Ring achieved important intelligence coups on behalf of George Washington and the Continental cause, the members of the Secret Six did not anticipate one of the most significant and notorious acts of defection during the entire Revolutionary War—that of America's most famous traitor, General Benedict Arnold. The how and the why behind the turning of one of General Washington's most successful and gallant field commanders is both complex and yet simple, one that threatened not only the future of the Culper Ring, but the American cause itself.

Arnold was an officer of extraordinary bravery during battle, yet an insecure man at heart. Born in 1741, he grew up in a household with little money or social standing, enduring the failures of an alcoholic father. When the French and Indian War opened, young Arnold (he was only fourteen in 1755) tried to enlist in a local militia unit, but had to wait another two years before taking up arms. Even then, he only served a year before he deserted.

As a young man in his twenties, the black-haired Arnold went into business as an apothecary, operating a dual storefront of pharmacy and bookshop in New Haven, Connecticut. He opposed oppressive taxation and trade duties laid on the colonies by the British, beginning with the Sugar Act of 1764, so he began supporting Patriot politics and policies. He married above his social rank in 1767, taking Margaret Mansfield as his wife, the daughter of a prominent family in New Haven. Even as colonial opposition to British policy continued to expand into the 1770s, Arnold remained a struggling businessman, one who accumulated more debts than he could manage to pay without difficulty. When the war opened in 1775, Arnold enlisted, taking the rank of captain in a Connecticut militia unit. He rose quickly, leading the attack on a key British post in eastern New York, Fort Ticonderoga, a great masonry fortress situated on the banks of Lake George. But Arnold's success in the field was overshadowed soon by the death of his wife.

Over the next two years, Arnold continued to distinguish himself as a field officer, participating in several important battles and rising to the rank of general. But his successes never led to the appointments the Connecticut commander believed he should have received. He often felt underappreciated, even passed over for plum assignments and commands. His men typically held opinions of him resting on both extremes. Some thought him a noble leader, while others thought he was an egotistical glory seeker. And he still had money problems, as one American officer, Colonel John Brown, once noted in 1777: "Money is this man's God, and to get enough of it he would sacrifice his country."[195] Perhaps Brown spoke about more than he even knew at the time.

Arnold's greatest leadership moment in the field came in the fall of 1777 with the Battle of Saratoga. During the engagement, Arnold rode back and forth between the lines, placing himself repeatedly in exposed positions, even as he rallied his men. But at least one British musket ball managed to find its mark, as Arnold received a severe wound in his left leg. Although doctors suggested the limb be removed, Arnold would have none of it. In time, the leg healed, if imperfectly, for he walked with a limp ever after.

Given his wound and its aftereffect, Arnold was soon removed from field duty by General Washington himself, who greatly admired his gallant officer. In the early summer of 1778, with the British evacuation from Philadelphia, Washington gave Arnold an assignment he hoped would make him feel appreciated and noticed at last—he was to serve as the military commander of the City of Brotherly Love.

But it would prove to be an assignment that placed Arnold on a path leading to corruption, scandal, intrigue, and defection from the Patriot cause. Still struggling to pay off old debts, Arnold's new position of power provided him with financial opportunities. Some of his business engagements were dubious, though, drawing criticism from various circles. When one of his subordinate officers, Captain Allen McLane, complained to General Washington about Arnold's shady dealings, His Excellency would have none of it. He stuck up for Arnold, for Washington admired him greatly, considering him something of a personal protégé. (Neither Washington nor McLane could know in 1778 that one day, nearly three years later, McLane would be tapped to kidnap Arnold after he turned traitor.)

In Philadelphia, Arnold found his station in Philadelphia's social stratosphere. He had more money than he had ever seen before, he was wined and dined by the city's upper crust, and soon became infatuated with a young socialite barely half his age, the daughter of a Loyalist family, one accustomed to wealth, the finest of everything, male attention, and getting her way. Margaret "Peggy" Shippen represented, for the darkly handsome Arnold, a starry beauty and a possible step up on the social ladder. Even as Philadelphia had hosted both the First and Second Continental Congresses and served as the birthplace of the Declaration of Independence, the Shippens had remained in the city—and remained Tories to boot. Before she met Arnold, Peggy Shippen, then only seventeen years old, had met Major John André, and the two had engaged in flirtatious overtures. But André had other admirers, and he had since moved on to New York. Peggy had also moved on in other ways and found herself charming yet another officer, the Patriot hero Benedict Arnold. He soon fell under her spell. The wife of Robert Morris, signer of the Declaration of Independence and superintendent of finance during the war, noted: "Cupid has given our little general a more mortal wound than all the host of Britons could."[196] (Mrs. Morris's mention of "our little general" refers to his height, as Arnold was only five feet, seven inches tall.) Everyone could see that Arnold had fallen hard for Peggy. She would help ruin him in the end.

In April 1779, Arnold and Peggy married. During the ceremony, his leg wound was acting up, so a soldier had to help him stand. (At the reception, he rested his leg on a campstool.) The marriage meant both love and money for Arnold, for his business connections brought him financial success, and his wife's family had money as well. But he always seemed to serve as a lightning rod for criticism and doubt, especially from his fellow officers who questioned his honesty. Such critics from within the ranks of the Continental Army prompted Arnold, just prior to his wedding, to send a letter to Washington complaining about the accusations against him: "If your Excellency thinks me criminal, for Heaven's sake let me be immediately tried, and, if found guilty, executed. I want no favor; I ask only for justice. . . . Having made every sacrifice of fortune and blood, and become a cripple in the service of my country, I little expected to meet the ungrateful returns I have received from my countrymen."[197]

Arnold presents himself as an exasperated commander, one tired of his critics and fighting back, even as he seems to be nursing a martyr complex. But, his psychological hang-ups aside, General Benedict Arnold *had* sacrificed, more than many others in the ranks of the Continental Army. The question was, of course, were his accusers merely expressing jealousy or were they correct about Arnold's alleged venal side?

REACHING OUT TO THE ENEMY

Only Arnold and a handful of British officers could have known the answer to that question by the spring of 1779. Within weeks of his marriage to Peggy, Arnold put out feelers to General Henry Clinton in New York, through a London-born, Loyalist third party, a Philadelphia merchant named Joseph Stansbury, asking the British commander if he could be of service to him. In Stansbury's words, General Arnold "communicated to me, under a solemn obligation of secrecy, his intention of opening his services to the commander in chief of the British forces."[198] (When Arnold sent the query to Clinton, Major John André had just been appointed chief of intelligence in New York.) The hero of the Battle of Saratoga was prepared to talk treason with the British.

André was not initially enthusiastic at the opportunity. Such an offer, from a high-status American officer, could represent a trick. But André responded, perhaps through Peggy, but more likely through Stansbury. Arnold was drawn in, and André began receiving reports from him. He was provided invisible ink and André's code, (see "André's Code System," page 236). The American general passed information to André through the summer of 1779. Stansbury continued to serve as the cutout connection between Arnold and André, so the two men would not have to meet in person and expose one another. In August, communications between the two officers were suspended, as accusations swirled across Philadelphia concerning the activities of several well-placed Loyalists in the city. (That Arnold had married the daughter of a Loyalist that May only made him more suspect in the eyes of those who already doubted his loyalties.) Arnold was becoming too hot for André to handle.

Washington had apparently taken Arnold at his word and given the green light for an investigation of the general and his finances, one that led to a court-martial in January 1780. Arnold defended himself vigorously, and the court found him guilty of only a couple of minor charges, which were subsequently allowed to disappear. But Arnold's vindication did not last long, for, in April, a congressional investigation discovered that he had bilked the government out of £1,000 pounds for expenses from the disastrous Quebec Campaign back in 1775–76, but for which he had no receipts or other documentation. Given the practice of the time, if Arnold could not produce the needed evidence to authenticate the expenses, he would not be reimbursed.

This time, Arnold was found guilty, even as he was once again mired in debt. (Peggy's lavish spending during their first year of marriage had not ultimately improved his financial situation.) A desperate Arnold was in contact a second time with General Clinton to offer his services. But Clinton was more interested in what the American general might be able to do for him in New York, rather than Philadelphia. The city and the Hudson River Valley to the north had always been an important focus of the British during the American Revolutionary War and Clinton was ready to pay if Arnold could provide information concerning the region. André told the American general to ask for a transfer.

Clinton's main interest in the region was a beehive complex of fortifications surrounding West Point, located fifty-five miles north of New York City, near a hairpin turn in the Hudson River. The larger fort at West Point commanded a bluff above the curve in the river, with smaller forts lining both the eastern and western banks. A great iron chain stretched across the river at this location, preventing any British war vessels from sailing any farther north. With three thousand men maintained at the local garrison, West Point was considered impregnable and extraordinarily vital to Washington who utilized this strong point on the Hudson to move men and materiel from New England to New York and back again. Whoever held West Point theoretically controlled much of the region flanked on the east by New England and on the west by New York.

By midsummer, the French fleet had arrived at Newport, and Washington turned to Arnold to lead a mission. Believing his general to be fully recovered from his wounds, despite his limp, he requested Arnold lead a raid against some of Clinton's forces stationed outside New York City. Arnold had other ideas already in the offing. He begged off, as he had back in the spring, and then deftly began campaigning for the appointment as commander of the West Point facilities. Washington relented, and Arnold was at his new post at West Point by early August.

⌘ ※ ⌘

André's Code System

Codes are an essential part of the world of spies, and espionage during the American Revolutionary War was no exception. The Culper Ring used a three-digit code system for more than seven hundred key words, and Major John André relied on a numeric code as well.

The technical term for such a system is an alphanumeric substitution code. But, while Tallmadge based his code on a codebook of his own design, André used a slightly different source, a book common to many at the time—William Blackstone's legal tome, *Commentaries on the Laws of England*.

For the code to work, obviously, both the sender and the recipient needed a copy of Blackstone's work. Also, each person needed the *exact* same edition of the book, since the code was based on words located on specific pages and in specific paragraphs.

As André himself wrote concerning the code system: "Three numbers make a word, the 1st is the page the 2nd the line the third the word."[199] Using this system, then, the word "general" would be written in code as 35.12.8, since the word is located on page 35 in the twelfth line, the eighth word.

While the system was a simple one, and the codebook could be left in plain sight on an agent's desk or on his bookshelves and not draw suspicion, it had a couple of problems, too. Obviously, if someone discovered the book being used, the code was a bust. Another problem was that the word needing coding had to be somewhere on the pages of Blackstone's book. Place names could be a problem. The word "Setauket," for example, never appears, so the person coding the message would have to fall back on spelling the word out, using a numeric code for each letter. Sometimes André just utilized a different sourcebook for some words, such as the twenty-first edition of Nathan Bailey's *Universal Etymological English Dictionary*.

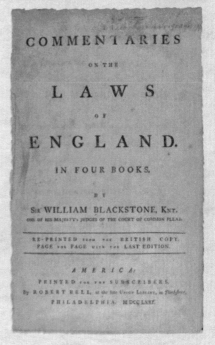

Another difference between André and Tallmadge's code was in how André named agents, as well as some of the more prominent locations referred to in his communiqués. André was fond of biblical names, so the Susquehanna River became "Jordan," Congress was "Synagogue," and Carlisle, Pennsylvania, was "Rome."

Arnold Sends Out Feelers

With a plum assignment dropped in his lap, one with extraordinary implications, the traitor Arnold went into full swing, with all the conniving of an American Richard III. He negotiated with the British over the surrender of the fortifications, agreeing to a payment of £20,000 pounds, close to $1 million in today's money. At the same time, Arnold was aware that his clandestine negotiations might become known through Washington's New York City spy network. Completely in the dark about their names, he began sending out feelers to Washington, telling him that, since he was now operating in the New York region, he would need to be privy to the spies plying the local intelligence game. But he was stymied at every turn. Washington could not tell him anything, since Tallmadge was their handler, a layer of security that had always worked in favor of the Culper Ring's anonymity. Arnold then asked the Marquis de Lafayette for names; he, too, declined, knowing nothing. Arnold then requested the information from Major General Robert Howe, whom Arnold had replaced as West Point commander, writing him a letter on August 5 (after only having taken command of West Point a mere forty-eight hours earlier!), explaining that "as the safety of this post and garrison . . . depends on having good intelligence of the movements and designs of the enemy . . . I must request (with their permission) to be informed who they are, as I wish to employ them for the same purpose. I will engage upon honour to make no discovery of them to any person breathing."[200] While Howe did respond to Arnold with the name of an agent he relied on over in Long Island, the spy was not part of the Culper Ring. Again, Arnold's attempt to learn the identities of the Secret Six had yielded no fruit.

As for Benjamin Tallmadge, he was not about to cooperate with Benedict Arnold, even though he was unaware of the general's plans to turn over West Point. Tallmadge's dislike of him extended back many years, their paths having crossed during their (and Nathan Hale's) days at Yale. Tallmadge wrote to a friend that he had been introduced to Arnold "while I was a member of Yale College & he residing at New Haven, & I well remember that I was impressed with the belief that he was not a man of integrity. The revolutionary war was coming on soon after I left college, & Arnold engaging in it with so much zeal, and behaving so gallantly in the capture of [General] Burgoyne, we all seemed, as if by common consent, to forget his knavish tricks."[201]

Still, Tallmadge had enough of the spy in him that, when Arnold began making inquiries, the dragoon officer kept his own counsel, refusing to turn over names. Then Tallmadge received a letter from Arnold informing him that he was expecting a visitor, a Mr. James Anderson, whom Arnold noted as "a person I expect from New York."[202] Arnold requested Tallmadge to provide Anderson with a cavalry escort between the American and British lines. (John Anderson was, in fact, John André. Why André chose an alias so close to his actual name is beyond knowing, but it certainly was a poor choice for a spymaster.)

It should be said again that in the previous year Tallmadge had managed to put together one of the most successful spy rings of the entire war. By comparison, even though the British had engaged in spying long before the American war, both on the European continent and in the colonies, the British Secret Service, including the likes of Major André, rarely achieved the same level of success as its American counterpart. Perhaps the British suffered from operating a spy network as strangers in a foreign land. They ran agents, but more often relied on military scouts—army officers disguised as civilians who spied on American troops and their movements, just as General Gage had done while in Boston prior to Lexington and Concord. Unfortunately for the British, this sort of operation rarely yielded significant, long-range intelligence. The Culpers, on the other hand, managed just that, and it was something they did well.

Since no American officer—Washington, Lafayette, Howe, Tallmadge—was willing to reveal the names of the Culpers, a frustrated Arnold simply went forward with his plans to betray West Point to the British. In negotiating his treachery, he had managed to convince Major André of the necessity of the two duplicitous agents meeting face-to-face. Why André would agree to such a meeting is unclear. As the director of British intelligence in the New York region, to meet with an American traitor, especially one as high-profile as General Arnold, represented a serious breach of protocol and standard operating procedure, while offering a potentially damning security risk. Such a meeting would be complicated logistically and would likely have to include other agents, deliveries of secret coded messages, and at least one remote location—a potential safe house—where the two men could rendezvous. But André agreed nevertheless. It would prove a fatal slip.

With Arnold's price established by late August, he and André wasted little time preparing for the transfer of West Point into British hands. André and Beverley Robinson, who operated a limited Tory spy ring along the Hudson River, scheduled their meeting with Arnold for September 11, but the rendezvous was interrupted when a British gunboat fired on Arnold's river craft as he floated downriver. They laid low for a week, then Arnold sent out word again to reschedule, informing the British spy handler that General Washington was scheduled to pay a call soon to West Point. He suggested that André might be able to receive the fort's plans and, per-haps—just perhaps—capture Washington as well. A new meeting was slated for September 20.

~ ※ ~

SOMETHING BIG IN THE WIND

As Arnold and André nailed down the details of the hand-off of the West Point plans and, thus, the transfer of this strategic New York fortification system from American control to British, members of the Culper Ring were picking up a vague scent regarding something big in the wind.

Townsend saw it firsthand while strolling down to the docks in Manhattan. There, the British seemed busy in preparations, but for what? Naval personnel were fitting out ships and Culper Jr. thought they were doing so perhaps in response to the arrival of the French fleet in New Haven. Engaging in conversation with British officers in his coffeehouse, he could not find a specific thread to unravel. Several seemed vague about what was being planned. But things had been extremely quiet in New York City the previous month; the British were planning something.

Then, on September 5, Abraham Woodhull sent a report to Tallmadge informing him that the British were pulling large numbers of troops out of Setauket for reasons that were unclear. As Woodhull wrote: "For God's sake attack them, you'll certainly be successful, if you are secret about it. . . . Setauket is exceedingly distressed. Pray offer some relief."[203] Perhaps ironi-cally, both Woodhull and Tallmadge responded to the removal of Redcoats

OPPOSITE:
*A French-made map
of the fortifications at
West Point, c. 1780.*

from Setauket by considering what the move might mean for liberating their hometown, rather than asking themselves *why* the British were shifting forces out of Setauket and, thus, where those troops might be bound.

Information was swirling around the Culper Ring, but the agents were never able to attain the specifics they needed to interpret what they saw. Without hard evidence that Arnold was in the process of turning traitor, that possibility likely seemed remote, even unthinkable.

Setauket: A Town Under Occupation

Several members of the Culper Ring shared a hometown—Setauket, Long Island. The British had first entered the Setauket area during their campaign to seize New York City in the summer of 1776. In 1777, a three-hour battle between Patriots and British Redcoats had ended with few casualties and a Patriot retreat to safety in Connecticut.

Located in Suffolk County, Setauket was a tiny, but close-knit community. Several of the town's citizens were related by blood and marriage. At nearly the same time the Culper Ring was being organized, the British occupied the town. Soon, the residents were living under conditions similar to martial law. They suffered greatly at the hands of one British officer in particular, Lieutenant Colonel John Simcoe of the Queen's Rangers.

Simcoe was a terror. The dragoon commander commandeered the Townsend house for his lodgings, forcing the family into cramped quarters in the rear of their own home. Simcoe ordered their orchard cut down to provide apples for his men and wood for a fort. Other buildings around town were stripped of wood as well. In 1778, Simcoe argued with Reverend Ebenezer Prime, a local minister, and punished him by ordering his men to destroy the parson's furniture, burn his books, and ransack his church. Reverend Prime died soon thereafter.

Simcoe commanded nearly five hundred troops occupying Setauket, including German Hessians who were especially hated by the locals. He organized enforcement squads among their ranks, and anyone caught outside at night was likely to receive a public lashing at German hands.

In the spring of 1779, Simcoe had ordered his Rangers to beat Abraham Woodhull's father, after he had arrived at the Woodhull house to arrest Abraham for spying. (Simcoe had no real proof at the time and was operating on a long-shot hunch.) While the raid at the family house rattled the often-nervous Woodhull, it also provided him with one more personal reason to continue spying on the British.

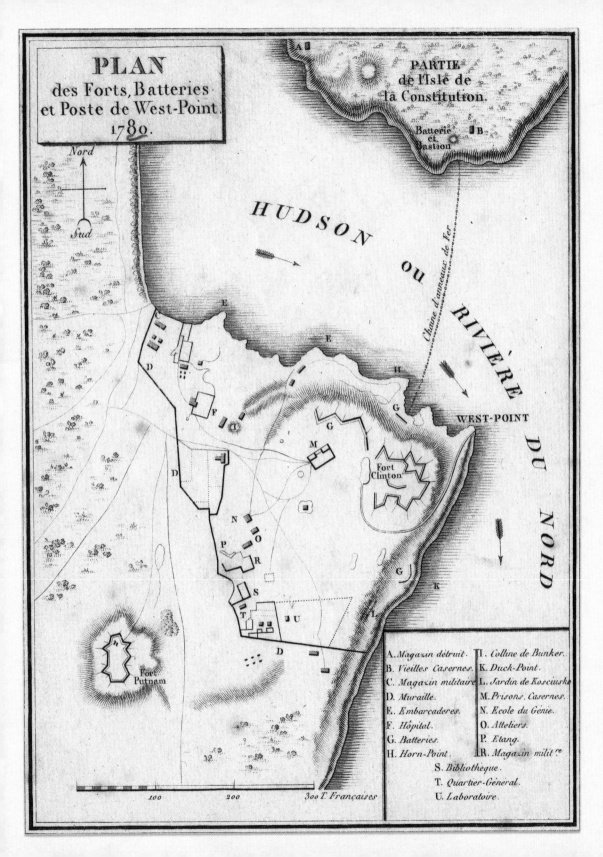

PLAN
des Forts, Batteries
et Poste de West-Point.
1780.

Nord

Sud

PARTIE
de l'Isle de
la Constitution.

Batterie
et
Bastion

HUDSON

ou

RIVIÈRE DU NORD

WEST-POINT

Chaine d'anneaux de Fer

Fort
Clinton

Fort
Putnam

A. *Magazin détruit.*	I. *Colline de Bunker.*
B. *Vieilles Casernes.*	K. *Duck-Point.*
C. *Magazin militaire.*	L. *Jardin de Kosciusko*
D. *Muraille.*	M. *Prisons, Casernes.*
E. *Embarcaderes.*	N. *Ecole du Génie.*
F. *Hôpital.*	O. *Atteliers.*
G. *Batteries.*	P. *Etang.*
H. *Horn-Point.*	R. *Magazin milit.re*

S. *Bibliotheque.*
T. *Quartier-Géneral.*
U. *Laboratoire.*

100   200   300 T. Françaises

An Unfortunate Series of Events

When the day for Arnold's handover of the plans for West Point arrived, it did not go smoothly. Nearly everything that could have gone wrong managed to do just that. André and Robinson were delivered upriver onboard the HMS *Vulture*, but failed to meet up with Arnold that night. The next day, André did make contact with a cutout Arnold had sent. Strangely, André was still dressed in his uniform, even though his plan was to claim he was a merchant on business. He was then delivered ashore on the west bank of the Hudson, near Haverstraw, New York. Here, Arnold met the British major and the two men discussed the layout of West Point and its strength as a military outpost. As the sun inched above the horizon that morning—September 22—the conspirators moved to the safe house of Arnold's accomplice, Joshua Smith.

It was here that André finally realized that he had passed through the American lines—still dressed in his regimental uniform. As Arnold prepared to leave, he handed André the papers the British military had bargained for so desperately—plans for West Point, including artillery maps and drawings of the fortress, along with a pass issued by Arnold to allow André to pass through the American zone and across the no-man's-land border separating the British and American dividing lines. André closely studied the drawings, memorized them, then tried to hand them back to Arnold. But the American traitor was too concerned that he might not receive his payment for his treason, so he forced André to retain the papers as evidence of a completed deal. Knowing the risk he was taking as an intelligence agent, André hesitated, but placed the incriminating papers in his boots.

André then shed his uniform and donned a disguise, one that included a bluish-purple coat and large-brimmed, round civilian hat. Smith was to remain with André until nightfall, then sneak him the six miles back to the spot along the Hudson where the *Vulture* would be waiting to pick him up.

However, André would never reconnoiter with the British gunboat. Before Arnold and André parted, they heard cannon fire along the Hudson, in the direction of the *Vulture*. An American patrol had spotted the British craft and opened fire with a howitzer, sending the British vessel downriver a dozen miles. André had lost his much-needed contact. Getting back through

American lines would be tricky, now that the *Vulture* was out of the picture. It was out of the question that he might commandeer a rowboat and paddle downstream for eighteen miles, so it was decided that André, Smith, and a black servant would ride through the back roads on horseback to Verplanck's Point, then cross the river, and ride until André reached British lines.

But the plan did not go accordingly. Along the way, André and his associates were stopped by an American sentry who warned them not to travel farther south to the British perimeter, since the area was thick with irregulars, gangs supporting both sides, including Tory "Cowboys" and Patriot "Skinners." The men stayed the night near the sentry post and the next morning—September 23—Arnold's man Smith handed André $40 to help him on his way, then bade him farewell. With British lines at White Plains only fifteen miles away, André started on his way fairly certain that he had achieved an intelligence coup that would be unmatched by any other for the remainder of the war.

But early that morning, around 9:30, the road for Major André reached its end. Three American militiamen—John Paulding, Isaac Van Wart, and David Williams—spotted the oddly dressed André emerging from bushes along the road, and they raised their muskets at the stranger. Why André did not present his pass from Arnold is an unanswerable question. The militiamen would likely have let him go immediately. (Even if André's opponents were Tory "Cowboys," they would have arrested the British agent and the matter would have been eventually sorted out at White Plains where he could prove his identity. But he did not.) Perhaps André was misled by the old British redcoat one of the men wore, the major stating: "My lads, I hope you belong to our party." Paulding then put the obvious question to his captive: Which side is that? When André answered, "the lower," he was doomed.[204]

Realizing they had captured a British sympathizer, the three men ordered André to dismount, as he blustered that he was "an officer in the British service on particular business in the country."[205] When André belatedly thought of showing Arnold's pass, it was too late. His cover was blown, and, when the men began frisking him for money—the capture devolved into a simple mugging in quick order—the freebooting Patriots made the fateful discovery of incriminating papers in his boots. As one of the men would testify later: "I searched his person effectually, but found nothing until I pulled off his boot, when we discovered that something was concealed

in his stocking . . . I pulled off his stocking, and inside of it, next to the sole of his foot, found three half sheets of paper enclosed in another half sheet which was endorsed 'West Point'; and on pulling off the other boot and stocking, I found three like paper."[206] Finally understanding the import of the prisoner they had in their possession, one shouted out: "This is a spy!"[207]

Soon, the path of Major André crossed that of a Culper Ring member directly. The militiamen hauled André to a nearby American sentry post, where "Mr. Anderson" was expected, per Arnold's orders, but hardly under such circumstances. Soon, the captured papers were on their way to General Washington and André—as Anderson—was sent to West Point. After all, General Arnold would want to be informed of the capture of a British agent! In the meantime, Major Benjamin Tallmadge was present at another American outpost not far away, where he was informed that "Mr. Anderson" had been captured and trundled off to Arnold. The suspicious spy handler felt something was fishy, and he sent out an order for "Anderson" to be delivered to him directly.

When André and Tallmadge faced one another, it was the American espionage officer who held the upper hand. André attempted to distance himself from the accusation of his being a spy, insisting he was a simple

The Mystery and Myth of Agent 355

One of the most enigmatic members of the Secret Six was the only female, the one whose codename "Agent 355" merely referred to the word in Tallmadge's code system for "lady." Why was her name not listed in the code as the other members were? We may never know. Perhaps because they believed she was not a full-fledged member or her contributions were not significant enough. After all, Agent 355 is only mentioned one time in the ring's correspondence, in a coded report sent to General Washington.

Possibly the members of the Culper Ring were intent on protecting her identity, because she was the only woman in the group. As a female, her risks were likely unique. Or maybe she was so strategically placed within the highest of social circles in Manhattan that she would have been completely ruined if her identity were known to her social peers.

One story about Agent 355 has been found to be completely ungrounded. During the 1920s, while researching the Culper group, Long Island historian Morton Pennypacker uncovered the names of some of the members of the group, names that had remained shrouded in mystery for nearly 150 years. During the 1940s, Pennypacker began relating a strange, previously untold tale of Agent 355 having a child by Robert Townsend (Culper Jr.). As the story continued, the female member of the ring was exposed, her identity revealed, she was subsequently arrested and was placed on a prison ship where she died giving birth. In the meantime, her child, also named Robert Townsend, lived and was eventually elected to the New York State Legislature.

Half a century later, this story was disproven. Historians came to believe that the child allegedly born to Agent 355 and Robert Townsend was, instead, the offspring of an affair between Townsend and his housekeeper. In fact, the child in question was not born until after the Revolutionary War was concluded.

So, who was Agent 355? Whether she was Anna Strong, who hung out her laundry at her hilltop home in Setauket, leaving a coded message for Caleb Brewster; a high-placed Manhattan socialite, or someone else, the truth is that the historians do not agree, and her real identity may remain as it has for more than two centuries—a mystery.

merchant, but his constant pacing and bearing—the Culper Ring handler wrote later that "as soon as I saw Anderson and especially after I saw him walk (as he did almost constantly) across the floor, I became impressed with the belief that he had been *bred to arms*"[208]—told Tallmadge he was dealing with a British officer. For a while, the captured British agent remained emphatic in his denial of being a spy.[209] But, soon, realizing his predicament, André then wrote a letter for General Washington's eyes only, which revealed to Tallmadge the name of his prisoner, one the Secret Six member knew all too well—Major John André, Adjutant-General to the British Army.[210]

Back at West Point, Benedict Arnold soon realized his treason was already catching up with him. He received a report that "Mr. Anderson" had been captured and that he had been carrying incriminating papers. With General Washington due any minute for an inspection of the West Point facilities, Arnold wasted no time making his escape. Washington soon arrived—this was on the evening of September 24—along with his aide, Alexander Hamilton, and he was irritated that Arnold was not present to greet him. Writing later, Washington noted: "The impropriety of his conduct when he knew I was to be there struck me very forcibly, and my mind misgave me; but I had not the least idea of the real cause."[211] The American commander soon understood everything. He was made aware of André's capture, was handed the incriminating documents, and only then realized the import of the information—that one of his favorite officers, General Benedict Arnold, was a traitor. Washington is said to have exclaimed: "Great Arnold has stolen off to the enemy!"[212] Although he immediately dispatched Hamilton in search of Arnold, he knew he was too late. Only then did Washington's shock give way to disappointment, as he went off to a room to be alone and erupted in an "uncontrollable burst of feeling."[213] Prior to that agonizing moment, none of his officers had ever witnessed George Washington weeping.

The following day, the head of the Culper Ring delivered the head of British intelligence in New York to General Washington's headquarters, then located at Tappan, New York. By accounts, the ride Tallmadge and André shared was pleasant, as the two men talked with one another, leading the American spy to later note that he "never saw a man whose fate I foresaw, whom I so sincerely pitied. He is a young fellow of the greatest accomplishments. . . . He has unbosomed his heart to me, and indeed, let me know almost every motive of his actions so fully since he came out on his late mission that he has endeared himself to me exceedingly. Unfortunate man!"[214]

During their ride to meet Washington, André queried Tallmadge concerning his possible fate. The Culper Ring leader answered firmly and clearly, reminding André of another captured spy from earlier in the war, Nathan Hale, with whom Tallmadge had shared a youthful friendship. André did remember Hale, and Tallmadge then said: "Do you remember the sequel of this story; 'Yes,' said André; 'he was hanged as a spy; but you surely do not consider his case & mine alike.' I replied, 'precisely similar, and similar will be your fate!' He endeavored to answer my remarks, but it was manifest he was more troubled than I had ever seen him before.[215]

(Recalling this conversation as an eighty-year-old veteran, Tallmadge may have embellished, or even fictionalized, this particular exchange. As André was a prisoner in Philadelphia at the time of Hale's arrest in New York, it is unlikely he had any memory of the young Connecticut spy.)

Strange Bedfellows

In late 1775, John André and several other captured British officers were being delivered to Philadelphia where they were to be paroled. He and the others had been taken prisoner during the Siege of Fort St. Jean (September–November, 1775). One evening, with a fierce snowstorm howling around New York's Lake George, the prisoners stayed at a local inn for the night. The twentysomething André shared a bed with a rather large gentleman, one who easily tipped the scales somewhere well above three hundred pounds. The ferocity of the storm kept the strange bedfellows awake much of the night, and they passed the time sharing a lengthy conversation.

The next morning, each man rose to don his respective uniform. Only then did they realize they represented two different sides of the war. André had spent the night with Colonel Henry Knox, a former Boston bookstore owner who was self-trained in artillery. Knox was at that time engaged in hauling cannon from the captured British Fort Ticonderoga to Boston to aid Washington in removing General Gage from the city.

What neither officer could then know was that, five years later, Henry Knox would sit on the tribunal of Washington's officers in judgment of John André for his role in Benedict Arnold's defection to the British.

Regardless of the story's veracity, André's fate was destined to mirror that of Nathan Hale, and other spies captured on both sides during the American Revolutionary War. In the few days that followed, a trial was held, one convened by Washington. As several of His Excellency's officers listened, André pleaded his innocence, claiming he was a prisoner of war, not a spy. But the tribunal was unmoved. By September 29, André was a condemned man. He then penned a letter to his commander, General Henry Clinton, in which he claimed "I am perfectly and tranquil in mind and prepared for any Fate to which an honest Zeal for my Kings Service may have devoted me."[216]

Major André's sentence was carried out on October 2. He made a request beforehand that he be executed by firing squad, rather than by hanging. His request was summarily denied. The day of his hanging, André climbed on top of his own coffin, which rested in the back of a horse-drawn cart painted black. As the hangman prepared to place the noose around the British spy's neck, André took the rope from him and did it himself. Then, he took a handkerchief and draped it over his eyes. An American officer assisting in the hanging asked André if he had any final words. He did: "Only that you all bear witness that I die like a soldier and a brave man."[217]

The moment had arrived, and, against the reverberations of beating drums, the hangman delivered a whip to the horse team, the cart slipped out from under André, and he fell toward earth, his neck breaking immediately.

Following the execution, he was cut down from the scaffolding and buried at that very location, under the same tree from which he had dangled. His body rested peacefully in the ground for forty years, but his remains were eventually exhumed and moved to a grander setting, that of Westminster Abbey, with all the honors of war.

Even as young Major André, co-conspirator in Benedict Arnold's duplicitous treason, swung from a gallows outside Tappan, New York, the American traitor was already behind British lines, stowed away on a ship in New York City, contemplating his next move. He was fighting for the British now. As for the members of the Culper Ring, they could rest easy that the head of British intelligence in New York had been removed from any further operations. What they did not know with certainty was whether Arnold knew their names and could compromise them further.

～ ※ ～

CHAPTER NINE

The Traitor
Benedict Arnold

FEARS CONCERNING ARNOLD

PREVIOUS PAGE:
Thomas Hart's painting
Colonel Arnold Who
Commanded the
Provincial Troops
Sent Against Quebec,
through the Wilderness
of Canada and was
Wounded in that
City, Under General
Montgomery, *1776.*

ith Benedict Arnold's deceptions and his defection to the British in September 1780, the members of the Culper Ring found themselves in a high state of anxiety. Each was uncertain as to what Arnold knew of their operations.

The fact that Arnold and André's plans had been thwarted did not mean the British were through with the American general. Arnold was commissioned as a British brigadier general, and one of his first post–West Point objectives was to uncover as much of Washington's spy network as he could manage. Somehow he determined that Hercules Mulligan had connections to the Secret Six, and he had him arrested and held for a time. But evidence against Mulligan was scant to nonexistent, so he had to let him go free.

Tallmadge was certainly made aware of the concerns of his agents, and he sent a report on the subject to Washington dated October 11. During the previous two weeks following André's capture, the Culper Ring nearly went dormant, not wanting to draw attention to itself or even to make contact with potentially compromised subagents, such as Mulligan. Tallmadge wrote:

> *The conduct of Arnold, since his arrival at N.Y. has been such, that though he knows not a single link in the chain of my correspondence, still those who have assisted us in this way, are at present too apprehensive of Danger to give their immediate usual intelligence. I hope as the tumult subsides matters will go on in their old channels.*
>
> *Culper, Junr. has requested an interview with me on Long Island on the 13th inst[ant], but in the present situation of affairs I believe it would be rather imprudent.*[218]

Given the circumstances, with Arnold representing a wild card, Washington understood that the work of the Culpers would need to be shelved for the time being.

Townsend seems to have been the agent among the Secret Six most concerned about exposure. After all, he was operating out of New York City, a location that typically made him the linchpin of the Culper Ring's efforts and the agent most directly under the nose of the British command. Washington was disappointed when Townsend almost completely shut down operations in late September and early October, but, by midmonth, as he noted in a letter dated on the 15th to Samuel Huntington, then-president of the Continental Congress, he had his hopes:

"Unluckily, the person in whom I have the greatest confidence is afraid to take any measures for communicating with me just at this time, as he is apprehensive that Arnold may possibly have some knowledge of the connection, and may have him watched. But as he is assured, that Arnold has not the most distant hint of him, I expect soon to hear from him as usual."[219]

In fact, Washington had to wait longer than he liked for Townsend to feel the coast was clear—literally—for him to resume his intelligence gathering. Even as late as mid-November, Townsend was still avoiding service with the Culper Ring. Woodhull wrote a letter to Tallmadge on November 12 indicating that Townsend was quite depressed about the situation in New York City, where "[s]everal of our dear friends were imprisoned, in particular one that hath been ever serviceable to this correspondence. This step so dejected the spirits of C. Junr. that he resolved to leave New York for a time."[220] Woodhull also reported that Brewster had recently been chased across the sound and nearly captured. These were dark times for the Secret Six.

To whom, exactly, Woodhull was referring in this letter—"several of our dear friends"—as having been "imprisoned" is unknown. Obviously, they were closely associated with Townsend. But the identities remain a mystery. Townsend became so gravely depressed and anxious over being exposed that he even left his businesses in other hands and went to Long Island for several weeks. While Townsend did not completely drop out of the Culper Ring during the winter of 1780–81, he did little on behalf of the intelligence operation until spring. In the meantime, Woodhull continued to feed information to Washington as he could and, in late November, Tallmadge and Brewster engaged in a raid on a British outpost operating outside Fairfield, Connecticut, as part of the so-called "Whaleboat War." The Culpers were down that winter, but they were not out.

An Awkward Encounter

Following his failed attempt to kidnap Benedict Arnold in late 1780, Sergeant John Champe left military service at Washington's insistence, even though he would have preferred to retain his place among General "Light-Horse Harry" Lee's dragoons.

After the war, a curious encounter took place when a lost traveler showed up unexpectedly at Champe's farm door in Loudon County, Virginia. The night was dark and stormy, with lightning flashing across the sky, and Champe's small house was the first the visitor had seen in many miles. Hearing a knock on the door, Champe unlatched it and suddenly two men who had once known one another stood face-to-face.

The visitor was Angus Cameron, a Scot who had served in Benedict Arnold's unit when Champe, an alleged deserter from Lee's ranks, had been recruited in. Cameron's last memory of Champe was that he had deserted a second time, but from Arnold's ranks. As Cameron wrote later, "Sergeant Champe stood before me,"[221] and for a desperate moment he was uncertain how he would be received.

He need not have worried, for as he recognized Champe, so Champe recognized him and offered up a hearty greeting: "Welcome, welcome, Captain Cameron, a thousand times welcome to my roof."[222] Champe had thought well of Cameron while he served under him and, of all Arnold's men to show up unannounced, none could have satisfied him more than Cameron.

That evening, the former Sergeant Champe explained all to the former Captain Cameron, and the next morning the two men bade one another well.

WASHINGTON SEEKS REVENGE

Few events that Washington experienced as commander of the Continental Army hit him harder than the defection of Benedict Arnold to the enemy. With Arnold posing a threat to his spy network, and given his anger at being deceived by an officer he had supported when others were not inclined to trust him, Washington decided to go on the offensive. Rather than wait for Arnold to commit further damage in the name of his British collaborators, he decided to have him tracked down and kidnapped. Washington wanted Arnold to pay for his treason, and the idea of having him brought before his former commander to account for himself gave the American general some hope for revenge and ultimate justice.

ABOVE:
Currier & Ives'
**The Escape of Sergeant
Champe**, *c. 1876.*

Washington threw the responsibility for the kidnapping to a fellow Virginian, Major Henry "Light-Horse Harry" Lee—he would one day father the famed Confederate general Robert E. Lee—one of his best cavalry commanders. Based on Washington's own plan, Lee recruited a new spy for the operation, one John Champe, a Continental Army sergeant. Champe was a fellow Virginian, as described in Lee's future memoirs, one who was "rather above the common size, full of bone and muscle, with a saturnine countenance, grave thoughtful and taciturn—of tried courage and inflexible perseverance," a description that leaves one with an imposing impression.[223] The twenty-three-year-old Champe volunteered for the mission to capture Arnold, asking nothing but a promotion in rank for his special services.

The plan was based on a simple deception. Champe was to pretend to be a deserter from Lee's Second Partisan Corps and, in the style of Arnold, add his name to the ranks of the British army. He was to then claim Arnold's defection was his inspiration and that he would like to meet his hero in the flesh. Once that happened, Champe was to kidnap Arnold and then deliver him to designated agents waiting in New Jersey. It was of utmost importance Arnold be taken alive. The general emphasized this point in a letter to Lee dated October 20: "No circumstance whatever shall obtain my consent to his being put to death. The idea which would accompany such an event would be that Ruffians had been hired to assassinate him. My aim is to make a public example of him, and this should be strongly impressed upon those who are employed to bring him off."[224]

The secret plan was set in motion in late October 1780. To provide cover for Champe's defection to the British, Lee provided him with documents the sergeant was to have "stolen." He was then to desert on horseback, with Lee waiting a decent interval before alerting Champe's fellow dragoons of their comrade's "treachery." But no sooner had Champe lit out from Lee's encampment than he was spotted by a patrol just a half mile down the road. Champe spurred his horse with his fellow cavalrymen on his tail. Giving them the slip on a fresh horse, Champe escaped, but his confused comrades returned to their camp to inform Lee that one of his own had likely deserted. Lee tried to put off ordering another dragoon unit to chase after Champe, but after stalling for an hour or so, he finally gave the command. Unable to warn his undercover operative, Lee knew that Champe was on his own.

Even if Champe understood that another unit of his fellow cavalrymen would likely soon be on his tail, he could not exactly gallop through the countryside toward the British without raising additional suspicion. The second patrol nearly caught up with him, but he managed to reach Paulus Hook, the site of a British fortification hugging the New Jersey shoreline, a key locale guarding the entrance to New York Harbor. With his pursuers less than a mile behind him, spurring their horses toward their deserting comrade, Champe threw off all extra weight—including his coat, sword, and other nonessentials—to lighten his horse's load, hastily pulled up short at the shore, and hit the ground running, calling toward a pair of

British ships anchored a mile away. With one of his pursuers having also dismounted and only two hundred yards away, Champe jumped into the water and began a frantic swim toward the British. From the ships, roused Redcoats fired at the American dragoons to ward them away.

Believing they had the latest American deserter on their hands, the British delivered an exhausted Champe into the city where he was given an audience with General Clinton. As Champe told his hair-raising story, Clinton was intrigued. The sergeant represented only the second man to ever desert Lee's command, so Clinton saw the possibilities in dampening American morale. Clinton then did exactly what Washington's plan had called for—the commander sent Champe to see General Arnold, who took an immediate liking to a fellow American deserter, and in short order recruited him into a new unit he was forming, its ranks filled with Loyalists and American deserters, called the "American Legion."

During the following weeks, Champe watched Arnold closely, noting his comings and goings, monitoring how the general regularly took a late-night walk in the garden outside his house before retiring. Champe saw his opportunity. The agent made contact with two operatives whose names Lee had given him, informing them to send word to Lee to have a boat and a unit of dragoons ready on a designated night—December 21—when he would kidnap Arnold. It would be simple: Champe and one of his contacts would sneak into the garden, coldcock Arnold, gag him, then haul his body down to the river where a boat would be waiting. Then, Champe and his fellow dragoons would bring the traitor Arnold to Lee, then to Washington.

The night of the planned kidnapping came, and General Lee delivered his men to the New Jersey side of the Hudson River with three spare horses in tow—one for Champe, one for Arnold, and one for Champe's accomplice. But the Americans waited as "hour after hour passed, [and] no boat approached" from the New York side.[225] As luck would have things, Arnold had chosen to order his men and their mounts onto a ship bound for Virginia where he intended to launch a cavalry assault on Richmond. Champe was, of course, caught up in the movement, unable to warn Lee what was transpiring. Arnold was not to be kidnapped, and Champe now had to desert for real from his British company and escape

A Possible Fate for Benedict Arnold

After Benedict Arnold's desertion to the British, he formed a new unit of Tories and deserters and was transferred south to harass George Washington's native state of Virginia. Soon, Arnold's forces were rampaging Virginia and even managed to attack Richmond, setting the capital on fire.

On one occasion, General Arnold was questioning a captured American captain and asked him tauntingly: "What do you think would be my fate if my misguided countrymen were to take me prisoner?" The captain responded without missing a beat, handing Arnold's attitude right to him: "They would cut off the leg that was wounded at Saratoga and bury it with the honors of war, and the rest of you they would hang on a gibbet."[226]

back to New Jersey. Months would pass before he found his way back to Washington's headquarters, where he arrived worn out and heavily bearded. Through no fault of his own, Champe had simply chosen the wrong night to seize Arnold. When Champe did return, Washington chose to discharge him from all service, fearing his life might be endangered, even as Champe protested.

Despite the failure of his first plot to capture Benedict Arnold, Washington recruited another would-be kidnapper, one of his New Jersey intelligence agents. Allen McLane was sent to Virginia where Arnold was based, in and around Richmond, the capital, in March 1781, under disguise as a local farmer. McLane carried out reconnaissance for several weeks, from an advanced American signal station along the James River, observing, as had Champe, that General Arnold was a man of habits. Just as he had taken nightly walks in his garden in New York, so too did the American deserter take morning horseback rides out of his post along the banks of Chesapeake Bay. McLane made plans to capture Arnold on one of these rides, but, alas, the plot failed again. Just prior to the attempted kidnapping, British warships appeared in the bay within sight of the planned abduction point, so McLane called it off. The intrepid McLane may have failed on this mission, but he had already proven valuable to Washington for years as a spy, and his greatest intelligence coup was still months ahead of him.

Yet another attempt was planned for the abduction of Benedict Arnold, this one at the hands of then-governor of Virginia, Thomas Jefferson. With Arnold cutting back and forth across Virginia on raids, he represented a specific threat to the Commonwealth. A scheme was put together, but little came of it. Arnold was simply too slippery, too inaccessible for anyone to get close enough to capture. He remained in the field, fighting for the British, through the remainder of the war and, with the final British defeat, he left America permanently for England. Due to the leg wound he received during the fighting at Saratoga, New York, in 1777, Arnold walked with a cane for the rest of his life. He died June 14, 1801, following four days of delirium, at the age of 60.

Cato, the Black Courier Who Would Not Talk

Hercules Mulligan proved to be one of the most effective subagents to work with the Culper Ring. Washington would eventually visit Mulligan at his clothing shop and make purchases from him, a sign that the clandestine agent was respected and appreciated by the general. As with other Culper agents, Mulligan tried to keep a degree of separation between himself and the Culpers, so he relied on Cato, one of his black servants. Cato worked as a courier, delivering messages to and from Mulligan. Although the British typically considered black servants as little threat, during one mission, Cato found himself in real jeopardy.

While delivering a report, he was intercepted by British officials who became suspicious of his movements in the New York area. He was eventually arrested, and the British tried to beat a confession out of him.

But Cato proved unbreakable, as he did not surrender information about the ring, even though his beating was quite severe. Following the beating, British authorities clapped Cato in jail. Fortunately Mulligan was able to wield significant influence, and he facilitated Cato's release. After that experience, Cato decided to call an end to his days as a courier.

Lafayette, He Is Here (to Capture Arnold)

As Washington ordered troops to march south to capture General Cornwallis at Yorktown in the fall of 1781, those forces included units under the command of the young, aristocratic French commander, General Lafayette. As he prepared to send Lafayette on his way south, Washington gave him secondary orders—to try and capture Benedict Arnold. Where others had failed, perhaps the French commander might succeed.

To that end, twenty-three-year-old Lafayette dispatched a Virginia slave named James Armistead behind British lines to find Arnold. (Armistead had joined Lafayette's unit after he was granted permission by his owner.) The newly recruited agent did manage to find Arnold's headquarters, where he claimed to be an escaped slave, one ready to serve the British in exchange for his freedom. The British took him on and turned him into a spy, not realizing this would actually turn Armistead into a double agent.

Lafayette planted false information on Armistead and sent him back to the British. There, the Virginia slave-spy turned a wadded-up piece of paper over to British officials, one that indicated that some American troops were in the process of marching south to join with Lafayette. This was just one more piece of disinformation the Americans created to confuse and mislead the enemy.

As for Arnold, he, once again, managed to give American agents the slip. He later surfaced in Connecticut where he engaged in the same type of depredations he had carried out in Virginia, including raids and setting ablaze warehouses, ships, and a great deal of New London, Connecticut.

RIGHT:

A certificate from the Marquis de Lafayette honoring James Armistead Lafayette's service as a double agent for the Continental Army.

WASHINGTON'S NEW PLAN

By 1781, the British were tiring of their war with America. Throughout the early years of the conflict, much of the action had centered in the North, in Boston, New York City, and Philadelphia, and across states including Pennsylvania, New Jersey, and New York. The British had anticipated that, once they captured the major cities, the Americans would capitulate. However, this strategy had not panned out. Controlling cities never translated into ultimate victory.

In late 1778, General Henry Clinton had shifted the focus of the war to the South, believing large numbers of Loyalists would provide needed manpower and help bring down the rebels. (Clinton did not sail south himself, though, until late 1779, deciding to remain in the comfort of New York City.) Savannah fell almost immediately, even though Charleston managed to hold out until the spring of 1780. At that point, Clinton returned to New York City, never venturing into the South again. When he arrived back in New York, the British commander placed a capable, experienced general in command in the field—Charles Cornwallis. His army numbered eight thousand, and they were reinforced by thousands of Loyalists.

Through 1780, Cornwallis and his men experienced alternating victories and defeats. August brought a significant win against General Horatio Gates, the hero of Saratoga, deep within rural South Carolina at Camden. Washington soon replaced the unreliable Gates—the general had abandoned the battlefield in the midst of the fight, leaving on horseback and surfacing in Charlotte, North Carolina, some sixty miles away—with an effective and skilled commander, General Nathanael Greene. In October, Greene's men defeated a portion of Cornwallis's army and a large number of Loyalists at King's Mountain, a site situated near the South Carolina–North Carolina border. Another American win unfolded in January 1781 at Cowpens, a few dozen miles west of King's Mountain. The victory was thanks to Brigadier General Daniel Morgan and his Virginia riflemen who carried deadly accurate Kentucky long rifles. (Lining up British officers in their sights and picking them off one by one was their specialty.)

Although Cornwallis gained a victory in March at Guilford Court House in central North Carolina, all these battles were leading to the same conclusion: the war in the South was one of attrition. Cornwallis, despite winning some battles, was running out of Redcoat troops and his lines were not receiving an equivalent number of Loyalists to fill the gaps. Believing his days in the South were numbered, Cornwallis made a fateful decision, one that infuriated Clinton—he marched to Wilmington, North Carolina, and from there, continued north toward Virginia, finally reaching a tiny tobacco port called Yorktown.

A Gap in Security

During the summer of 1781, General Washington kept a tight lid on any and all information regarding his plans to march south to capture Cornwallis at Yorktown, rather than advance on New York City as Clinton and his commanders anticipated. Fortunately, security proved airtight, allowing Washington and his men to march toward Virginia without warning. Well, almost airtight.

One person in the know actually did spill his information to another. He was none other than General Rochambeau's son, who served as a colonel in the French commander's forces. The son told his girlfriend many of the details concerning the planned march on Yorktown and that they would reconnoiter with French warships once arriving in Virginia. What Colonel Rochambeau did not know was that his girlfriend was a field agent for the British—and one of their best.

However, when she reported her intelligence to General Clinton, he was incredulous, believing so fervently that Washington must be planning to attack New York City that he discounted her claim altogether and failed to take any steps that might have blocked Washington's southern march to Yorktown and ultimate victory

ALL EYES ON CORNWALLIS

Even as Cornwallis arrived in Yorktown, where he would remain for much of 1781, the Americans wasted little time gathering intelligence on him and his forces. Leading the pack was a Continental Army colonel named James Innis, a native Virginian, who created his own limited spy network. His agents helped to observe the movements of Cornwallis's forces as they situated themselves along both sides of the York River. Civilian agents even crossed British lines disguised as peddlers, merchants, and other tradesmen ready to sell anything the British army might need. They returned to Innis with intelligence, which he collected and passed on. Although none of his reports still exists—as far as is known—he was credited later for the quality of his agents' information.

Once Cornwallis reached Yorktown, the end of the war was nearly set, and a British defeat was soon in the offing. Here, the typical history written concerning the steps taken by General Washington and his French counterpart, Comte de Rochambeau, tells of Washington wanting to attack New York City, with French military and naval support, as the combined armies would be large enough to challenge the British in the city. The usual version of events also says that in early June Rochambeau ordered De Grasse's French fleet to Virginia toward Cornwallis's army instead. Rochambeau believed New York, after years of British occupation, would be too heavily fortified—too tough a nut to crack—and that Cornwallis and Yorktown offered greater potential for a decisive victory. A diary entry of Washington's, dated August 14, 1781, even seems to confirm this interpretation of events: "Matters having now come to a crisis and a decisive plan to be determined on, I was obliged . . . to give up all idea of attacking New York, and instead thereof to remove the French Troops and a detachment from the American Army to the Head of the Elk (River) to be transported to Virginia for the purpose of co-operating with the force from the West Indies against the Troops in that State."[227]

Accordingly, on September 5, the French fleet engaged an inferior British squadron at the entrance to Chesapeake Bay, in the Battle of the Capes. The British were sent scurrying back to New York, leaving Cornwallis trapped and defenseless, which allowed American and French forces to surround him on an isolated peninsula near the Virginia coast by the end of September. The following month would deliver victory for Washington and his allies.

While some of this scenario actually did take place, a few facts do not exactly reflect reality. What is usually left out is the real backstory, the intelligence operation based on deception that General George Washington carried out, an operation that stretched back nearly a year prior to the October Battle of Yorktown.

In fact, by 1780, George Washington had no intention of storming New York City with his French counterparts and driving Clinton out of the boroughs. In 1788, in a letter to writer Noah Webster, who is remembered today for his early version of an American dictionary, Washington explained his true strategy:

> *It was determined by me (nearly twelve months before-hand) at all hazards to give out and cause it to be believed by the highest military as well as civil Officers that New York was the destined place of attack, for the important purpose of inducing the Eastern and Middle States to make greater exertions in furnishing specific supplies than they otherwise would have done, as well as for the interesting purpose of rendering the enemy less prepared elsewhere . . .*

> *I only add that it never was in contemplation to attack New York, unless the Garrison should first have been so far disgarnished to carry on the southern operations, as to render our success in the siege of that place as infallible as any future military event can ever be made.*

> *That much trouble was taken and finesse used to mis-guide and bewilder Sir Henry Clinton in regard to the real object, by fictitious communications, as well as by making a deceptive provision of Ovens, Forage and Boats in his neighborhood, is certain. Nor were less pains taken to deceive our own Army; for I had always conceived, when the imposition did not completely take place at home, it could never sufficiently succeed abroad.*[228]

The import of Washington's letter, written years after the war, is that the commander of the Continental Army and a handful of others spun a complicated web of subterfuge, deception, and misinformation, aimed not only at confusing the British, but also misdirecting his own troops, all in the name of keeping his ultimate goal a secret. Never in the course of the entire war would Washington go to such elaborate lengths to surround his intentions with a veil of secrecy. Among those who provided support for his plans were several intelligence agents, including some of the members of the Culper Ring. Security was so tight regarding his intentions, it is likely that, even today, historians have not yet put together all of the puzzle pieces of Washington's deception, even as many salient details are known.

One of Washington's concerns about the Yorktown operation related to British counterintelligence operations. That they had spies everywhere went without saying, but it would only take one double agent to sink the entire plan. Thus, Washington moved cautiously. By early 1780, the first bit of intelligence reached Clinton indicating the supposed American plans to attack New York City once the French fleet arrived; this was delivered by a British agent operating in Connecticut. But the significant avalanche of reports began in early 1781. In early February, Dr. John Halliburton, a British agent in Newport, Rhode Island, reported to Clinton that French troops were on the move and headed south. Unfortunately for the British, the courier who delivered the message was a double agent named Caleb Bruen, who conveniently left out the intelligence regarding French troop movements. Later in February, Clinton was "disinformed" that the Americans were attempting to set up a new intelligence operation in New York City, an effort led by Colonial Elias Dayton, one of Washington's intelligence chiefs in New Jersey. Everything Washington did was meant to keep Clinton focused on New York.

In March, a double agent codenamed "Hiram" (his real name was William Heron) sent a report to Clinton saying that the French were, indeed, *not* on the move in any direction. The American commander who fed him the information knew Hiram was working both sides, and the intelligence he handed the British spy was meant to give Clinton the wrong picture.

Washington upped the ante in April, setting a situation in motion whereby the British would catch an American courier carrying supposedly sensitive intelligence claiming Washington still intended to target New York City. This established even firmer in Clinton's mind the idea that New York was Washington's target.

In early May, General Clinton's agents intercepted additional intelligence, all fed to the British to disinform, that the French troops were moving out of Rhode Island and headed to newly prepared encampment sites in the hills outside New York City. The information alarmed Clinton to the point that he sent messages to Cornwallis, who was in Virginia by then, to deliver some of his forces to New York to augment Clinton's men. Through yet another ingenious feint, in late May, documents were allowed to fall into the hands of a British operative named James Moody. The captured intelligence detailed an alleged meeting between Washington and Rochambeau (the information forwarded to generals John Sullivan and Lafayette), stating emphatically that the Americans and French had agreed to attack New York. In some of the papers, to make the information more plausible, Washington had inserted personal information about himself, since he was making contact with fellow officers with whom he shared private relationships, including that the general was having trouble with his false teeth.

For months, Washington fed such information to Clinton, and the British general took the bait with little suspicion. He believed Washington was planning to attack New York City and these documents only provided proof positive that his hunch was correct.

At times, General Washington himself acted as a field agent of sorts. By August, he sent American troops from New Jersey to New York's Staten Island. Washington was there as well, and he even met with a local farmer he knew to be a Tory to question him about the island's geography, telling the local resident that he must not repeat any information to the British, as the plans underway should be viewed with "the most profound Secrecy."[229] Washington did not have to guess that the local Loyalist would waste little time telling the British everything he knew.

As Clinton sifted through intelligence reports, all roads appeared to lead to New York City. Washington left no stone unturned to convince Clinton. He actually did send several hundred troops toward the city in

August to test the strength of perimeter defense lines. He ordered supplies to be stockpiled at Trenton and Princeton, over in New Jersey. Given such efforts, it seems Washington's deception could not possibly have failed to impress. By the end of August, Clinton had his men hunkered down in New York, with no intention of budging or heading south to provide support for Cornwallis. By the time Washington, Rochambeau, and Admiral de Grasse moved in unison toward Yorktown, it was too late for Clinton to do anything strategic. He had simply been outfoxed and outspied.

Even members of the Culper Ring became involved in the activities that pointed toward Yorktown. No sooner had the Americans opened the siege against the small tobacco port and headquarters of Cornwallis's army, than a valuable piece of information fell into the hands of the Secret Six through the efforts of Washington's agent, Allan McLane. Washington had dispatched McLane to Long Island to collect any actionable intelligence he could regarding British plans to move troops, ships, or both in response to Washington's moves. In particular, he was assigned to discover, if possible, the British navy's code signals. If such information could be routed to the French navy, then, theoretically, any flag instruction sent up during a fight by a British naval commander could be interpreted and responded to immediately, even peremptorily. The possibilities of McLane discovering such information were highly unlikely. However, sometimes miracles do happen.

During McLane's time on Long Island, he was directed to make contact with James Rivington, who was still doing business on Manhattan's East Side, printing newspapers and dispensing coffee and rubbing shoulders with British commanders. Somehow—no one is exactly sure how—Rivington had managed to gain possession of a copy of the entire British naval codebook. Maybe someone had routed the information to him; maybe someone carelessly left a copy lying on a table in his coffeehouse; maybe he had printed copies of the book on his own printing presses for the British. No matter. Rivington forwarded the copy to McLane, and it was soon delivered to General Washington.

Perhaps few single pieces of acquired intelligence would have a greater impact on the outcome of the American Revolutionary War than this codebook. Washington made certain Admiral de Grasse had the precious naval codes by mid-September. Over the following four weeks, Cornwallis faced a relentless attack from combined American and French forces on land. He was unable to be relieved by sea, as every move made by the British fleet in the Chesapeake Bay was effectively countered by well-informed French commanders and their crewmen. (It should be noted, however, that some historians do not believe French access to the signal book had much effect on the actual encounter between the French and British fleets in the bay.) Cornwallis could not break out, withstand the siege, or evacuate the Yorktown Peninsula. His surrender on October 19 would represent the grandest of victories.

The Intrepid Private Charles Morgan

General Lafayette relied on several individuals to distract Cornwallis and his forces on the Yorktown Peninsula. One such agent was Private Charles Morgan who volunteered for special service when a request went out from Lafayette's Virginia headquarters for someone to pose as a deserter to the British for the purpose of spreading incorrect information.

Morgan's only special request was that, if he failed and was hanged as a spy, Lafayette was to see that newspapers in New Jersey ran stories explaining that he had not actually deserted, but had been on a mission.

Morgan, a member of a New Jersey light battalion, soon "defected" to the British. Under interrogation—including at the hands of General Cornwallis and his cavalry commander, Colonel Banastre Tarleton—Morgan spun a story, warning Cornwallis that General Lafayette had access to a large number of boats that would allow him to follow the British army if Cornwallis chose to cross the James River (which Cornwallis was contemplating). At that time, Lafayette would not have had enough men or boats to pursue Cornwallis, which might have allowed the British general and his men to escape.

The wily undercover operative managed to convince Cornwallis to remain exactly where he was, and his mission proved a success, but in more ways than one. In time, Morgan, now dressed as a Redcoat, escaped from the British lines, having talked a half-dozen British soldiers into deserting. He also returned to Lafayette's army with a Hessian prisoner in tow.

LAST DAYS OF ESPIONAGE

The year 1781 proved to be the last for serious intelligence gathering by the Culper Ring. Rivington may have provided special agent McLane with a key piece of intelligence by handing off a copy of the British naval codes, but there were few additional coups for the Secret Six after that. Even by early summer, Culper contributions were few and far between. The flow of Woodhull's letters fell to a trickle. In fact, between June 1781 and April 1782, no reports were delivered from his pen. In the meantime, Tallmadge, the spy handler, remained preoccupied with military movements afoot rather than with intelligence gathering. He was working cavalry, not codes. Townsend did submit a few reports, but his personal life was redirecting him. On November 24, 1781, Townsend married. With a new bride, he was no longer willing to take any significant risks as a spy.

During the spring of 1782, Washington took serious steps to try and resuscitate the Culper Ring. The new British commander in New York, Sir Guy Carleton—his official title identified him as "Commander-in-Chief of His Majesty's Forces between Nova Scotia and the Floridas"—was dragging his feet concerning the evacuation of New York City. Surprisingly, Washington managed to get members of the Secret Six on their feet and into action, sending Austin Roe into the city to observe British movements. Soon, Townsend sent a report through Woodhull describing the British presence in the city as limited and their positions only defensive. "They have a number of ships ready to sink in the river if an enemy should appear," noted Townsend. "There's only two ships of any consequence in the harbor."[230] Back in late summer of 1776, the British had delivered hundreds of naval vessels to surround Manhattan and the boroughs. Now, the force holding New York was skeletal, at best.

Washington kept a communication channel open with the Culper Ring for a few more months. Little information passed from agent to general, for there was simply so little to report. The last of Woodhull's messages to reach Washington was dated February 21, 1783. By then, the British had accepted the reality of American independence. The spy business was no longer a valuable commodity to Washington or to the revolution. The Culpers and a myriad of other agents who had reported to Washington over the years had served their purpose.

FOLLOWING:
John Trumbull's 1820 painting Surrender of Lord Cornwallis *is currently on display in the Rotunda of the United States Capitol.*

Washington, Triumphant Spymaster

When Major John André was hanged in 1780, following his capture during Arnold's treason, Major Oliver De Lancey of the Seventeenth Light Dragoons was selected as his replacement as spymaster. Among De Lancey's key lieutenants in the intelligence service were two British officers, Colonel Beverley Robinson and Captain George Beckwith. By the summer of 1782, De Lancey stepped down due to poor health and Beckwith became the new head of the British secret service. As a spy, Beckwith was privy to the successes of the Culper Ring and the work of

Clinton and Cornwallis: Feuding Commanders

Once American and French forces toppled Cornwallis's defensive positions at Yorktown, the war was effectively over. The British had lost, and the commanders in the field, including Clinton and Cornwallis, soon began blaming one another for the British defeat. Cornwallis left for England in January 1782, sailing on the same ship as Benedict Arnold. From London, Cornwallis could launch attacks against Clinton's leadership.

As for Clinton, he sailed for England in May 1782. By the following year, he had written a book presenting his version of events as they related to the Yorktown campaign, and he naturally placed all blame at Cornwallis's feet.

Regardless of whether either or both were to blame for the loss at Yorktown, the battle signaled the end. By March 1782, the British House of Commons voted to cease all offensive operations in North America. Troops were retained in America until a treaty could be negotiated.

As for Washington, he could have continued his offensive campaign and headed south to liberate the Carolinas and Georgia, as well as Charleston and Savannah. (The British abandoned Savannah on their own in July 1782.) But he instead chose to cease offensive operations, taking the majority of his forces back to the Hudson River Valley region north of New York City where he remained at Newburgh until the war was officially negotiated to a conclusion in 1783.

General Washington as a spy handler. Captain George Beckwith would leave America after the war, but would return during the early 1790s, causing as much trouble for the fledgling American republic as he could muster, as an agent provocateur out of Canada. By the end of the decade, his star shot into the heavens, as he was appointed governor of Bermuda in 1797 and knighted in 1808. (By the end of the Napoleonic Wars, he had made general.)

Secret Identities Well Kept

Not only were the identities of the members of the Culper Ring a well-kept secret during the American Revolutionary War, but some agents' names were not known until many years later. Even the existence of the ring was not commonly known until the 1930s.

In 1929, Long Island historian Morton Pennypacker, after years of research and examining documents, including various handwritings, identified Robert Townsend as "Samuel Culper Jr." Pennypacker made the connection after reading letters Townsend had written and materials uncovered in the Townsend family home. Then he compared the handwriting with other missives sent by Culper Jr. to Washington. The signatures on both sets of documents were a match.

Some agents, such as James Rivington, were not revealed until the 1950s.

After the Revolutionary War, Beckwith was soon quoted in London newspapers, expressing one of the greatest compliments one spymaster can offer regarding another, even if he meant it as a back-handed acknowledgement. Speaking bitterly, Major Beckwith said of his nemesis, General Washington: "Washington did not really outfight the British, he simply outspied us." George Washington, general and spymaster, had fought a two-front war, one on the battlefield and the other through intelligence. In the end, by engaging in the latter he had managed to win the former.

~ ※ ~

What Happened to the Secret Six?

When wars end, the victors typically bestow honors and recognition on their own. Soldiers receive medals and special commendations. But spies usually remain on the sidelines, out of sight, anonymous to all. The members of the Culper Ring were no exception to the rule. They had operated together on cloak-and-dagger missions and most were not eager to have their names revealed once the war was over. But life went on for each after the war.

BENJAMIN TALLMADGE married the daughter of a signer of the Declaration of Independence. He and his wife, Mary (Floyd), had seven children and lived in Connecticut. For all his clandestine activities during the war, he led an extremely public life, including serving sixteen years in the House of Representatives (1801–17). While a congressman, he led an effort to deny pensions to the three militiamen—John Paulding, Isaac Van Wart, and David Williams—who had captured John André back in 1780. Having inside information as to their motives, Tallmadge asserted that "when Major André's boots were taken off by them, it was to search for plunder, and not to detect treason."[231] Tallmadge died at age eighty-one, on March 7, 1835. Today a facility at Fort Huachuca in Arizona, which serves as the base for U.S. Army military intelligence, is named in honor of Tallmadge (Tallmadge Hall) and the service he gave to his country as a cavalryman and spy during the American Revolutionary War.

CALEB BREWSTER, the excitable boatman, was married by 1784 and retired to a farm at Black Rock, then outside Bridgeport, Connecticut, close to where he had run whaleboats across the sound before and during the war. He had several children and died in 1827, his tombstone reading: "He was a brave and active officer of the Revolution."

JAMES RIVINGTON was one of those recognized directly by Washington in the latter days of the war. Washington visited Rivington's bookshop in Manhattan, where he allegedly handed Rivington a bag of gold for his services. (At least this is the story told years later by Washington's step-grandson, George Washington Parke Custis, who, of course, was not actually present in Rivington's shop that day.) Since many New Yorkers believed he had remained loyal to England during the war, his newspaper business declined. Over the years, he fell into debt and eventually served time in debtors' prison. He died at age seventy-eight, on July 4, 1802. Recognition for his spying accomplishments would come later. Today, Rivington Park and nearby Rivington Street in Lower Manhattan are named for him.

ROBERT TOWNSEND remained much the man he had been before and during the war, if even more reclusive. He never spoke of his work as a spy for the Culper Ring. He didn't marry, but may have fathered a child by his French-Canadian housekeeper (although his brother, William Townsend, could have been the boy's real father). Nevertheless, Robert raised the child, who was named Robert Townsend Jr. In his later years, Townsend became a staunch abolitionist, calling for slavery's end. He died at age eighty-four, on March 7, 1838, the same date, plus three years, as Tallmadge's death.

AUSTIN ROE gained the rank of captain during the war. He and his wife had eight children. By 1798, the family moved from Setauket to a village on the south shore of Long Island where they opened an inn for local visitors. Those who stayed at Roe's hotel might find the proprietor regaling them with stories of his spying exploits, even as he kept the names of the other members of the Secret Six, well, a secret. He was eighty-one when he died in November 1830.

AGENT 355 remains a mystery. Whether she was Anna Strong of Setauket, Long Island, or an unidentified Manhattan socialite, or someone else entirely remains a matter of historical debate. As she was unnamed during her service to the Culper Ring, so she remains anonymous even today. One may only hope that someday an intrepid historian will stumble across the necessary information, triangulate the documentation, and name her once and for all.

ABRAHAM WOODHULL married in 1781. He and his wife Mary, (Smith), remained in Setauket, raising three children. After his wife died, Abraham married again, this time to Lydia Terry. He rarely spoke about his spying during the war, but served in several capacities in the Suffolk County government. He died on January 23, 1826, and his gravestone still stands in the Setauket Presbyterian Church cemetery. One hundred and ten years after his death, the Mayflower Chapter of the Daughters of the American Revolution placed a second marker next to his gravestone, one noting his service as an agent of General Washington's: "Friend and confidant of George Washington, Head of the Long Island Secret Service During the American Revolution he operated under the alias Samuel Culper, Sr. To him and his associates have been credited a large share of the success of the Army of the Revolution."

Messages in Plain Sight

Exactly how spy Allen McLane and James Rivington first made contact with each other remains a mystery. But at least one historian believes he has discovered the answer.

Historian John A. Nagy, who has extensively researched the subject of espionage and intelligence gathering during the American Revolutionary War, has suggested that Rivington may have left coded messages embedded in advertisements printed in his *Royal Gazette*.

Although Nagy's theory is based on speculation, a closer look suggests that he might just be on to something. One such advertisement appeared in the July 11, 1781, issue of the *Gazette*:

> *The person to whom Mr. Lemuel Nelme wrote a letter dated Fish-Kill, April 27 . . . takes this earliest opportunity to desire he will immediately obtain permission to come to New York, where he will receive intelligence of matters momentous and interesting to himself, and be enabled directly to return to his native country, and enjoy the happiness of meeting his parents, proper information; and directions are left with the printer, to whom Mr. Nelme will be pleased to repair as soon as he shall have met with this advertisement.* [232]

To Nagy, the ad appears a bit cryptic and mentions important "intelligence." Also, the name Lemuel Nelme may be a coded reference to the author Lemuel Dole Nelme who had penned a book in 1772 about the origins of language and alphabetic symbolism, something on which codes are often based. Since McLane and Rivington left no other written correspondence, historians such as Nagy continue to scratch their heads and wonder whether the two agents' messages may have been written in plain sight.

Afterword

*There is nothing more necessary than good intelligence to frustrate
a designing enemy, & nothing requires greater pains to obtain.*[233]

—*George Washington*

Within the steel- and glass-lined corridors of the Central Intelligence Agency's headquarters, nestled in the woods outside Langley, Virginia, a trio of meeting rooms connects America's modern intelligence agency with its Revolutionary-era counterparts. In 1997, the CIA opened a new operational wing, the Liaison Conference Center, which includes three meeting rooms used for coordinating visits from foreign officials to CIA headquarters. The rooms are named after three men the agency considers the "Founding Fathers of American Intelligence"[234]: Benjamin Franklin, John Jay, and George Washington.

꩜ ※ ꩜

AMERICA'S FIRST SPYMASTERS

Not only does the CIA recognize the general contributions each revolutionary leader made to the development of American intelligence gathering, but it also associates each man with a specific type of intelligence work. Franklin is recognized as the founding father of covert action, Jay for his work in American counterintelligence, and Washington for the acquisition of foreign intelligence. This singular tribute by the agency most responsible for the nation's modern intelligence gathering suggests that the work done by these men is recognized as having been effective at the time and worthy of professional appreciation by modern-day spies.

Textbooks on the American Revolution are filled with stories of battles and political events, but traditionally, little notice is given to those clandestine activities of America's spies. Dozens of men and women carried out missions and gathered information on behalf of the American cause. These undercover supporters of the revolution made contributions that historians are still attempting to discover, document, and bring to light.

Although Franklin's intelligence efforts were broader than romancing the French into supporting the American cause—first covertly, then overtly—those efforts were crucial to the ultimate success of the revolution. Franklin utilized as many variant tricks of the trade as imaginable to gain the French alliance, including propaganda, backroom diplomatic intrigue, the formation of a dummy corporation for funneling money and other support to the Americans, and subtle arm-twisting. Had the French not fallen into the American camp, the outcome of the revolution might have been completely different. Additionally, Franklin (and Silas Deane) supported, in the modern parlance, paramilitary raids and other operations against British facilities, such as boatyards, dock sites, and warehouses.

Due to the later trajectory of his life, John Jay is remembered first and foremost for his legal legacy, including his service as the first chief justice of the United States Supreme Court. But Jay initially served his country as the founding father of American counterintelligence. Effectively, he became the first counterintelligence chief on a national level. His efforts predate the early days of Tallmadge's recruitment of the Culper Ring by two years, beginning in the autumn of 1776. While Jay's operation was focused largely on the region of the Hudson River Valley—the state of New York would utilize Jay before Washington did, placing him at the head of the

RIGHT:
This statue of Nathan Hale was erected in 1973 at the Central Intelligence Agency's headquarters in Langley, Virginia.

newly formed Committee and First Commission for Detecting Conspiracies—he ran an efficient counterintelligence system, handling more than a dozen agents, including the dashing Enoch Crosby. It was under Jay's leadership that the use of codes and other elements of spy craft became more commonplace for the Americans. (His brother, Dr. James Jay, helped to develop invisible ink formulas for the Patriot cause.)

As considerable as the contributions of Franklin and Jay were to American spying and intelligence gathering, George Washington remains the most important American spymaster of the Revolutionary War era. An examination of his activities helps to explain why Washington's legacy during the British-American conflict rests on more than his military skills as a general. His field record is less than stellar: Washington engaged directly in a dozen or so battles between 1776 and 1781, and won, at best, only one out of three. However, historians often credit Washington as a general who, despite losing battles, served as a rallying post, managing to keep the Continental army intact and willing to fight another day.

But further credit lies in his skills as a coordinator of intelligence and counterintelligence activities. This often unsung element of his leadership may have accomplished more than his military efforts in keeping the American Revolution on a course that ultimately carried the young republic to its final victory over king and mother country. Washington chose well those who served under him as spy handlers and field agents. He put civilians and military personnel to good use as informants, saboteurs, go-betweens, cutouts, and couriers. Did Washington make mistakes? Were there failures on his part concerning espionage? Of course, and no better example exists than the infamous treachery of Benedict Arnold. No one was more surprised by Arnold's turning to the British than Washington. Still, his mastery of the fine art of espionage—including skills he first honed in the wilds of western Pennsylvania during that snowy winter mission of 1753–54—served him well.

~✕~

REASONS FOR AMERICAN SUCCESS

Beyond the leadership provided by these three Founding Fathers, the American intelligence system operated under several specific and, perhaps, unique circumstances that may have helped those efforts succeed. Some of these should be obvious. First, the revolution and the war took place on American soil, often centered in

American cities. And second, the British were, essentially, fighting a war on foreign soil, in the midst of a population where distinguishing friend and foe was often difficult. These elements alternately helped the Americans and hindered the British. Patriotism fed the Americans while paranoia dogged the British.

Other reasons might be less obvious. For one, the ultimate scope of American intelligence gathering typically remained small and rather focused. Agents may have come and gone with regularity, but espionage always continued and rarely became so complicated or involved that spymasters such as George Washington were unable to manage it. And Washington managed this effort even though he was, first and foremost, a general who juggled many other responsibilities, including overseeing the Continental Army and its various needs, maintaining political connections with the Continental Congress as well as thirteen state governments, and—one must not forget—running his plantation back at Mount Vernon. Washington was able to remain consistently "hands-on" with his agents, or at least their handlers, such as Tallmadge, Jay, and others.

Another important aspect of America's spy networks was that they operated, despite having their ranks filled with little more than ill-trained amateurs, within a nearly hermetically sealed system. Even Washington was careful not to know the names of more agents than necessary. Washington knew Tallmadge, but only Tallmadge knew the names of his agents. Yet the American system often relied on the fact that one agent could vouchsafe for another. Spymasters recruited, as often as possible, from the ranks of their friends, particularly from among those they knew and trusted, including those they had known since childhood. Thus, Tallmadge knew Abraham Woodhull, Woodhull knew Caleb Brewster and Robert Townsend, and Townsend knew James Rivington. The circle of spies that became the Culper Ring was, at its center, a circle of friends.

Of course, the British had agents, some quite skilled, and they experienced their own successes. However, it must be said that even though the British were adept in the ways of espionage—Franklin and Deane, remember, were always under the watchful eye of British agents, even as their ranks were infiltrated by a double agent—they still managed to make serious mistakes. Perhaps their greatest problem was their collective blindness. Sometimes, British officers elected to ignore intelligence simply because they took a shortsighted view of their opponents. British arrogance often kept their officials from taking the Americans seriously, causing them to underestimate the rebellious colonials, perhaps especially in the area of intelligence gathering.

General Gage remained more concerned about the day-to-day acts of sabotage and subversion by Patriot night raiders than he was about any organized spy efforts the colonials might be operating. At its core, British conceits concerning the Patriots were typically misplaced and astonishingly cursory. Both British commanders stationed in America and those politicians making decisions in London rarely conceived of the Americans as anything more than, well, colonials—amateurs trying to cobble together a political future while trying to defend their goals with armies filled with militia misfits. The American spirit, the level of American tenacity, was something the British never seemed to get their finger on. That the Americans could manage to pull together an intelligence network with any capacity for sophistication was simply beyond their mindset. The British never won the hearts and minds of their American opponents, because they did not believe it was an effort worth bothering with.

This presumption caused the British to minimize the capacity of American intelligence gathering, even while choosing to ignore the reports of their own agents or at least failing to adequately respond to those reports. One of the most glaring examples of this failure lies in Sir Henry Clinton's inability to detect Washington's plans in 1781 to evacuate New Jersey and head south to Virginia where a vulnerable General Cornwallis sat trapped at Yorktown. While Washington engaged in a marvellously orchestrated series of intelligence moves, all designed to convince Clinton that Washington intended to attack him and his forces headquartered in New York City, Clinton had his own agents informing him otherwise. Still, the British commander remained fixed in his belief that New York had always been Washington's goal, when, in fact, it never had been. Such failure to accurately consider the intelligence reports of one's own agents, while looking past the false leads planted by one's opponent, indicates either a failure of good judgment or a prejudicial arrogance. Clinton may have been guilty of both.

～ ※ ～

CONTINUING AMERICAN ESPIONAGE

Today, the U.S. government maintains multiple, sophisticated government programs involving electronic eavesdropping, aerial drones, and even spy satellites orbiting the earth. But between early Revolutionary War spying efforts and now, the United States continued to engage in some element of espionage, even if it was sometimes extremely limited. Throughout the nineteenth century, the U.S.

generally operated outside of an organized, official spy network or government agency. Most spying or intelligence gathering was carried out by diplomats and the military. Communication and transportation remained slow and, given America's general reluctance to involve itself in foreign intrigues, the need for spies remained minimal. During the Civil War (1861–65), civilian and government spies and informants provided intelligence to both the North and the South and, by war's end, the Union Army's Bureau of Military Information was one of the foremost intelligence agencies in the world. The agency, however was considered unnecessary and was summarily disbanded at the conclusion of the war.

By the twentieth century, American intelligence gathering was becoming the responsibility of specialized units, but those efforts fell short of their European counterparts. During World War I (1914–18), the Europeans were much better equipped to engage in spying, relying on military and naval intelligence operatives, as well as small, clandestine offices. Modern spy innovations included an increasing reliance on aerial photography and "signals intelligence," which involved the interception of other nations' electronic communications, including telegraph cables and radio messages. Just as revolutionary-era American and British agents had relied on codes and various ciphers to keep the content of messages and communiqués secret, codes remained important.

Such activities helped push the United States into World War I. In early 1917, British naval intelligence operatives intercepted a coded telegraphic cable sent from the German foreign secretary, Arthur Zimmerman, to the German minister in Mexico City. The minister was to propose an alliance between Germany and Mexico in case war broke out between the U.S. and Germany. Along with an offer of financial aid to Mexico, the Germans promised to help them recover "the lost territory in Texas, New Mexico, and Arizona."[235] The intercepted and decoded "Zimmerman Telegram" was handed off to President Woodrow Wilson, who subsequently released the bombshell missive to the Associated Press. Soon, Americans across the country were clamoring for war with Germany. Within two months, Wilson asked for a declaration of war.

By World War II (1939–45), espionage played a vital role in the conflict, including various code-breaking successes by the Allies. U.S. Army Intelligence managed to break the Japanese code by 1940, more than a year before the United States entered World War II, following the Japanese attack against Pearl Harbor in December 1941. It was during the war that the United States formed one of its earliest, freestanding intelligence organizations, the Office of Strategic Services (OSS).

ABOVE:
An aerial view of the CIA headquarters complex in Langley, Virginia, which was completed in 1961 but only given an official name (the George Bush Center for Intelligence) in 1999.

President Franklin Roosevelt established the OSS in 1942 to operate under the coordination of the U.S. Joint Chiefs of Staff. Led by a longtime Republican friend of FDR, William "Wild Bill" Donovan, the organization worked closely with British intelligence, tasked with analyzing strategic intelligence information and running agents from Moscow to Shanghai. Although the OSS sometimes took a backseat to its British counterpart, it experienced fairly dramatic success with its agents in Germany. Yet the signals intelligence services of the U.S. Army and Navy actually proved more crucial to the war effort than the OSS, and the organization was shut down in September 1945. When the Central Intelligence Agency (CIA) was established two years later, through the National Security Act of 1947, several former agents of the OSS made the transition to the new agency.

Much of the intelligence gathering carried out by the CIA through the following decades was done within the context of Cold War espionage. Other intelligence offices were also established, including the National Security Agency (NSA), which began operation in 1952, taking on many of the activities formally carried out by the signals intelligence services. While agents on the ground remained vital, the 1960s also brought advancements in technology, including satellites. With the Soviet Union deploying missiles by the hundreds, America's ability to keep track of their proliferation was crucial. In 1967, President Lyndon Johnson noted this very element: "Before we had the [satellite] photography our guesses were way off. We were doing things we didn't need to do. Because of the satellites I know how many missiles the enemy has."[236] As early as 1962, American aerial reconnaissance carried out by high-altitude U2 spy planes had detected Russian plans to place missiles in Cuba. American spies were in the skies.

Today, American intelligence gathering continues to rely on these same elements, including both human and technological. Field agents gather essential information while desk-bound analysts pore through electronic and photographic data, sifting through endless streams for clues that might prove valuable.

Given the complicated nature of the modern world, with foreign leaders engaging in overheated rhetoric and Islamic terrorists committing themselves to acts of violence against the West in general and the U.S. specifically, it seems that the United States is as dependent on intelligence gathering and the efforts of field agents and analysts as ever in its history. While government intelligence services such as the NSA and the CIA carry out endless surveillance and intelligence operations—including electronic eavesdropping, the enlistment of agents to carry out clandestine missions, the dispatching of killer drones across foreign skies, and the interrogation of suspects using methods that challenge the nation's moral center— some critics wonder whether the very rights and freedoms Americans have fought for since the revolution of 1776 have been compromised, if not actually threatened. One may only hope that, despite the march of international terrorism and other foreign intrigues that represent existential threats to America, the work carried out by the nation's intelligence services will help keep alive the nation's ideals of freedom, allowing the legacy of those American Patriots of centuries past—including those who first spied for their young country—to remain alive, perhaps representing the last great hope for the world and its future.

Bibliography

Allen, Thomas. *George Washington, Spymaster: How the Americans Outspied the British and Won the Revolutionary War.* Washington, D.C.: National Geographic, 2004.

Anderson, Fred. *Crucible of War: The Seven Years' War and the Fate of Empire in British North America, 1754–1766.* New York: Vintage, 2001.

———. *George Washington Remembers: Reflections on the French and Indian War.* Lanham, NY: Rowman & Littlefield, 2004.

Annals of Congress. House of Representatives, 14th Congress, 2nd Session, January 13, 1817, Column 474.

Bakeless, John. *Turncoats, Traitors & Heroes: Espionage in the American Revolution.* New York: Da Capo Press, 1998.

Bemis, Samuel Flagg. *The Diplomacy of the American Revolution.* Bloomington: Indiana University Press, 1957.

Borneman, Walter R. *The French and Indian War: Deciding the Fate of North America.* New York: HarperCollins Publishers, 2006.

Boylan, Brian Richard. *Benedict Arnold: The Dark Eagle.* New York: W. W. Norton & Company, 1973.

Butterfield, L. H. ed. *The Adams Papers: Diary & Autobiography of John Adams.* 4 vols. New York: Athenaeum Press, 1964.

———. *Adams Family Papers, an Electronic Archive (Autobiography and Diary).* Massachusetts Historical Society. http://www.masshist.org/digitaladams/.

Clary, David A. *George Washington's First War: His Early Military Adventures.* New York: Simon & Schuster, 2011.

Clinton, George. George Clinton to the Council of Safety, October 11, 1777. In *Public Papers of George Clinton, First Governor of New York, 1777–1795, 1801–1804*, edited by H. Hastings and J. A. Holden. Albany, NY, II, No. 836. Albany: State of New York, 1900. Digitized 2005. http://www.historyisfun.org/pdf/tea-overboard/RoadtoRevolution.pdf.

Commager, Henry Steele and R. B. Morris, eds. *The Spirit of Seventy-Six: The Story of the American Revolution As Told by Its Participants.* 3rd ed. New York: Da Capo Press, 1978; reprint 1995.

Crocker, Thomas E. *Braddock's March: How the Man Sent to Seize a Continent Changed American History.* Yardley, PA: Westholme Publishing, 2009.

Daigler, Kenneth A. *Spies, Patriots, and Traitors: American Intelligence in the Revolutionary War.* Washington, D.C.: Georgetown University Press, 2014.

Fischer, David Hackett. *Washington's Crossing.* New York: Oxford University Press, 2004. Flexner, James Thomas. *George Washington: The Forge of Experience (1732–1775).* Boston: Little, Brown and Company, 1965.

Force, Peter. *American Archives*, Ser. 4, 2: 151–154. 1837–1853. New York: Johnson Reprint, 1972.

French, Allen. *General Gage's Informers.* New York: Greenwood Press, 1968. First published 1932 by University of Michigan Press.

———. *Thomas Gage Papers, American Series.* William L. Clements Library. University of Michigan, Ann Arbor.

"History of American Women," Margaret Kemble Gage. http://www.womenhistoryblog.com/2009/05/margaret-kemble-gage.html.

Howell, T. B. "Trial of James Hill alias John the Painter." In *Complete Collection of State Trials and Proceedings for High Treason and Other Crimes and Misdemeanors (1771–1777).* Vol. 20. London: Longman, Hurts, Rees, Orme, & Brown, 1814.

Hughes, Ben. *The Siege of Fort William Henry: A Year on the Northeastern Frontier*. Yardley, PA: Westholme Publishing, 2011.

Huntoon, Daniel T. V. "An Old Bostonian, Robert Twelves Hewes," *Weekly Transcript*, January 26, 1886 (Boston Public Library).

Irving, Washington. *Life of George Washington*. Vol. 2. London: Henry G. Bohn, 1856.

Isham, Charles, ed. *Deane Papers, 1737–1789*. 5 vols. New York: New York Historical Society Collections, 1886.

Jackson, Donald and Dorothy Twohig, eds. *The Diaries of George Washington*. Vol. 1. Charlottesville: University Press of Virginia, 1976.

Kilmeade, Brian and Don Yaeger. *George Washington's Secret Six: The Spy Ring That Saved the American Revolution*. New York: Sentinel, 2013.

Kitman, Marvin. *George Washington's Expense Account*. New York: Grove Publishing, 2001.

Koestler-Grack, Rachel A. *Nathan Hale: Courageous Spy*. New York: Chelsea House, 2006.

Labaree, Leonard, et al., eds. *The Papers of Benjamin Franklin*. 39 vols. Vol. 22. New Haven: Yale University Press, 1982.

Longfellow, William Wadsworth. "The Midnight Ride of Paul Revere."

Macrakis, Kristie. *Prisoners, Lovers & Spies: The Story of Invisible Ink from Herodotus to al-Qaeda*. New Haven: Yale University Press, 2014.

Manley, Sean. *Long Island Discovery: An Adventure into the History, Manners, and Mores of America's Front Porch*. New York: Doubleday, 1966.

Massachusetts Historical Society Archives. Vol. 50. Massachusetts House of Representatives, November 11, 1775, 5360.

McNeese, Tim. *Revolutionary America*. St. Louis: Milliken Publishing Company, 2002.

Nagy, John A. *Dr. Benjamin Church, SPY: A Case of Espionage on the Eve of the American Revolution*, Yardley, PA: Westholme Publishing, 2013.

———. "Appendix A." In *Invisible Ink: Spy Craft of the American Revolution*. Yardley, PA: Westholme Publishing, 2010.

———. *Spies in the Continental Capital: Espionage Across Pennsylvania During the American Revolution*. Yardley, PA: Westholme Publishing, 2011.

Paltsits, Hugo. "The Use of Invisible Ink for Secret Writing During the American Revolution." *Bulletin of the New York Public Library* 39 (1935).

Paul, Joel Richard. *Unlikely Allies: How a Merchant, a Playwright, and a Spy Saved the American Revolution*. New York: Riverhead Books, 2009.

Pellew, George. *John Jay, American Statesmen*. New York: Chelsea House, 1997.

Pennypacker, Morton. *General Washington's Spies on Long Island and in New York*. Cranbury, NJ: Scholar's Bookshelf, 2005.

Peyser, Joseph L., ed. *Jacques Legardeur de Saint-Pierre: Officer, Gentleman, Entrepreneur*. East Lansing: Michigan State University Press, 1996.

Purvis, Thomas L. *Colonial America to 1763, Almanacs of American Life Series*. New York: Facts on File, 1999.

Rhodehamel, J., ed. *The American Revolution: Writings from the War of Independence*. New York: Library of America, 2001.

Rose, Alexander. "The Spy Who Never Was: The Strange Case of John Honeyman and Revolutionary War Espionage." *Studies in Intelligence* 52, no. 2 (June 2008).

———. *Washington's Spies: The Story of America's First Spy Ring*. New York: Bantam Dell, 2006.

Ross, John F. *War on the Run: The Epic Story of Robert Rogers and the Conquest of America's First Frontier*. New York: Bantam Books, 2009.

Schaeper, Thomas J. *Edward Bancroft: Scientist, Author, Spy*. New Haven: Yale University Press, 2011.

———. *France and America in the Revolutionary Era: The Life of Jacques-Donatien Leray de Chaumont, 1725–1803*. New York: Berghahn, 1995.

Seymour, George Dudley. *Captain Nathan Hale and Major John Palsgrave Wyllys*. New Haven, CT: Tuttle, Morehouse & Taylor, 1933.

Documentary Life of Nathan Hale: Comprising All Available Official and Private Documents Bearing on the Life of the Patriot. Whitefish, MT: Kessinger, 2006.

"The Mad Scientist May 6, 1775—Benjamin Thompson to Gage's Staff." Spy Letters of the American Revolution. William L. Clements Library. University of Michigan, Ann Arbor. http://clements. umich.edu/exhibits/online/spies/stories-networks-2. html.

Stevens, Benjamin F. *B. F. Stevens' Facsimiles of Manuscripts in European Archives Relating to America 1773–1783, with Descriptions, Editorial Notes, Collations, References and Translations, No. 235*. London: Matby & Sons, 1889–95.

Stout, Neil R. "The Spies Who Went Out in the Cold." *American Heritage*, February 1972.

Stuart, Isaac William. *Life of Captain Nathan Hale, the Martyr-Spy of the American Revolution*. Hartford: F. A. Brown, 1856. Facsimile reprint by HardPress Publishing.

Tallmadge, Benjamin. *Memoir of Col. Benjamin Tallmadge Prepared by Himself at the Request of His Children*. New York: Thomas Holman, 1858. Reprint, New York: New York Times, 1968.

Taylor, Robert J., ed. "To John Adams from James Warren, 1 October 1775," Founders Online, National Archives (http://founders.archives.gov/documents/ Adams/06-03-02-0089 [last update: 2014-12-01]). Source: *The Adams Papers*, Papers of John Adams, vol. 3, *May 1775–January 1776*. Cambridge, MA: Harvard University Press, 1979, pp. 177–180.

Traister, Bryce. "Criminal Correspondence: Loyalism, Espionage and Crevecoeur." *Early American Literature* 37, No. 3 (2002).

Van Doren, Carl. *Secret History of the American Revolution: An Account of the Conspiracies of Benedict Arnold and Numerous Others, Drawn from the Secret Service Papers of the British Headquarters in North America, Now for the First Time Examined and Made Public*. New York: Viking Press, 1941.

Walker, Jeffrey. *The Devil Undone: The Life and Poetry of Benjamin Church, 1734–1778*. New York: Arno Press, 1982.

Washington, George. George Washington to Noah Webster, July 21, 1788. In *Papers of George Washington*, edited by William Wright Abbot, Mark A. Mastromarino, and Jack D. Warren. Charlottesville: University Press of Virginia, 2000.

Notes

CHAPTER ONE

1   Walter R. Borneman, *The French and Indian War: Deciding the Fate of North America* (New York: HarperCollins Publishers, 2006), 14.

2   Donald Jackson and Dorothy Twohig, eds., *The Diaries of George Washington: Volume I* (Charlottesville: University Press of Virginia, 1976), 126.

3   James Thomas Flexner, *George Washington: The Forge of Experience (1732–1775)* (Boston: Little, Brown and Company, 1965), 54.

4   Clary, 54.

5   Ibid.

6   Ibid., 53.

7   Fred Anderson, *Crucible of War: The Seven Years' War and the Fate of Empire in British North America, 1754–1766* (New York: Vintage, 2001), 41.

8   Flexner, 60.

9   Ibid.

10   Jackson and Twohig, 44.

11   Fred Anderson, ed., *George Washington Remembers: Reflections on the French and Indian War* (Lanham, NY: Rowman & Littlefield, 2004), 16–17.

12   Thomas L. Purvis, *Colonial America to 1763, Almanacs of American Life Series* (New York: Facts on File, 1999), 128.

13   Clary, 55.

14   Ibid., 57.

15   Flexner, 66.

16   Ibid., 67.

17   Clary, 62.

18   Joseph L. Peyser, ed., *Jacques Legardeur de Saint-Pierre: Officer, Gentleman, Entrepreneur* (East Lansing: Michigan State University Press, 1996), 201.

19   Clary, 63.

20   Ibid., 63.

21   Ibid.

22   Flexner, 72.

23   Ibid., 74.

24   Clary, 66.

25   Ibid.

26   Ibid.

27   Ibid.

28   Ibid., 75.

29   Kenneth A. Daigler, *Spies, Patriots, and Traitors: American Intelligence in the Revolutionary War* (Washington, D.C.: Georgetown University Press, 2014), 7.

30   Clary, 69.

CHAPTER TWO

31   "Stamp Act of 1765, Original Text," StampAct, http://www.stamp-act-history.com/stamp-act/stamp-act-of-1765-original-text/.

32   Nagy, Church, 39.

33   Nagy, 55.

34   Peter Force, American Archives, Ser. 4, 2: 151–154 (Reprint of 1837–1853 edition by New York: Johnson Reprint, 1972).

35   Allen French, General Gage's Informers (Reprint of 1932 University of Michigan Press by New York: Greenwood Press, 1968,) 156–57.

36   Taylor, Robert J., ed. "To John Adams from James Warren, 1 October 1775," Founders Online, National Archives (http://founders.archives.gov/documents/Adams/06-03-02-0089 [last update: 2014-12-01]). Source: The Adams Papers, Papers of John Adams, vol. 3, May 1775–January 1776. Cambridge, MA: Harvard University Press, 1979, pp. 177–180.

37   Ibid., 13.

38   Bakeless, 13.

39   Bakeless, 22.

40   The term "en croupe" refers to the use of a crupper, which includes a loop and an adjustable strap (the crupper strap or back strap) that is designed to attach to the crupper portion of the back of a saddle. To hold the contraption in place, a loop is run beneath the horse's tail.

41   Washington Irving, Life of George Washington (London: Henry G. Bohn, 1856), 2:400.

42   Ibid.

43   Carl Van Doren, *Secret History of the American Revolution: An Account of the Conspiracies of Benedict Arnold and Numerous Others, Drawn from the Secret Service Papers of the*

British Headquarters in North America, Now for the First Time Examined and Made Public (New York: Viking Press, 1941), 21–22.

44 Nagy, Church, 105.

45 Bakeless, 18.

46 Ibid.

47 Nagy, 116.

48 Massachusetts Historical Society Archives, Massachusetts House of Representatives, vol. 50, November 11, 1775: 5360.

49 John Adams to Abigail Adams, October 28, 12775, Adams Famiily Papers, Massachusetts Historical Society.

50 Bakeless, 20.

51 Nagy, Church, 144.

52 Bakeless, 21.

53 Ibid., 23.

54 Ibid.

55 Bakeless, 22.

56 Ibid.

57 Massachusetts Historical Society Archives, 216: 217–218.

58 Ibid.

59 Benjamin Church to Thomas Gage, May 24, 1775, Gage Papers, vol. 129.

60 Bakeless, 68.

CHAPTER THREE

61 No evidence exists today to indicate that Dr. Church ever revealed the names of the Mechanics to British authorities, including General Gage, to whom he reported regularly. Why he chose not to do so is unknown. Perhaps he thought turning in the group's names would expose him.

62 Thomas B. Allen, *George Washington, Spymaster: How the Americans Outspied the British and Won the Revolutionary War* (Washington, DC: National Geographic, 2004), 33.

63 Allen, 32.

64 Ibid., 34.

65 Bakeless, 70.

66 The "Emerson" referred to by Gage's spy in Concord was the Reverend William Emerson, a Congregationalist minister, and the father of Ralph Waldo Emerson, well-known American transcendentalist leader and essayist.

67 Bakeless, 29–30.

68 "History of American Women," Margaret Kemble Gage, http://www.womenhistoryblog.com/2009/05/margaret-kemble-gage.html.

69 Bakeless, 31.

70 "The Mad Scientist May 6, 1775—Benjamin Thompson to Gage's Staff," *Spy Letters of the American Revolution,* http://clements.umich.edu/exhibits/online/spies/stories-networks-2.html.

71 Bryce Traister, "Criminal Correspondence: Loyalism, Espionage and Crevecoeur," *Early American Literature 37,* no. 3 (2002): 469.

72 Bakeless, 39.

73 Neil R. Stout, "The Spies Who Went Out in the Cold," *American Heritage,* February 1972, http://www.americanheritage.com/content/spies-who-went-out-cold.

74 Ibid.

75 Ibid.

76 Ibid.

77 Ibid.

78 Ibid.

79 Bakeless, 56.

80 Ibid.

81 Ibid., 57.

82 Ibid.

83 Ibid., 66.

84 Ibid., 67.

85 Ibid., 76.

86 Ibid.

87 Henry Wadsworth Longfellow, "The Midnight Ride of Paul Revere," http://www.paul-revere-heritage.com/poem.html.

88 Tim McNeese, *Revolutionary America* (St. Louis: Milliken Publishing Company, 2002), 93.

CHAPTER FOUR

89 Bakeless, 119.

90 Daniel T. V. Huntoon, "An Old Bostonian, Robert Twelves Hewes," *Weekly Transcript,* January 26, 1886.

91 Ibid.

92 Marvin Kitman, *George Washington's Expense Account.* (New York: Grove Publishing, 2001), 119.

93 Bakeless, 86.

94 Ibid., 93–94.

95 Ibid., 103.

96 Ibid., 107.

97 Ibid.

98 Ibid., 108.

99 *George Dudley Seymour, Captain Nathan Hale and Major John Palsgrave Wyllys* (New Haven, CT: Tuttle, Morehouse & Taylor, 1933), 25.

100 Ibid.

101 Daigler, 96.

102 George D. Seymour, *Documentary Life of Nathan Hale: Comprising All Available Official and Private Documents Bearing on the Life of the Patriot* (Whitefish, MT: Kessinger, 2006), 39.

103 Seymour, 317–18.

104 Rose, 29.

105 Ibid.

106 J. Rhodehamel, ed., *The American Revolution: Writings from the War of Independence* (New York: Library of America, 2001), 229.

107 Bakeless, 118.

108 Rose, 33.

109 Rachel A. Koestler-Grack, *Nathan Hale, A Courageous Hero* (New York: Chelsea House Publishing, 2006), 105.

CHAPTER FIVE

110 George Pellew, John Jay, *American Statesmen* (New York: Chelsea House, 1997), 24–25.

111 Pellew, 63.

112 Bakeless, 139.

113 Ibid., 140.

114 Daigler, 122.

115 Bakeless, 167.

116 David Hackett Fischer, *Washington's Crossing* (New York: Oxford University Press, 2004), 423.

117 Alexander Rose, "The Spy Who Never Was: The Strange Case of John Honeyman and Revolutionary War Espionage," *Studies in Intelligence* 52, no. 2 (June 2008).

118 Daigler, 129.

119 Bakeless, 145.

120 Ibid., 146.

121 Bakeless, 146.

122 Ibid., 148.

123 Bakeless, 149–50; Allen, 170.

124 Letter, George Clinton to the Council of Safety, October 11, 1777, Public Papers of George Clinton, First Governor of New York, 1777–1795, 1801–1804, eds. H. Hastings and J. A. Holden, Albany, NY, II, No. 836, 412–14.

125 Henry Steele Commager and R. B. Morris, eds., *The Spirit of 'Seventy Six: The Story of the American Revolution as told by Participants*, 3rd ed. (New York: Da Capo Press, 1978; reprint 1995), 587–88.

126 Ibid.

127 Allen, 100.

CHAPTER SIX

128 George Clinton to the Council of Safety, October 11, 1777, in Public Papers of George Clinton, First Governor of New York, 1777–1795, 1801–1804, H. Hastings and J. A. Holden, eds., Albany, NY, II, No. 836. Albany: State of New York, 1900, digitized 2005, http://www.historyisfun.org/pdf/tea-overboard/RoadtoRevolution.pdf.

129 Samuel Flagg Bemis, *The Diplomacy of the American Revolution* (Bloomington: Indiana University Press, 1957), 14–15.

130 Leonard Labaree et al., eds., *The Papers of Benjamin Franklin* (New Haven: Yale University Press, 1982), 22: 373–74.

131 Thomas J. Schaeper, *France and America in the Revolutionary Era: The Life of Jacques-Donatien Leray de Chaumont, 1725–1803* (New York: Berghahn, 1995), 137–44.

132 Charles Isham, ed., *Deane Papers, 1737–1789* (New York: New York Historical Society Collections, 1886), 5: 237–43.

133 Allen, 89.

134 Thomas J. Schaeper, *Edward Bancroft: Scientist, Author, Spy* (New Haven: Yale University Press, 2011), 25.

135 Benjamin F. Stevens, B. F. Stevens' Facsimiles of Manuscripts in European Archives Relating to America 1773–1783, with Descriptions, Editorial Notes, Collations, References and Translations, No. 235 (London: Matby & Sons, 1889–95).

136 Daigler, 84–85.

137 Kristie Macrakis, *Prisoners, Lovers, & Spies: The Story of Invisible Ink from Herodotus to al-Qaeda* (New Haven: Yale University Press, 2014), 84.

138 Hugo Paltsits, "The Use of Invisible Ink for Secret Writing During the American Revolution," *Bulletin of the New York Public Library* 39 (1935): 362.

139 Deane to Edward Bancroft, undated, probably March 1777, in *The Deane Papers, 1737–1789*, ed. and trans. by Charles Isham, 5 vols. (New York: New York Historical Society Collections, 1886), 2: 9–10.

140 Isham, 6–7.

141 T. B. Howell, "Trial of James Hill alias John the Painter," in *Complete Collection of State Trials* and *Proceedings for High Treason and Other Crimes and Misdemeanors* (1771–1777) (London: Longman, Hurts, Rees, Orme, & Brown, 1814), 20: 1335.

142 Allen, 86.

143 Ibid., 91.

144 Allen, 54.

CHAPTER SEVEN

145 Bakeless, 170.

146 Ibid., 172.

147 Ibid.

148 Ibid.

149 Ibid., 173.

150 Ibid., 241.

151 Ibid.

152 Ibid., 242.

153 Ibid., 176.

154 Ibid., 178.

155 Ibid.

156 Ibid., 178–79.

157 Ibid., 6.

158 Bakeless, 179.

159 Brian Kilmeade and Don Yaeger, *George Washington's Secret Six: The Spy Ring That Saved the American Revolution* (New York: Sentinel, 2013), 38.

160 Allen, 50–51.

161 Rose, 45.

162 Benjamin Tallmadge, *Memoir of Col. Benjamin Tallmadge Prepared by Himself at the Request of His Children* (Reprint of 1858 Thomas Holman by New York: *New York Times*, 1968), 19.

163 Ibid., 19.

164 Morton Pennypacker, *General Washington's Spies on Long Island and in New York* (Cranbury, NJ: Scholar's Bookshelf, 2005), 34.

165 Rose, 173.

166 Kilmeade, 93.

167 Tallmadge, 26–27.

168 Ibid.

169 Kilmeade, 83.

170 Tallmadge, 26.

171 Rose, 175.

172 Ibid., 86.

173 Ibid., 87.

174 Rose, 226.

175 Ibid., 225.

176 Allen, 64–65.

177 Sean Manley, *Long Island Discovery: An Adventure into the History, Manners, and Mores of America's Front Porch* (New York: Doubleday, 1966), 83.

178 Rose, 228.

CHAPTER EIGHT

179 Ibid.

180 Ibid., 232.

181 Rose, 170.

182 Kilmeade, 104.

183 Ibid., 107.

184 Ibid., 106

185 Ibid.

186 Kilmeade, 122.

187 Ibid., 115.

188 Rose, 223.

189 Kilmeade, 115.

190 Ibid., 116.

191 Kilmeade, 122.

192 Ibid., 122–23.

193 Ibid., 123.

194 Ibid., 124.

195 Ibid., 129.

196 Brian Richard Boylan, *Benedict Arnold: The Dark Eagle* (New York: W. W. Norton & Company, 1973), 153.

197 Kilmeade, 133.

198 Allen, 114.

199 Van Doren, 440.

200 Rose 214.

201 Ibid., 196.

202 Allen, 121.

203 Kilmeade, 148.

204 Rose, 205.

205 Ibid.

206 Allen, 124.

207 Rose, 205.

208 Rose, 208.

209 Ibid., 208.

210 Rose, 208.

211 Boylan, 221.

212 Allen, 127.

213 Ibid.

214 Rose, 209.

215 Ibid., 210.

216 Kilmeade, 171.

217 Boylan, 236.

CHAPTER NINE

218 Kilmeade, 176.

219 Ibid.

220 Kilmeade, 177.

221 Rose, 222.

222 Ibid.

223 Bakeless, 305.

224 Kilmeade, 181.

225 Allen, 131.

226 Carney Rhinevault, *Hidden History of the Lower Hudson Valley: Stories from the Albany Post Road* (Charleston, SC: The History Press, 2012), 61.

227 Fitzpatrick, Diaries of George Washington, 2:253–54.

228 George Washington to Noah Webster, July 21, 1788, Papers of George Washington.

229 Allen, 140.

230 Rose, 260.

231 *Annals of Congress,* House of Representatives, 14th Congress, 2nd Session, January 13, 1817, Column 474, http://memory.loc.gov.

232 John A. Nagy, *Invisible Ink: Spy Craft of the American Revolution* (Yardley, PA: Westholme Publishing, 2010), appendix A.

AFTERWORD

233 Paul S. Boyer, ed., *The Oxford Companion to United States History* (New York: Oxford University Press, 2001), 390.

234 P. J. Rose, "The Founding Fathers of American Intelligence," Central Intelligence Agency, accessed March 9, 2015, https://www.cia.gov/library/center-for-the-study-of-intelligence/csi-publications/books-and-monographs/the-founding-fathers-of-american-intelligence/art-1.html.

235 George Brown Tindall and David Emory Shi, *America, A Narrative History,* 4th ed. (New York: W. W. Norton & Company, 1997), 770.

236 Boyer, Oxford Companion, 390.

Image credits

Bridgeman Images: 9

Courtesy Concord Museum, www.concordmuseum.org: 93

Getty Images: Leemage 16, Universal History Archive 161

Heritage Auctions: 220

Library of Congress: ii–iii, 1, 35, 36, 40, 65, 74–75, 80–81, 94, 95, 100, 118, 119, 126, 148, 152, 153, 162, 170, 176, 177, 178, 210, 213, 232, 250, 255, 283

National Portrait Gallery: 6, 149

New York Public Library: 211, 215

Paramount Press Inc: Artist Robert Griffing: 15, 30–31, 32–33

West Point Museum: 2, 103

Courtesy Wikimedia Foundation: 11, 26, 30 (lower left), 41, 76, 87, 236, Architect of the Capital 270–271, Boston Public Library 68, Boston Public Library Digital Map Collection 241, Brandywine River Museum 145, Anne S. K. Brown Collection at Brown University 251, Central Intelligence Agency 278, Geographicus Rare Antique Maps, 114, Litchfield Historical Society 188, Massachusetts Historical Society 39, Metropolitan Museum of Art, 132–133, Museum of Fine Arts, Boston 44, 66, Museum of Fine Arts, Houston 113, National Portrait Gallery, Washington 122, New York Public Library 90, Palace of Versailles 227, Virginia Historical Society 260, Yale University Art Gallery 19, 96–97

William M. Clements Library: 55, 136–137, 139, 164, 192, 244, 248

Courtesy the private collection of Roy Winkelman: 21

Yale Center for British Art: 49

Index